THE SPANISH INQUISITION

THE SPANISH INQUISITION

A HISTORY

Joseph Pérez

translated by Janet Lloyd

YALE UNIVERSITY PRESS
NEW HAVEN & LONDON

First published in the United States in 2005 by Yale University Press

First published in Great Britain in 2004 by Profile Books

First published in France in 2002 by Librairie Arthème Fayard as *Brève Histoire de L'Inquisition en Espagne*

Copyright © Librairie Arthème Fayard, 2002

This translation copyright © Janet Lloyd 2004

Printed in the United States of America

Library of Congress Control number: 2004114614
ISBN 0-300-10790-0 (cloth : alk. paper)

A catalogue record for this book is available from the British Library.

The paper in this book meets the guidelines for permanence and durability of the Committee on Production Guidelines for Book Longevity of the Council on Library Resources.

10 9 8 7 6 5 4 3 2 1

Contents

Preface

This book is designed to set the record straight on the form taken by the Inquisition in Spain, that is to say in but one part of the states ruled by Ferdinand and Isabella, then the Hapsburgs, then the first Bourbons. It will therefore allude only rarely and briefly to the activities of the Holy Office in the many other territories under the crown of Castile (the Canaries and the territories ruled by viceroys in New Spain and Peru) and the crown of Aragon (Sicily). This is not an arbitrary choice. The Inquisition was created, in the late fifteenth century, in order to resolve the particular problem presented by the presence of thousands of converted Jews in the Iberian peninsula. It therefore seems justifiable to concentrate chiefly on how the Inquisition tackled this problem in Spain, even though, from the sixteenth century onward, it did extend its authority to other minoritites and become implanted in other geographical regions.

Introduction: From the Spain of three religions to inquisitorial Spain

etween 1478 and 1502, Isabella of Castile and Ferdinand of Aragon took three complementary decisions. They persuaded the pope to create the Inquisition; they expelled the Jews; and they forced the Muslims of the kingdom of Castile to convert to Catholicism. All these measures were designed to achieve the same end: the establishment of a united faith. The sovereigns thus seem to have broken with earlier policies. Tolerance of non-Christian confessions appears to have been replaced by intransigence and persecution. However, in reality that tolerance had been no more than a semblance. We need to challenge the preconception of a Spain in which the three religions based on sacred books – Christian, Muslim and Jewish – existed tolerantly together throughout the first centuries of Muslim domination and continued to do so in the Christian Spain of the twelfth and thirteenth centuries. Tolerance presupposes an absence of discrimination against minorities and respect for the points of view of others. In the Iberia of the eighth century to the fifteenth, such tolerance was nowhere to be found. The Christians and the Muslims were equally convinced that it was they who held the truth and that their own respective faiths were incompatible with the faiths of all others. If they acted with tolerance, that was because they could not do otherwise: unwillingly, they accepted what they had no means of preventing. It was the force of circumstances that made possible the presence of Christian communities in Islamic territory and Mudejars (Muslims) in the Christian kingdoms – not to mention the Jews, who were to be found everywhere. The idea of a tolerance peculiar to medieval Spain thus calls for qualification. It was a *de facto* tolerance, suffered rather than desired.

It is true that in Islamic territory the pact known as the *dhimma* laid down special provisions for 'people of the Book', that is to say Jews and Christians. They were not forced to convert, and they had an official status – which, however, is not to say that they were placed on an equal footing with the Muslims. On the contrary, Jews and Christians were subjected to both civil and legal forms of discrimination. Their status did, nevertheless, allow them to preserve not only their possessions but also the freedom to practise their respective cults, as well as a relative legal autonomy. On the other hand, non-believers were subjected to heavy taxation. The Jews rapidly integrated themselves into Muslim society. A minority of them had specialised in trade, finance and money-lending. Since many Jews had adopted Arabic as their language of communication and culture, the authorities gladly assigned them unpopular administrative tasks such as tax-collection. In a number of cases, Jews came to hold high-ranking State responsibilities, but these were personal and exceptional promotions. The vast majority of their fellow-Jews lived in much more modest conditions. Furthermore, the social position of these Court Jews exposed them to popular resentment and vindictiveness when times were hard. The high responsibilities that they discharged explicitly contravened the *dhimma* pact, which forbade non-believers to exercise authority over those of the Muslim faith. So they tended to fall as rapidly as they had risen, for no guarantee protected them against the possible reversals of fortune. The Jews' prosperity in this period was possible only thanks to the negligence and laxity of the Muslim authorities, so it was extremely precarious. Far from being the consequence of a deliberate policy of openness and tolerance, it depended entirely upon the goodwill, and hence the arbitrary whims, of their rulers.

The second Muslim wave of invasion, at the end of the eleventh century and in the mid-twelfth, put an end to this state of affairs. The Almoravids and, particularly, the Almohads proved intransigent with regard to non-believers. The persecuted Jews now found refuge in the Christian kingdoms of the north, whose rulers welcomed them because they hailed from a region – al-Andalus – whose civilisation was, at this time, far superior to that of Christian Spain, they spoke Arabic, they understood the political, economic and social organisation of the Muslim territories, and they were familiar with the most advanced commercial techniques. The rulers of Christian Spain therefore encouraged the Jews to settle in their territories in spite of the Catholic Church which, ever since the fourth Council of Lateran (1215), had been seeking to limit contacts between Jews and Christians solely to economic transactions. Mixed marriages were banned; Jews were forbidden to employ Christians and to assume posts that gave them authority over Christians, and so on. In Spain itself, the Council of Zamora (1312) repeated and increased the severity of such injunctions: Christians could not share meals with Jews, nor employ Jewish wet-nurses, nor have sexual relations with Jews or Jewesses; it was also proposed that Jews should wear a distinctive sign. The sovereigns avoided following any such recommendations. As they saw it, the Jews constituted valuable auxiliaries in diplomatic relations and in the rehabilitation of the territories that they had reconquered. However, in Christian Spain, as previously in Muslim Spain, they were certainly not on the same footing as those faithful to the dominant religion. The famous legal code promulgated by King Alfonso X of Castile (reigned 1252–84) (known as the *Partidas*) was explicit in this respect. The Jews were allowed to live among Christians in a kind of perpetual captivity, 'so that their very presence should be a reminder that they are descended from those who crucified our Lord Jesus Christ'. This was certainly in conformity with the spirit of the liturgical texts which, from the seventh century right down to 1959, invited the faithful to pray, on Good Friday, for the perfidious Jews (*pro perfidis judaeis*). To be sure, that word 'perfidious' referred to a lack of faith, disbelief or infidelity, but with the passing of time it acquired the sense of deceitfulness, and it thereby fuelled the hostility of Christians.

In medieval Spain, three religions (Muslim, Christian and Jewish) thus more or less coexisted, but only two were ever dominant: initially the Arabic civilisation, then the Christian. The Arabic civilisation was the richer and the more brilliant until, from the twelfth century on, the Christian civilisation definitively acquired the upper hand. The Jews assimilated each in turn and, at the turn of the eleventh to twelfth centuries, this enabled them to act as intermediaries, without renouncing their own religious traditions.

Such were the conditions in which, in medieval Spain, Jewish communities (known as *aljamas*) that enjoyed relative autonomy became established. They administered their own affairs, under the authority of their own magistrates. They had their own synagogues, schools and cemeteries. These *aljamas* were not ghettos, for the Jews could live wherever they pleased. If they favoured certain areas it was for reasons of convenience, so as to be closer to the synagogue, the Talmudic school and the kosher butcher where they bought their food supplies. The one to two hundred thousand Jews of Spain were dispersed among scores of *aljamas*, the most important of which, in Castile, were those of Toledo, Burgos, Segovia, Avila, Valladolid, Cordova and Seville, and in Aragon those of Saragossa, Barcelona and Valencia. They enjoyed an official status that guaranteed them a legal existence and, in theory, protected them from arbitrary acts of aggression. In this micro-society, as in the dominant Christian society, the poor far outnumbered the rich. Most led a modest existence as artisans (tailors, cobblers and so on) or as shopkeepers. A small minority of Jews practised trade on a major scale and possessed fortunes which, when the opportunity arose, enabled them to lend money to kings, prelates, lords and other individuals. Sovereigns, prelates and great feudal lords were happy to leave the management of their own affairs in Jewish hands and likewise the collection of taxes, tithes and other dues. It was this aspect of their activities that fuelled ordinary people's hatred of the Jews.

As a general rule, anti-semitism is linked to the prevailing circumstances. Persecutions and expulsions 'always stem from downturns in economic life; they accompany the latter ... Their major cause is recession' (Fernand Braudel). The Jews' experience is that of Joseph: when too many cows are thin, as in the Egypt of the Pharaohs, they know that they will be the first to suffer. That is borne out by what happened in fourteenth-century Spain, when a new social climate spread through the Iberian peninsula. The period of relative openness and tolerance was replaced by a time of conflicts. What changed was not people's mentalities, but the circumstances. The golden age of the Spain of three religions had coincided with a phase of territorial, demographic and economic expansion. Jews and Christians had not had to compete in the work market. Both groups had contributed to the general prosperity and had shared its profits; and the militant anti-Judaism of the Church and the monks had found few supporters. But the social, economic and political upheavals of the fourteenth century, and the wars and natural catastrophes that preceded and followed the Black Death, created a new situation. They ushered in a phase of recession, hardship and tensions when, for both Christians and Jews, everything changed. The phenomenon was not restricted to the Iberian peninsula. Not only in Spain, but in France and Germany, and throughout Europe, populations were in a state of disarray, faced with misfortunes that they could neither understand nor arrest. They believed themselves cursed, punished for sins that they had committed. The monks urged the faithful to repent, change their ways and return to God. Now the presence of a 'deicide people' among the Christians was felt to be scandalous. On all sides, people turned against the Jews. They were even accused of, for instance, propagating the plague by poisoning the water wells. The first wave of persecutions, the 'Pastoureaux' crusade, began in

France and reached Navarre in 1321. In Pamplona, Jews were assassinated. In Estella, in 1328, the sermons preached by a Franciscan provoked a riot; the houses of Jews were sacked and Jews were killed. Twenty years later, there were similar scenes in Barcelona and other Catalan localities. Eventually things returned to normal, but a new note had been struck. From that time on, anti-semitism was established in Spain. Jews now started to be accused of profaning consecrated communion hosts and committing ritual crimes. It was also at this point that Jewish usury was first perceived as a problem.

The medieval rule was to charge no interest on money lent to fellow-believers, that is to say on money lent by a Christian to a fellow-Christian or by a Jew to a fellow-Jew. But a Christian could charge a Jew interest on a loan, and vice versa. Recourse to credit is an essential element of economic life. In the absence of specialist institutions, a number of Jews would advance money to those with financial difficulties. Money-lending was not a reprehensible activity, and was regulated by a law that set the authorised rate of interest: 20 per cent in the kingdom of Aragon, 33.3 per cent in the kingdom of Castile.[1] Any charge above those rates was considered to be usury. Most loans involved small sums and were very short-term – six months or a year. After six years, the debt was considered to be extinguished. Creditors were consequently eager for prompt repayment. In times of recession, debtors were unable to pay up and the law courts were flooded with complaints: lenders clamoured for repayment, while borrowers claimed that they were victims of usury. The Cortes sympathised with the difficulties of the debtors and demanded damages or even that part of the debts be annulled.

The king would be required to arbitrate. But he himself would also have cash-flow problems. Without loans from the Jews, he would be unable to resolve them. To advance those loans, the Jews needed money, so had to be repaid by their individual creditors. Furthermore, the king's royal power depended on an effective State apparatus – a bureaucracy, military means and so on – and this presupposed rising taxes. It was still the Jews who collected those taxes. The stereotype of the Jew who sucked the blood of the poor and was both the instrument and the beneficiary of fiscal oppression thus took shape. In reality, the *aljamas* were also suffering from the crisis: the Jews too were crippled by taxation, even more so than the Christians, for they were more vulnerable. Only a tiny minority of them became wealthy; the vast majority were impoverished. However, the Christians believed the opposite, or rather they were encouraged to believe it.

The opposition seized upon the problem and exploited it for political ends. Anti-semitism became a propaganda weapon for the nobles of Castile who challenged the authority of King Peter I and, in order to win the support of the Christian people, supported its complaints. Henry of Trastámara accused his half-brother Peter I of surrounding himself with infidels – Moors and Jews – and of favouring them by every possible means. There was nothing spontaneous about the first massacres of Jews (in Toledo, in 1355). They were perpetrated by Trastámara's partisans when these entered the town. In the spring of 1366, it was again the soldiers of Trastámara (together with French mercenaries under the command of Duguesclin) who destroyed the Jewish quarter of Briviesca. In April 1366, Henry of Trastámara himself entered Burgos and demanded a huge ransom from the town's Jews; those who could not pay would be reduced to slavery and sold. In 1367 the populace of Valladolid fell upon the Jewish quarter with cries of 'Long live King Henry!' There were no casualties, but the synagogues were looted.

Following his victory, Henry II of Trastámara modified the open anti-semitism of the civil war. He promulgated a general annulment of debts. However, he again made some Jews responsible for the collection and administration of taxes, although not such a high proportion as before; so from this time onward the public finances were no longer monopolised by Jews. The civil war had altered the position of Jews in the kingdom of Castile. For the first time anti-semitism had been exploited for political ends; for the first time it had taken violent forms and had led to murder and looting. It had been presented as an ideological justification for a social conflict which, initially, had not been rooted in religion. Famine, rising prices and heavy taxation had provoked tensions and clashes, in which the poor were pitted against the rich, and anti-semitism was used to deflect the violence towards the Jews. Another point is also worth noting: the Jews needed a strong and respected royal power, for it alone could act in their defence. They were well aware of this and that is why they were loyal to the crown. The best service the Court Jews could render their fellow-Jews was to strengthen the throne, as was confirmed by the tragic events of 1391.

Ever since 1378, Fernand Martínez, the archdeacon of Ecija, in Andalusia, had been preaching a stream of anti-semitic sermons, in the midst of particularly difficult social circumstances in which inflation and soaring prices had plunged modest folk into deep poverty. Acting solely on his own initiative, the archdeacon was urging the faithful to break off all contacts with Jews and to destroy the synagogues. In March 1382, at the request of the archbishop of Seville, King John I ordered him to moderate his behaviour. Martínez took no notice of this warning, nor of others that followed. He pretended to believe that these pleas for moderation did not reflect the king's true intentions. The archbishop eventually decided to suspend Martínez and lay charges against him, but at this point (July 1390), the prelate died, and the agitator Martínez, as a leading cleric, became the provisional administrator of the diocese. A few months later, the king also passed away, leaving a young child, Henry III, as his heir. The two deaths, only a few months apart, gave the archdeacon a free hand. He made the most of the power vacuums at the head of the State and in the diocese of Seville to intensify his provocations. He had synagogues demolished and confiscated Jewish prayer books. The first riot, in January 1391, was repressed by the municipal authorities, but nothing could prevent the second, in June of that same year.

Synagogues were now turned into churches, houses were looted and Jews were assassinated. Others, terrified, asked to be baptised or took flight.

From Seville, the rioting spread to the whole kingdom of Castile. In Cordova, Ubeda, Baeza, etc. similar scenes of looting and murder were repeated. The *aljama* of Ciudad Real was wiped out, and those of Toledo and Cuenca were sacked. To the north of the Guadarrama, events took a less dramatic turn. Signs of panic among the Jews were noted in Burgos, and there was sporadic looting, but few casualties. The territories of the kingdom of Aragon had been spared the anti-semitic hysteria, possibly thanks to the fact that the royal power here commanded more respect than that of Castile. Here, few protests had been voiced against the presence of the Jews in the fiscal administration and the theme of usury had hardly been mentioned. However, the violence soon spread to Aragon. In the month of August 1391, Saragossa, Barcelona, Lerida, Gerona, Valencia and Majorca were all affected. The same scenes were repeated everywhere – massacres, rape, looting – and the same consequences followed: many Jews converted, others fled. Only Navarre was spared. It now served as a refuge for Jews from Castile and Aragon.

The events of 1391 must be interpreted as an explosion of class hatred deflected against the Jews and encouraged by the weakness of the ruling power. Everywhere the same process is detectable. The sermons of mendicant monks inflamed people's minds. Saint Vincent Ferrer, for example, preached on the theme of the Apocalypse. For centuries, Christians had been encouraged to hate the Jews. With preachers telling them, Sunday after Sunday, that the Jews were perverted and guilty of complicity in the death of Christ, the faithful ended up by detesting them with a hatred that was bound one day to express itself in violence. The idea that all Jews were money-lenders took a general hold. From there it was but one step to believing that the Jewish usurers were responsible for, and benefited from, the poverty of the Christian people; and in the fourteenth century that step was taken. Small groups of agitators had no difficulty in turning against the Jews the resentment of sections of the population driven to despair by a seemingly endless distress the causes of which they could not understand. They were shocked by the opulence of a minority of Jews and became convinced that they were the victims of an injustice.

The number of victims is hard to calculate. Some estimates are clearly excessive, in particular those provided by chroniclers who speak of thousands of assassinations. Wherever more precise details are available, the numbers are much lower: 400 victims in Barcelona, 250 in Valencia, seventy-eight in Lerida, for example. The unleashing of such hatred terrified the Jews even more than the assassinations. Those who could, fled abroad, most to North Africa, the rest to Navarre, France and Portugal. Others found refuge with nobles who took them under their protection, in which case they left the large towns and installed themselves in smaller settlements where they thought they would be safer.

But it was the conversions, even more than the massacres and the emigration, that impoverished Spanish Jewry. This movement had begun in the fourteenth century but at that time concerned only a small number of cultivated or rich Jews. The most spectacular of those conversions was that of a rabbi of Burgos, one year before the 1391 massacres. Salomon ha-Levi, from an old family of Talmudists, had himself baptised, along with his entire family. As he was descended from the tribe of Levi and claimed to belong to the same stock as the Virgin Mary, he took the name Pablo de Santa María, and a while later became the bishop of Burgos! From 1391 on there were many more conversions. Now thousands of Jews were requesting baptism, appalled by their experiences and anxious to spare their families more persecution. This movement peaked around 1415. Twenty years after the massacres, the civil authorities decided to make life impossible for the Jews and so force them to convert. In 1412, Catherine, the Queen Mother, who was regent of Castile until John II came of age, decided to confine the Jews to ghettos. Thenceforward they had to let their beards and hair grow long and sew a red disc on their clothing. Outside the ghettos, a number of professions were barred to them. They could no longer practise as doctors, chemists, drug-sellers, blacksmiths, carpenters, tailors, butchers, cobblers, traders, tax-collectors ... In 1415 this legislation was extended to Aragon, with the addition of further aggravating clauses: possession of the Talmud was declared illegal; Jews were allowed only one synagogue for each *aljama*; they were ordered to attend three Christian sermons every year: one on the second Sunday in Advent, one on Easter Monday and a third on a day left to the discretion of the local authorities. In the event, these rules were not applied, but they were indicative of a particular state of mind. People were no longer prepared to resign themselves to the presence of Jews. They wanted to force them to convert.

Monks skilfully exploited the terror felt in Jewish communities and embarked on an intense campaign of proselytisation. Vincent Ferrer (1350–1419) was the most famous of these preachers ambitious for success. This Dominican from Valencia, who preached in Italy and France as well as in Spain, possessed the art of inflaming the crowds by his eloquence and the settings that he chose for his performances. He liked to preach as night was falling, in cemeteries, surrounded by penitents and flagellants. He claimed that he did not wish to force conversion upon anybody and was merely 'helping grace to produce its effects'. In 1407, he took charge of the evangelisation of the territories of the kingdom of Aragon. His connections with Pope Benedict XIII and the Infante Ferdinand of Antequera (whom he helped to install on the throne of Aragon in 1412) facilitated his work. He was credited with thousands of conversions. The evangelisation campaign culminated in what was inaccurately known as the Dispute or Controversy of Tortosa (1413–14), brainchild of Pope Benedict III. This was designed to establish the truth of Christianity on the basis of the Jewish texts and to show that the rabbis had deliberately falsified the Talmud on fundamental points such as the coming of the Messiah. Jews were ordered to attend these sessions: eight rabbis were appointed to speak in the name of their community, their role being to ask questions. But as soon as they began to argue and to defend the orthodox Jewish point of view, the pope would suspend the session: they were there not to argue their case, but to recognise publicly that they were in error.

Hardly surprisingly, in these circumstances, there were thousands of conversions. Between 1391 and 1415 more than half of the Jews in Spain are said to have been baptised, among them many rabbis and figures of note. This 'betrayal by the clerics' (Leon Poliakov) encouraged humbler folk also to turn to apostasy. Spanish Judaism was never to recover from this catastrophe, which was a prelude to the expulsion that took place a century later.

Spanish Judaism emerged from the terrors of the years 1391–1415 profoundly shaken. In the whole of the Iberian peninsula, no more than 100,000 individuals still faithful to Judaism remained. In the kingdom of Aragon, many *aljamas* had disappeared or were much reduced – those of Barcelona, Valencia and Palma, for example. Only the *aljama* of Saragossa remained intact. A similar situation obtained in the domains of Castile. The numbers in formerly flourishing *aljamas* (Seville, Toledo, Burgos) had fallen considerably. On the other hand, a few new ones appeared – one in Talavera, for example. Andalusia now contained fewer Jews than the northern *meseta* and the large towns contained fewer than the smaller villages. Between 1419 and 1422, the kings John of Castile and Alfonse V of Aragon abrogated most of the discriminatory measures taken by their predecessors. The Jews now repossessed the synagogues that had been confiscated from them; they were again allowed to practise professions from which they had been banned; and they no longer had to display a red disc on their clothing. On these foundations, Abraham Benveniste set about rebuilding Judaism in Castile. In 1432, in Valladolid, this wholesaler, who had arrived at the Court of John II in

1420, gathered together representatives from all the Jewish communities in the kingdom in order to elaborate a document designed to organise and regulate life in the *aljamas*. These preserved their internal autonomy, with special taxes to finance their cult and religious education. These rulings were submitted to the king for his approval, which he gave. They were thus officially sanctioned, which meant that the Jewish community was recognised as an integral part of the kingdom. In Castile, at least, Judaism now recovered a legal existence and was relatively vigorous. However, let no mistake be made about it: Spanish Judaism was no longer what it had been. In political and economic life, in particular, Jews no longer played anything but a minimal role. In the kingdom of Aragon, not one now held a State post of major importance. In Castile, Jews now collected barely one quarter of the taxes.

From the fifteenth century on, new terms were introduced to refer to Jews, so as to distinguish between those who continued to profess Judaism and were Jews in the strict sense of the term and those who had converted: the latter were known as New Christians or *conversos*.

The positions that Jews abandoned were now occupied by *conversos*. Geographically, that was certainly the case. In Barcelona, Valencia and the large towns of Andalusia and Castile (Seville, Cordova, Toledo, Segovia, Burgos ...), the *conversos* formed numerous groups, all drawn there by business: trade, both wholesale and retail, financial services and craft industries. Many were bourgeois in both senses of the word: they lived in urban communities and they belonged to the emerging middle class. Veritable dynasties of merchant *conversos* thus came to hold dominant positions in Burgos, the centre of the international wool-trade. What was new was that their conversion made it possible for them to join professions that had been, and remained, closed to Jews. Relatively large numbers of them now held public posts. In the course of the fifteenth century they invaded the municipalities, becoming magistrates or aldermen. Others entered the clergy or the religious orders where, thanks to their high level of culture, they rapidly rose to posts of responsibility and prestige, becoming canons, priors and so on.

The social rise of the *conversos* did not pass unnoticed, and in popular circles it aroused antagonistic reactions. While the elite groups – the royal authorities, the aristocracy and the ecclesiastical hierarchy – encouraged the assimilation of the *conversos*, the masses remained hostile. Long-standing anti-semitism now condemned Jews and New Christians alike. People continued to believe that both groups were exploiting them and monopolising the best jobs, but, because many occupied high-profile positions, it was the *conversos* who attracted most of the popular anti-semitism. As in the fourteenth century, the combination of economic hardship and political crises lent itself to exploitation, as can be seen from the events of 1449 and 1474 in Castile. There can be no other explanation for the rioting in Toledo in 1449. A demagogue, Pero Sarmiento, exploited the discontent of the poor, already crushed by taxes, and turned it against the government. For several months he controlled the town, systematically looting the homes of his political opponents. He decided to exclude *conversos* from municipal responsibilities and ordered that, in principle, such posts should be reserved exclusively for Old Christians. This was the first of the statutes on blood purity that introduced discrimination between Christians based on the date of their baptism. This affair prompted a passionate polemic. Theologians condemned such discrimination. Lope de Barrientos, the bishop of Cuenca, denounced the troublemakers who stirred up discord. He said it would be to admit people into the community of the faithful, only then to deny them access to certain posts. Pope Nicholas V took a similar view: whatever the date when they became Christians, all the faithful formed a single flock; all had an equal right to the posts and benefits that society, both civil and ecclesiastic, might offer them.

Eventually order was restored in Toledo, at least for the time being. But in 1467 trouble broke out again. Again the excuse was provided by unpopular taxation and by rivalry between the supporters and the adversaries of Henry IV. Following veritable street-battles, the *conversos* were massacred and their houses looted and burned to the ground. And so it went on. The events of 1473 were reminiscent of those of 1391: they occurred in almost the same place and for similar reasons. This time it was not in Seville that the trouble started, but in Cordova. For several years harvests in Andalusia had been poor, and food shortages were rife and aggravated by steep price rises. The undernourished population was then struck by a series of plague epidemics. The masses hated the wealthy because they were protected from hunger and sickness. They accused them of stockpiling wheat so as to force prices up. The houses of many were looted, but *conversos* were particularly targeted. The various factions and demagogues exploited the people's exasperation and turned it against the *conversos*. In 1473, Cordova was the scene of looting and street-fighting in which *hidalgos* and great lords were to be found risking their lives to defend the *conversos* who were threatened with death. It was at the time of these scenes of violence that Henry IV's reign came to an end, leaving Isabella of Castile and Ferdinand of Aragon to confront the situation.

When they became the sovereigns of Castile in 1474, and then of Aragon in January 1479, the Catholic sovereigns were faced with the problem posed ever since the mid fourteenth century by the rise of anti-semitism. When the Cortes met in 1480, the sovereigns took two discriminatory measures against the Jews. In the first place, they ruled that Jews should live in separate quarters; they would be allowed to leave them in the daytime, but would have to return there for their meals and for the night. Secondly, they were obliged to display a coloured disc upon their clothing. Both were measures that had been passed in 1412 but had remained a dead letter, never applied. That discrimination was, however, compensated by the precautions that the Catholic sovereigns took to guarantee the security of the Jews. The restoration of public order in the kingdom of Castile benefited the Jews, as it did all the sovereigns' subjects. Attacks against individuals and property ceased; and the queen on several occasions declared that she personally guaranteed that order. On 6 September 1477, for instance, in a letter to the Jewish community of Seville, she wrote: 'I take under my protection the Jews of the *aljamas* in general, and each one of them in particular, both their persons and their possessions. I guarantee them against all attacks, of whatever nature [...]; I forbid anyone to strike them, kill them, or wound them; I also forbid anyone to turn a blind eye if they are attacked, killed, or wounded.' On 12 August 1490, in Burgos, she again affirmed her desire to see the Jews live peacefully in Castile as subjects of the crown. At about this time, the Jews of Spain, addressing their co-believers in Rome, congratulated themselves on their subjection to sovereigns who were so just and so well disposed towards them. As has sometimes been remarked, if Ferdinand and Isabella had died in 1491, the judgement passed on them by Jewish posterity would have been very different.

The situation had no doubt improved from the point of view of public order, but in people's minds it was no better. Anti-semitism diminished neither in popular circles nor in the mendicant orders. It was now directed more against converted Jews than against those who had retained their Jewish faith, because the converts – the *conversos* – were accused of being false Christians and of leading a double life. It was said that in public they conformed with their obligations as Catholics, going to mass, attending services, and distinguishing themselves as little as possible from other Christians; but in the privacy of their homes they observed the rites and practices of the law of Moses, and respected the Jewish sabbath and festivals. Some were even said to have been circumcised. It was proved that, among those who had converted to escape the blind fury of the crowds in 1391, or under the pressure of the proselytising campaigns of the early fifteenth century, some had secretly reverted to their former faith when the danger appeared to have passed. These, it was said, 'judaised'. This crypto-Judaism was the source of much psychological strain and many family tensions. One chronicler reports that in some cases a husband would judaise while his wife regarded herself as a true Christian. In 1510, one young woman described her family as living constantly on the *qui-vive*, 'never knowing whether it was day or night'. A number of widely reported scandals eventually convinced even the most hardened sceptics. One example was that of the powerful Caballería family, which had converted in 1414 in Saragossa. It was later learned that Pedro, the head of the family, who had died in 1461, had never ceased to recite Jewish prayers and to observe the sabbath. An even graver case was that of Father García Zapata, prior of the Hieronymite monastery of La Sisla, close to Toledo, who every year, in September, celebrated the Tabernacle Festival. Furthermore, when he officiated at mass, at the moment of the Elevation of the Host, instead of pronouncing the words of consecration, he whispered words that were blasphemous and irreverent. He later became one of the first victims of the Inquisition and was burnt at the stake. A relatively large number of *marranos*, after conversions forced upon them, continued secretly to live in Judaism, read the Bible, observe the sabbath, abstain from eating pork and so on.

Judaism was risky for New Christians. Canon law considered that baptism imprinted an indelible seal upon the souls of those who received baptism. Even when it was administered under constraint, it created an irreversible situation. Anyone baptised willy-nilly belonged definitively to the Church; there was no going back. Contemporaries may find such rulings shocking, but they are nevertheless part of official Church doctrine, as the most recent official edition of the catechism reminds us.[2] To assume that they are now forgotten and without effect would be mistaken. The Mortara affair, in nineteenth-century Italy,[3] and, closer to the present day, the affair of the Finaly children in immediate postwar France,[4] testify to quite the contrary.

If the rulings of canon law were reaffirmed not so very long ago in France, despite its official secularism and the separation between State and Church, it is hardly surprising that they were invoked in an Ancien Régime country such as Spain, which was deeply steeped in religious values. Converted Jews who, despite their baptism, returned to Judaism were judged guilty of heresy and the Church could demand the cooperation of the State in the punishment of that crime. From the mid fifteenth century onwards, in Castile, voices were raised, calling for such sanctions to be applied. Some of those voices even belonged to *conversos*. These seemed to bring the zeal of neophytes to their attacks upon both Jews and *marranos* (as those who reverted to Judaism were being called), targeting the former because they clung to their error, and the latter because they cast doubt upon the sincerity of all New Christians. In the fourteenth century already, Abner, who had converted in 1321, had specialised in denouncing the falsifications he believed he had detected in the Talmud and the blindness of rabbis to these; and he recommended strong-arm tactics to force Jews to change their religion. In the mid fifteenth century, two *conversos* were responsible for the most cutting pamphlets against their former Jewish co-believers. One was a Franciscan, Alonso de Espina, the other a Hieronymite, Alonso de Oropesa. In a text written in 1459 entitled *Fortalitium fidei*, Espina denounced the materialism of certain *conversos*. His view was that they should be punished and that Jews, by their presence alone, constituted an obstacle that prevented *conversos* from being fully assimilated. His remarks contained the seeds of the inquisition against judaising Christians and also of the expulsion of the Jews. Alonso de Oropesa, for his part, defended *conversos*, but only the better to attack Jews and crypto-Jews. He too thought that the very presence of Jews constituted a provocation and an invitation to judaise. In order to have done with this irritating problem, he too recommended rigorously severe measures against Judaisers. Henry IV responded by making a few overtures to the papacy, with a view to obtaining the creation of an inquisition, but soon lost interest.

Ferdinand and Isabella restored public order in their kingdoms and, at a stroke, put an end to the insecurity suffered by both Jews and *conversos*. But they did not manage to eliminate anti-semitism. On the contrary, the crypto-Judaism of certain *conversos* strengthened the animosity provoked by their social rise in the course of the fifteenth century. In 1475, Friar Alonso de Hojeda, prior of the Dominicans of Seville, presented the queen with an alarming report. It stated that incredulity was steadily increasing and many *conversos* made a show of their quality as Christians simply to accede to public responsibilities and ecclesiastical benefits but, even as they did so, they openly practised Judaism: they had their children circumcised, ceased all activities on the day of the sabbath, recited Jewish prayers, celebrated Jewish Easter and other festivals, buried their dead according to Jewish customs ... In a period deeply steeped in religion, such behaviour was bound to scandalise the masses and alarm the authorities. Increasingly detailed information of this kind reached the Court, where insistent demands were made for energetic measures to be taken against crypto-Jews. In 1477–78, the Catholic sovereigns visited Extremadura and Andalusia. They spent several months in Seville, where they were able to get a better view of the situation. But the queen was not convinced that violence was necessary; and members of her entourage, men who had won her confidence, such as her confessor Friar Hernando de Talavera, himself a *converso*, and Cardinal Mendoza, the archbishop of Seville, were even more reticent. Ferdinand, on the other hand, became committed to the idea; and it was he who won the day. Twenty years later, in 1507, he confirmed the importance of that stay in Seville: so worrying did the situation in Andalusia seem that it was impossible to act otherwise. Paradoxically enough, it is now fashionable in certain circles to criticise the fanaticism of Isabella whereas it was, in truth, King Ferdinand, rather, who was responsible for the persecution – a fact that tends to be forgotten.

The Catholic sovereigns turned to Pope Sixtus IV who, in a papal bull, *Exigit sincerae devotionis*, dated 1 November 1478, authorised them to appoint inquisitors in their kingdoms. But Ferdinand and

Isabella delayed two years before making use of this permission. The explanation for this seems to be the repugnance felt in the queen's entourage at the idea of engaging in violent repression. Cardinal Mendoza, the archbishop of Seville, produced a catechism that he sent to every church in the diocese. In a pastoral letter, he requested priests to devote themselves utterly to the instruction of their congregations, in particular that of New Christians. The queen's confessor, Friar Hernando de Talavera went to Seville, to preach there and to warn the *conversos* of the persecution that threatened them unless they changed their lives. Both men were convinced that the repressive programme could still be averted. The real scale of the problem did not escape them: many *conversos* had received very inadequate, if any, religious instruction, so how could they be expected to practise a faith about which they knew little or nothing? How could they be punished for errors due to ignorance? They would therefore make an effort to catechise the New Christians, in the hope of thereby reducing the number who also practised Judaism and averting the need for stringent methods.

The evangelisation campaign came too late and produced no more than mediocre results. As the chronicler Pulgar, himself a *converso* and extremely hostile to the Inquisition, admitted, 'It was not much use.' The New Christians of Seville did not seem to appreciate the danger they were in; they did not take this tardy catechism at all seriously. Such was their obtuseness that some had no qualms about publicly justifying their position, as in one anonymous defamatory pamphlet that circulated in Seville.[5] In this, the author expounded the idea that there was nothing to prevent one from practising Christianity and Judaism simultaneously; on the contrary, Judaism made it possible to improve Christianity; in fact, one was bound to conclude that Judaism was superior to Christianity. Nor did the anonymous author stop there. He expressed reservations as to the dogma of the Holy Trinity and likewise the cult of images and saints; he asserted the Jewish people's superiority over other peoples (since the Jews were too intelligent to be taken in by the nonsense that the priests purveyed); and he commented ironically on the superstitious practices of the Catholic masses. This pamphlet testified eloquently to the state of mind of some of the Andalusian *conversos* and it inevitably confirmed the advocates of strong-arm tactics. The Catholic sovereigns drew their own conclusions. On 27 September 1480, they appointed the first inquisitors, who promptly installed themselves in Seville. The Holy Office was born; it was not to disappear until 1834.

Ferdinand and Isabella thus resigned themselves to heeding the suggestions of the mendicant orders and others who recommended sanctions against judaising *conversos*. It was their belief that the Inquisition would force the *conversos* to become definitively assimilated: once all the New Christians had renounced Judaism, there would be nothing to distinguish them from other members of the society. Anti-semitism would disappear along with the reasons that had occasioned it. Such was the line of argument by which the Catholic sovereigns were persuaded, in 1492, to expel the Jews who had decided to remain Jews. Torquemada, the grand inquisitor, had convinced them that the Jews constituted an obstacle to the assimilation of the *conversos*: the two groups were linked by bonds of family, friendship and work. By their very presence, the Jews represented a constant temptation to revert to Judaism, and as long as Jews remained in Spain, the *conversos*, in contact with them, would find it hard to renounce their old ways and the faith of their fathers.

This was the official explanation, as spelled out in the expulsion decree of 31 March 1492. But a number of historians remain sceptical. Was not religion used as a pretext designed to hide the authorities' true intentions? Had they not created a false problem – that of the *marranos* and Judaisers – in order to eliminate a particular minority or social class? That is certainly the thesis of the historian B. Netanyahu. According to him, in 1480 the *marranos* were well on the way to assimilation, while the number of Jews was in steady decline. That process was brutally interrupted by the Inquisition, the creation of which prompted men and women to revert to the Judaism that they had been engaged in abandoning. The thesis is supported by decisions that the rabbis of North Africa made where the *marranos* were concerned. These rabbis, who had left Spain at the time of the persecutions of 1391–1415, inevitably took a severe line with those of their faith who had lacked the courage to stand by it and had instead preferred their material comfort or been won over by rationalist trends. However, in truth, the persistence of an orthodox Jewish minority and the reality of the crypto-Judaism of the *marranos* do seem well documented.

But supposing that Netanyahu is right, what could the intentions of the Catholic sovereigns have been? Two can be ruled out immediately: namely racism and cupidity. There were, without doubt, antisemites at every level in Spain, but they did not include the Catholic sovereigns. Both prior to and following the Inquisition, Jews and *conversos* were to be found in their entourage and occupying posts of the greatest importance. One *converso*, Hernando de Talavera was the queen's confessor. Between 1474 and 1492, he played an essential role in internal politics, and in 1492 he became the first archbishop of reconquered Granada. After the expulsion of the Jews, the situation remained unchanged, with *conversos* continuing to fill top-ranking posts. Might the sovereigns have been acting as demagogues in order to flatter an anti-semitism that they did not share? Such behaviour seems very out of character. In no less important domains, they never hesitated to impose their will upon powerful and well-organised groups, such as the nobility and the clergy. Why should they have cared what their subjects thought only in the case of the Jews and the New Christians? No, what they had in mind was not the elimination of the Jews, but their assimilation and the eradication of Judaism. Their hope was that, faced with a painful choice, most Jews would convert and remain in Spain. Antisemites would never have counted on this happening.

The argument based on cupidity, a desire to appropriate the fortunes of the *conversos* convicted by the Inquisition and of the Jews forced to depart, is equally shaky. If the Catholic sovereigns had been after immediate profit, they would certainly not have deprived themselves of docile taxpayers. As we shall later see, the finances of the Inquisition were never flourishing and the Catholic sovereigns themselves recognised that, from an economic point of view, the expulsion had been a bad business. The queen, in particular, was well aware of the consequences that their religious policies would entail for the country's economy: temporary stagnation, loss of revenue for the State and so on. But it was neither the first time in history, nor the last, that sovereigns put political or ideological objectives before economic interests.[6]

Did the Catholic sovereigns succumb to pressure from the nobility, anxious to be rid of an emerging bourgeoisie that would threaten their own interests? Was this an episode in the class struggle? Neither the Jews nor the New Christians constituted a homogeneous class. They included both rich and poor (but more poor than rich) and a wide variety of professions. Did solidarity bind them together? That is by no means certain. As we have seen, the Jews reproached the New Christians for their apostasy, and *conversos* were among the sternest critics of both Jews and *marranos*. Besides which, it would be necessary to prove that the Spanish bourgeoisie was chiefly composed of Jews and *conversos*. Finally, the nobility does not appear to have been particularly threatened at this time. It had certainly lost some of its political power, but it retained considerable economic clout and its social influence remained unimpaired. It was still one of the bases of the regime and it is hard to see how the Jews could have inconvenienced it. Even if the Jews and *conversos* did constitute elements in an emerging bourgeoisie, did that bourgeoisie stand in opposition to the nobility? It seems not. The interests of the great Castilian bourgeois and the aristocrats were complementary, not antagonistic. The two groups were associated in the exploitation of the wool market, the former as breeders and pasturage proprietors, the latter as export-ers.

All in all, it would seem that the explanation produced at the begin-ning of the expulsion decree is probably the correct one. The intention was to create an irreversible situation. By eliminating Judaism, it was hoped to discourage reversion to it. The creation of the Inquisition and the expulsion of the Jews should therefore not, I think, be inter-preted as manifestations of anti-semitism on the part of the Catholic sovereigns. All the same, the results of their policy were not what they expected. It did not put a stop to anti-semitism, in fact it probably prolonged and strengthened it. This was precisely what, from the very start, had been feared by the *conversos* in the queen's confidence such as Friar Hernando de Talavera and Pulgar, the chronicler. These, and others too, accepted the notion that, in a Christian society, heretics might be punished, but they reproached the inquisitors for inadmissibly discriminating between different kinds of heretic: on the one hand those of Jewish origin, on the other all the rest. By choosing to attack one particular type of heresy – that of the Judais-ers – and a single category of heretics – those of Jewish origin – the Holy Office contradicted Catholicism's principles of universality, according to which there could be only one flock and one shepherd. That discrimination caused doubt to hover over the intentions of the inquisitors. On the pretext of punishing Judaisers, they cast discredit upon all Christians of Jewish origin, whether or not they reverted to Judaism. As soon as they decided to track down that sole category of heretics, they made every *converso* a potential criminal, a suspect, a pariah. History was to confirm those fears. Spaniards of Jewish origin came to feel that their lives, their possessions and their honour were constantly under threat. It was not long before certain institu-tions – religious orders, diocesan chapters, establishments of higher education, military orders – began to refuse to accept *conversos*. First they insisted that postulants produce proof that they had never been pursued by the Holy Office; next they required such proof in relation to the postulants' parents and grandparents; to be on the safe side, all those with a Jewish ancestor fell under systematic suspicion. All this encouraged the development of the insidious prejudice of blood purity. It was a prejudice that eventually poisoned the very spirit of the Spanish public.

1   The eradication of Semitism

The first two inquisitors for the diocese of Seville were appointed on 27 September 1480. They were Juan de San Martín and Miguel de Morillo, both Dominicans. A secular priest, Doctor Juan Ruiz de Medina, a member of the Royal Council, soon joined them as a legal adviser. The municipal authorities and the nobility welcomed them with many reservations. In fact, their reception was so muted that on 27 December the Catholic sovereigns had to order the municipality to lend the inquisitors its assistance. The newcomers also provoked panic among the *conversos* of Seville, who reacted in two ways: some fled the town; others tried to remove the inquisitors by force.

According to contemporary chroniclers Andrés Bernáldez and Hernando del Pulgar, some 3,000 *converso* families now decided to exile themselves to Portugal, France or North Africa, where most of them reverted to Judaism. Others – 8,000 individuals, according to the same sources – apparently sought refuge in the domains of the great lords of the region: the Marquis of Cadiz, the Duke of Medina Sidonia, the Count of Arcos ... On 2 January 1481, the inquisitors urged these nobles to stop protecting the *conversos* on pain of themselves being charged with complicity and obstruction to the work of the Holy Office. These reactions confirm our earlier remarks on the attitude of members of the aristocracy towards Jews and *conversos*. Their strongest feeling seems to have been not hostility, but sympathy.

Other *conversos* planned to resist the inquisitors and intimidate them in order to force them to leave the town. A small group prepared for a popular demonstration, but their plot was rumbled as a result of the indiscretion and chatter of the daughter of its foremost leader, Suzanne, known as *la Hermosa Hembra* (the Pretty Woman). These plotters, who were forthwith arrested, tried and condemned to death, were among the very first victims of the Spanish Inquisition.

The inquisitors then made many more arrests among the *conversos* suspected of practising Judaism. The first auto da fé was organised on 6 February 1481; others soon followed. The court of Seville proved extremely severe and sentenced many to death. Between 1481 and 1488, 700 executions and thousands of other sentences, mostly to life-imprisonment, were recorded. Voices were raised, in particular those of Pulgar the chronicler and the protonotary Juan Ramírez de Lucena, demanding indulgence for the New Christians whose only crime, in many cases, was ignorance: they and their parents had converted in order to avoid persecution; would it not be in keeping with Christian charity to instruct them in the truths of the Christian faith, rather than send them to burn at the stake? Relatives of the victims turned to the pope, drawing his attention to the cruelty of the inquisitors. Sextus IV was horrified. In a letter dated 29 January 1482, he admitted that he had acted too hastily in acceding to the request of Ferdinand and Isabella, and claimed that he had not realised the scope of the concession he was granting to the sovereigns. He had thought that it was simply a matter of reviving the Inquisition as it had been in the Middle Ages, that is to say under the authority of the bishops. He now claimed that the inquisitors were abusing their power. An accused absolved by a civil court should not be pursued or condemned. Finally, he denounced the attitude of the inquisitors, who were refusing to allow those they condemned to appeal to the court of Rome.

The pope seemed to be on the point of revoking the authorisation to appoint their own inquisitors that he had granted the Catholic sovereigns in 1478. But heavy diplomatic pressure was brought to bear upon him. On 11 February 1482, he agreed that the inquisitors should remain in their posts, but the concession was accompanied by a number of conditions: the inquisitors were to provide the bishops with reports, the Holy Office should no longer keep the names of the accused secret, and those sentenced should be allowed to appeal to the court of Rome. Ferdinand of Aragon would accept none of these conditions. He insisted upon appointing the inquisitors himself and categorically refused to allow those sentenced to appeal to Rome. Tension again mounted between Spain and the Holy See. Eventually, in 1483, the pope bowed to the demands of the sovereigns. He tried to save face by maintaining the right of those found guilty to appeal against the sentence, not to Rome, but to the archbishop of Seville.

At the death of Sixtus IV, on 12 August 1484, the sovereigns reopened the whole matter with his successor, Innocent VIII who, however, finding himself under equal diplomatic pressure, agreed with little resistance to renew the existing dispositions regarding the Inquisition. Indeed, he went further: on 25 September 1486, Innocent VIII granted to Torquemada, who since 1483 had borne the title of grand inquisitor, the right to receive the appeals of those sentenced, in place of the archbishop of Seville, except in the case of bishops who, if they were found guilty on charges brought against them, could appeal to Rome against their sentences. In 1488, the same Innocent VIII gave the sovereigns permission to appoint Torquemada's successor at the head of the Inquisition, when the time came to do so.

Torquemada, Grand Inquisitor

The trial of strength with the papacy had thus turned to the advantage of the sovereigns. The papacy had ceded to them one of its essential prerogatives: in Spain, the defence of the faith and the battle against heresy were now the responsibility of a court with powers delegated by the papacy but answerable to the civil authority, which appointed its magistrates. This decisive period saw the appearance of the figure who was to give the Spanish Holy Office its quasi-definitive form. Tomás de Torquemada was one of the five new inquisitors appointed by Pope Sixtus IV, on 11 February 1482. He must have received the title and post of Grand Inquisitor soon after, at which point he acquired the right to appoint and delegate inquisitors himself. Torquemada (1420–98) was the nephew of the theologian Juan de Torquemada, the archbishop of Valladolid, who had distinguished himself at the Council of Basle in 1431. He was still very young when he was admitted to the Dominican order; then, in 1452, he became the prior of the monastery of the Holy Cross, in Segovia. Around 1475, Ferdinand and Isabella made him their confessor. Torquemada was renowned for his austerity: he never ate meat, wore clothing only of linen, and refused all honours, most famously the archbishopric of Seville which was offered to him. However, this did not prevent him from amassing a huge fortune, thanks to which he was able to expand the monastery of the Holy Cross in Segovia and to build another, named after Saint Thomas Aquinas, in Avila.

Torquemada is regarded as the prototype of the fanatical and cruel inquisitor. He undoubtedly did manifest extreme severity, although – as we shall see – the number of his victims was not as high as is claimed. It was Torquemada who structured the Spanish Inquisition, making it a strongly centralised institution and producing its first code of procedure. The Inquisition had been created to solve a specific problem, namely that posed by judaising *conversos* in the diocese of Seville. Torquemada extended the competence of the Holy Office to the entire territory of the kingdom of Castile by creating permanent courts in all the principal towns, first in Andalusia (Cordova and Jaen), then to the north of the Sierra Morena. Carrillo, the archbishop of Toledo, refused even to consider the implantation of the Inquisition in his diocese, which suggests that, had other bishops adopted the same attitude, the Holy Office might not have been able to develop as it did. However, most prelates were anxious not to displease the sovereigns. At Carrillo's death, his successor was Cardinal Mendoza, who raised no difficulties, and in 1485 the Inquisition was thus established in Toledo, albeit not without opposition: as in Seville, plotters had decided to resist by force and had determined to assassinate the two newly appointed inquisitors on the day of Corpus Christi, 2 June 1485. As in Seville, the authorities were warned in time and on 1 June the leading conspirators were hanged. In the meantime, Torquemada had created a court in Ciudad Real. In 1485 he set up a court in Llerena and one in Medina del Campo (later to be transferred to Salamanca). Courts in Segovia, Guadalupe, Valladolid (transferred to Palencia in 1493), Burgos, Cuenca, Avila, Siguenza, Jerez, Leon … followed. In fact, all the zones where relatively large groups of *conversos* were to be found were now under the inquisitors' surveillance.

The Inquisition in the kingdom of Aragon

It was also Torquemada who assumed the task of implanting the Inquisition in the kingdom of Aragon. This was not an easy matter, for two reasons. The papal bull that had authorised Ferdinand and Isabella to appoint inquisitors had been signed in 1478, at a time when their authority extended only to the kingdom of Castile, as Ferdinand did not become king of Aragon until January 1479. When, on 23 May 1481, Ferdinand requested permission to act in Aragon as he did in Castile, the pope expressed reservations. The second fact that threatened to obstruct the implantation of the Inquisition in the Aragonese territories was that, within the kingdom of Aragon, an Inquisition already existed: the 'medieval Inquisition'. This Inquisition, which lay within the authority of the bishops, had not become totally obsolescent: between 1460 and 1467, fifteen or so Judaisers had been brought to trial in Valencia. There had been an inquisitor in Barcelona ever since 1459, even if he showed little zeal; and in 1482 heretics had been sentenced in Saragossa. However, this did not suit Ferdinand at all, for he was determined to extend the institution of the Inquisition to the kingdom of Aragon in the form in which it already functioned in the Castilian domains – that is to say an Inquisition dependent upon not Church institutions, but the civil authorities, which alone had the power to appoint magistrates.

On 29 December 1481, Ferdinand attempted to force the issue. He replaced the diocesan inquisitors of Valencia by others of his own choice, then proceeded in the same fashion in Saragossa. In both cases, he behaved as though the papal bull of 1 November 1478 gave himself and Isabella the power to appoint inquisitors in all the domains that fell under their authority. On 18 April 1482, the pope reacted violently and in October of that year he suspended all inquisitorial activities in Aragon. The stand-off lasted until 17 October 1483, on which date Sixtus IV agreed to appoint Torquemada, who was already the grand inquisitor of Castile, as the supreme head of the Holy Office in the kingdom of Aragon, with the authority to appoint inquisitors.

Papal resistance had been overcome, but the sovereigns still needed to crush the opposition of the institutions of the kingdom of Aragon. Here, unlike in Castile, the sovereign had to take into account a number of legal dispositions that limited his powers: namely the local laws, or *fueros*. The subjects of the king of Aragon raised two objections: 1. the procedures of some of the proposed sanctions (for example, the confiscation of property) contravened the *fueros*; 2. the *fueros* were also opposed to foreigners occupying posts of authority, and most of the inquisitors, certainly Torquemada, were Castilian and therefore foreigners. Such were the objections raised by the Cortes of Valencia, in 1484, and the Cortes of Catalonia and Aragon in the years that followed. When the Cortes of Monzon met between 1510 and 1512 in order to vote on taxation, Ferdinand undertook to reform the Inquisition, but as soon as the session was closed, in 1513, he hastened to demand that the pope absolve him from a promise which, he claimed, had been extracted from him under constraint. Julius II did not dare to oppose him, for Ferdinand was not a man easily intimidated. He argued that faith was a sacred objective above and beyond all considerations of a temporal order, so the *fueros* should not be invoked in order to deliver a heretic from justice. Furthermore, the new Inquisition had been created by virtue of a decision of the Holy See, so national law could not override canon law. This was the argument subsequently systematically produced every time the Aragonese sought to invoke their *fueros* in order to limit the prerogatives of the Holy Office. The Inquisition was thus presented somehow as an institution of divine law that was superior to all human institutions. In 1518–19, the Cortes of Saragossa returned to the attack against the new sovereign. They obtained from Charles V a promise that the inquisitorial courts would pursue only cases of blatant heresy; and they demanded for the accused the right of appeal to the pope or to the grand inquisitor, to choose their legal representatives freely and to know the names of their accusers. Charles V committed himself only to show respect and exact respect for canon law, and this fooled the Aragonese. They did not spot that the formula came down to confirming earlier practices since, for Charles V, as for his grandfather, the documents issued by the Holy See were held to be superior to national laws. In 1563–4, Philip II responded in similar fashion when the Cortes of Monzon again accused the Inquisition of interfering in affairs outside its authority and of flouting the laws of the kingdom. Conscious that it would be impossible to suppress the Inquisition altogether, the Aragonese authorities demanded that it be reformed and that it limit itself to matters of faith. But even this claim was dismissed.

Legal objections thus proved unable to prevent the Inquisition from implanting itself in the kingdom of Aragon. Nor was active resistance at all effective. So the Inquisition was established in Catalonia without major incident. That was not the case in the other two components of the realm of Aragon – the kingdom of Aragon in the strict sense, and Valencia. In the latter town, the arrival of the first inquisitors, in November 1484, provoked a riot, at the instigation of not the plebs, nor Jewish circles, but the local nobility. Decidedly, nowhere do the aristocrats appear to have looked kindly upon the Inquisition. In Valencia, they were to continue to manifest their disapproval for many years.

Far more grave were the incidents that followed the arrival of the two first inquisitors for the kingdom of Aragon, Friar Gaspar Juglar and Canon Pedro Arbués. On 23 May 1484, the municipality of Teruel forced them to leave the town and kept to that decision despite all the ecclesiastical sanctions (such as excommunication) introduced against the municipal magistrates. Gaspar Juglar died in January 1485, poisoned by the *conversos*, according to rumour, although this was never proved. Arbués knew that he was under threat. He survived two attempts on his life, and he took precautions, always wearing a chain-mail vest and an iron helmet, concealed beneath his headgear. The hired assassins recruited to kill him were aware of this; they stabbed the inquisitor in the neck as he knelt in prayer in the cathedral of Saragossa on the night of 14 September 1485. Two days later, Arbués died. The assassins, their accomplices and their instigators (who included well-known *conversos*) were promptly arrested, judged and, on 30 June 1486, executed. The crime aroused horror and indignation among the population, which turned against the Jews and the *conversos*. King Ferdinand milked the situation for all it was worth and organised solemn obsequies for the victim, as if he were a martyr for the faith. In December 1487, the town of Saragossa built a magnificent tomb for Arbués's remains, adorned by a bas-relief representing the scene of the assassination. In 1490, the municipality financed two lamps of solid silver, to be placed before the tomb, in the cathedral; one of them was kept alight day and night.[1]

Neither violence nor recourse to the law had been able to prevent the Inquisition from becoming established in the kingdom of Aragon just as it had recently been in the domains of Castile. *Conversos* accused of judaising appeared in their thousands before the Holy Office's courts, and the sentences passed upon them were extremely heavy. This was by far the most murderous period in the entire history of the Spanish Inquisition (although it must be said that the number of its victims has often been exaggerated). The most numerous and the most severe sentences were those passed in Andalusia, where as many as 500 executions may have taken place. To the north of the Sierra de Guadarrama and in the territories of the kingdom of Aragon, the figures, though not so high, were still considerable: one hundred executions in Avila, fifty or so in Valladolid, several hundred in Valencia, for instance. In all, over 2,000 Judaisers, or those considered as such, must have perished at the stake throughout Spain between 1450 and 1500.

The expulsion of the Jews

To have done, once and for all, with the problem of Judaisers, in 1492 the sovereigns decided to expel the Jews. Since these had never been baptised, they could not be charged with heresy and were therefore not threatened by the Holy Office. But Torquemada was of the opinion that their expulsion was a corollary to the Inquisition. He convinced the Catholic sovereigns of this with an argument that is set out in the preamble to the decree of 31 March 1492: the assimilation of the *conversos* was hampered, indeed made impossible, by the presence of Jews linked to them by kinship, friendship and work. So long as Jews remained in Spain, the *conversos*, through contact with them, would be unable to forgo old habits and would be encouraged to revert to Judaism. And that probably is the correct explanation: the aim was to create an irreversible situation. By eliminating Judaism, it was hoped to discourage Judaisers. The climate of religious exaltation that followed the capture of Granada achieved the rest.

The religious argument was supported by reasons of a political nature. With the Reconquest completed, Spain aspired to become a country like those in the rest of Christendom which, by now for many years, had been willing to harbour only the Catholic religion. Besides, the creation of a modern State seemed to presuppose a united faith. Was it desirable to preserve Jewish communities with a special status that allowed them an administration of their own with its own particular laws, alongside the majority Christian society? On this point, the sovereigns did not favour originality on the part of Spain. The modern State was not prepared to recognise any right to be different or any different laws for religious minorities. The Spain of 1492 led the way along a path that other European countries were soon to follow; everywhere, sovereigns would soon consider themselves authorised to impose a particular faith upon their subjects.

The Jews were given four months to leave Spain. They were allowed to sell their possessions before leaving but were forbidden by law to take any gold or silver with them. They could, however, negotiate with bankers for bills of exchange to be cashed abroad. Given the situation and the time limit, it was extremely difficult for the Jews to call in money that was owed to them and to sell their possessions for a fair price. Many buyers waited until the last minute to come forward and purchased property for derisory sums. Meanwhile, bankers negotiated bills of exchange with the most unfavourable of conditions for the interested parties. It is not hard to see why many Jews preferred to convert rather than be defrauded and abandon the land of their ancestors. The sovereigns organised considerable publicity for some of these conversions, in the belief that they would encourage others. They stood as godparents at the baptism of Abraham Senior, the head of the Jewish community of Castile and his son-in-law, the rabbi Mayr. The baptism was celebrated with great pomp in the monastery of Guadalupe. The sovereigns were convinced that the vast majority of the Jews of Spain would prefer conversion to leaving their country. They were mistaken. Many Jews chose exile and loyalty to their faith.

How many did leave? Due to the many last-minute conversions

and changes of heart, followed by baptisms, the figure wavers between fifty and one hundred thousand, that is to say fewer than half the Jews of Spain. Some moved to Portugal; others went to Flanders, Italy or North Africa; most settled in the Ottoman Empire (in Thessalonika, Constantinople or the Greek islands) where, right up to the twentieth century, they preserved some of the traditions of their country of origin and the use of their language, a Judeo-Spanish derived from Castilian as spoken in 1492. This was the origin of the Sephardic communities of the East. It brought about not an economic catastrophe, but at the most a passing stagnation. The fact is that the role of the Jews was more limited than is sometimes claimed. Most of them were humble artisans, street-vendors or small-scale pawnbrokers. Only a very few were prosperous bourgeois engaged in international commerce; and most of these had converted at the end of the fourteenth century, so were not affected by the expulsion decree.

After the severe persecutions during the early years of the Inquisition, the number of convicted Jews diminished. Does this mean that, as the inquisitors and the Catholic sovereigns hoped, Judaism was eliminated in Spain? To make such an assertion would be to exaggerate. There were still *marranos* in Spain, Catholic in appearance but in reality of the Jewish faith, but they were now obliged to practise their faith in secret, living permanently in fear of betraying themselves or being denounced. For example, the Psalms of David were accessible to all Catholics through the Vulgate and they constituted a source of spiritual comfort to the Jews. But woe betide those who omitted to tack on a *Gloria Patri*, for the Inquisition would not fail to see this as a case of *marranos*. The habit of secrecy and fear of the Inquisition eventually created a particular kind of religion that was reduced to a set of rudimentary and deformed features. 'In this way the *marranos* established a cult of certain saints, a notion altogether foreign to Judaism. Esther, for example [...] became Saint Esther. Meanwhile Purim, considered by Jews as the festival of Esther, was reduced to a fast, which became a central feature of *marrano* ritual. The rite of circumcision, for its part, was seldom followed, given the danger that it represented [...] The funerary rites were only partially preserved. Although they were obliged to bury their dead according to Catholic ritual, *marranos* would try to do so in virgin earth and among other members of their community.' Certain festivals, such as the Great Pardon (Yom Kippur) and Easter, continued to be celebrated. Little by little, kosher meat ceased to be eaten, with one or two exceptions: the sciatic nerve continued to be removed before cooking the meat, oil was used for cooking so as to avoid the proscribed mixture of milk and meat products, and chickens were beheaded rather than having their necks wrung. The *bar mitzvah* ceremony (the religious coming of age, at thirteen) was turned into a kind of initiatory rite, when the young boy would be let into the family secret.[2]

The Portuguese Judaisers

The great persecutions of the late fifteenth century struck Judaisers extremely hard. The *marranos* (*conversos* who still practised Judaism in secret) did not disappear completely, but their numbers steadily declined. The records of sixteenth-century inquisitorial trials do still mention charges laid against Judaisers and sentences passed upon them, but they are increasingly rare. At the end of the sixteenth century, things changed. Since 1580, the kingdoms of Castile and Portugal had been placed under the authority of a single sovereign, Philip II, and through the reigns of Philip III and Philip IV, up until 1640, this situation continued unchanged. Many Jews of Spanish origin who had taken refuge in Portugal when they were expelled from Spain and had subsequently been forced to convert now took the opportunity to return to their native land. Portuguese Jews also moved to Spain, attracted by the prosperity then enjoyed by the monarchy. They mainly chose to settle in the regions that were the most highly developed, Andalusia and the capital, Madrid.

This movement began under the reign of Philip III (1598–1621), sometimes known as 'the king of the Jews': *Philippus Tertius Rex Iudaeorum*. If they could pay for it, Portuguese *marranos* could benefit from an amnesty for their past judaising. In 1602, for example, they paid 1,860,000 ducats to the king, 50,000 *cruzados* to his favourite, the duke of Lerma, and equivalent sums to members of the Council of the Inquisition. Philip III then agreed to engage in negotiations with the Holy See. On 23 August 1604, a papal brief authorised the Portuguese grand inquisitor to 'reconcile' New Christians of Portuguese origin, inflicting upon them no more than spiritual penances. In principle, *marranos* were forbidden to leave the country, but eventually, and always in return for hefty sums of money, derogations were granted. In 1601, in exchange for 200,000 ducats, Philip III gave New Christians the right to emigrate to the new Spanish and Portuguese colonies. That authorisation was retracted in 1610, then re-established in 1629. The numbers of Portuguese returning to Spain swelled under the government of the count-duke of Olivares (1621–43), who sought to attract them on account of the connections that some maintained with their Dutch fellow-believers. He was counting on them to break the hegemony of the Genoese bankers, despite the fact that the latter were Catholics.

In 1628, Portuguese 'businessmen' – in reality *marranos* – were authorised to move about freely and to engage in trade by both land and sea. The objective was to exclude foreigners from the lucrative trade with the West Indies. Julio Caro Baroja cites a memorandum written for the eyes of Philip IV, the author of which may well have been a member of the Council of the Inquisition. He pointed out that, in order to escape persecution by the Holy Office, Portuguese *conversos* were emigrating to countries where they could both practise their faith and make their fortunes. He deplored this situation, suggested recalling these *conversos*, promising them moderate punishments for their past sins, and he reckoned that, with the passing of time, the Portuguese *marranos* would eventually be assimilated, just as the Spanish *conversos* had been. It was not really all that surprising for an inquisitor to manifest such indulgence for, as we shall see, the Inquisition was as much a political institution as a religious one. It was placed under the power of the civil authorities, so its support for government initiatives was natural enough.

The Inquisition had been implanted in Portugal much later than in Spain and had been far less active, which explains how it was that *marranism* was so much stronger there. As Spinoza pointed out in the seventeenth century, most of the *conversos* in Spain had eventually become sincere Christians, unlike the *marranos* of Portugal, who were averse to becoming assimilated. They took fewer precautions and engaged in imprudent, if not provocative, behaviour, as is shown by two of many incidents that occurred in Madrid. The first, in 1629, concerned an episode known as the affair of the Christ of Patience. Several Portuguese *marranos* were accused of having whipped, then burnt a crucifix. Six of them were found guilty and perished at the stake after an auto da fé celebrated in Madrid, in the Plaza Mayor, in the presence of Philip IV. Four years later, on 2 July 1633, also in Madrid, posters written in Portuguese were discovered; they declared that the Hebraic religion was superior to Catholicism. In reaction, Quevedo composed his anti-Jewish pamphlet entitled *Execración contra los judíos*. Those were but two of the more spectacular incidents of blatant *marranism*. The Inquisition was regalvanised into action. Although its courts were less severe than those of the late fifteenth century, many death sentences were passed against Portuguese *marranos*, particularly after the count-duke of Olivares fell from power in 1643.

The persecution of *marranos* of Portuguese origin continued in the second half of the seventeenth century and beyond. The accession of the Bourbons affected it hardly at all. Detailed studies have been made of the courts of Logroño, Llerena and Valladolid.[3] In these three districts, as elsewhere in the country, fewer charges were laid against Judaisers during the War of Succession and the sentences passed on them were less harsh: fines, domicile bans or, in a few instances only, an obligation to wear the *sambenito* (penitential tunic) or a prison sentence. This relative leniency may be explained by the political circumstances: for one thing, the war hampered the inquisitors in their enquiries; furthermore, Philip V's entourage protected the wealthy Judaisers who had opposed the archduke of Austria.

In 1714, the figures who had up until then been the most influential in Spanish politics – the Orsini princess, Orry and Macanaz – fell from power. The king's new wife, Isabella Farnese, drew close to the Jesuits and the Inquisition. The *marranos* suffered from this change in the situation. Between 1720 and 1725, at least ninety individuals were burnt at the stake. People were no longer accustomed to so many death sentences. Antonio Domínguez Ortiz has noted that between 1718 and 1730 thirty-six death sentences were passed and followed by executions in Granada, fourteen in Seville and seventeen in Cordova, quite apart from all the minor sentences. He also cites the case of two doctors, Juan Muñoz Peralta and Diego Mateo Zapata, both of whom attended Philip V. In 1724 they were both denounced as Judaisers. As no proof could be found to support the accusation, Zapata, the founder of the Seville Society of Medicine, was acquitted, but was nevertheless disgraced; his colleague received a one-year prison sentence.[4] In Extremadura the scene was similar. On 30 November 1719, fourteen Judaisers appeared in an auto da fé held in Badajoz; one woman was released in effigy but the rest had their possessions confiscated and were sentenced either to wear the *sambenito* or to prison. In 1727, two living individuals and two in effigy were sentenced to death. On the second Sunday in May 1721, a man and a woman were burnt alive in Madrid while sixteen other detainees were sentenced to reconciliation. In the course of the same period, the Valladolid court tried 348 similar cases. It pronounced seven acquittals, fifty-two abjurations, 247 reconciliations and forty-two death sentences, thirty-five of which were carried out. Here too, most of those convicted were either Portuguese or of Portuguese origin. They were from Portugal's border dioceses (Zamora,

Salamanca. Astorga) and belonged to the second generation of the Portuguese who had come to Castile in the seventeenth century. Most were poor people – artisans, small shopkeepers and so on. In Logroño at least 320 arrests were made between 1712 and 1746. Most of the accused were sentenced to reconciliation, but in 1719 one was condemned to death and executed. Most of those convicted were foreign to the region – Portuguese who were passing through, trying to make their way abroad. All those found guilty were circumcised. Many were subjected to torture and the court pronounced not a single acquittal. It imposed a variety of penalties – mostly confiscations, *sambenitos*, domicile bans, imprisonment – but also passed three death sentences: two were carried out in effigy, but one, in 1719, that of Lorenzo González, was carried out for real. Despite being subjected to five years' imprisonment and torture as well as to heavy pressure, he had refused to repent. However, upon arrival at the place of execution, where the pyre had just been lit, Lorenzo González was struck by fear. He declared that he wished to die as a Christian and asked to make his confession. The executioner then garrotted him before consigning his body to the flames.

After 1730, fewer Judaisers were arrested. The Inquisition did still detain *conversos* sometimes, but it did not condemn them to death. One example is provided by the case of Lorenzo Beltrán, which has been studied by Julio Caro Baroja. This cobbler, a native of Arjona, had been arrested and detained for an infraction of common law. Along with the other detainees, he attended the prison Sunday mass. He took communion, but immediately spat out the host. When asked why he did so, he replied that he was a Jew. He was sentenced to 200 lashes, one month in prison, four years of forced labour, and a four-year domicile ban.[5] At the beginning of the century his sentence would certainly have been much harsher, perhaps even death at the stake.

Up until about 1750, a residual crypto-Judaism continued to be detectable in Spain, as is confirmed by the number of *conversos* who, as soon as they managed to flee and settle abroad, hastened to integrate themselves in Jewish communities there. In Bordeaux, for instance, most of the 'new Christians of the Portuguese nation' who reverted to Judaism when they arrived in France in the eighteenth century came from Braganza or Lisbon, but some had spent more or less protracted periods of time in Spain from which they had then fled, knowing that they were threatened by the latest wave of inquisitorial repression.[6] The Mexican monk Servando Teresa de Mier reports in his memoirs that in 1801, still, there were in Bayonne a number of Spanish Jews who had recently had themselves circumcised.[7] In the second half of the eighteenth century, however, everything changed. By then the Inquisition could be considered to have completed the mission for which it had been created, namely the eradication of Judaism in Spain. The Inquisition even came round to the view that there was no longer any point in prohibiting total or partial vernacular translations of the Bible. In the sixteenth century it had been thought that Judaisers might find encouragement for the perpetuation of their faith in such translations; but since there were now no Judaisers, why should those old prohibitions still be maintained? Times change, as Grand Inquisitor Beltrán recognised in 1782, in justification of his decree liberalising the rules applying to translations. In 1785 translations of Proverbs, the Gospels, and the Epistles of Saint Paul, appeared, to be followed in 1786 by Ecclesiastes, and in 1789 by the Psalms, The Book of Wisdom and Ecclesiasticus, and in 1798 by the Song of Songs (the cause of so many of the troubles of Fray Luis de León). In 1801 the Psalms appeared in the translation of Fray Luis de Granada.

It was not the case that hatred of the Jews had disappeared, but it no longer had any real object. In some regions and in some circles, the tendency was now to confuse Jews, Protestants, freemasons, atheists and free-thinkers. At the end of the eighteenth century there was a song in which Olavide, the man of the Enlightenment, was accused of every heresy imaginable: 'Olavide is a Lutheran, / a freemason, an atheist, / he is a pagan, a Calvinist, a Jew and an Aryan ...'. One may smile at incoherent amalgamations of this kind, but it is worth remembering that not so long ago General Franco still regarded 'the Judeo-Masonic conspiracy' as the source of all the misfortunes by which Spain was beset.

The chuetas of Majorca

The hounding of Judaisers of Portuguese origin indirectly brought about the disappearance of Spanish *marranos* who, up until this point, had more or less managed to survive. The best-known case is that of the *chuetas* of Majorca. The name is believed to be a diminutive of *jueu*, 'Jew' in Majorcan. In theory, the Jews of Majorca had all converted in 1435, well before the creation of the Inquisition. In truth, however, for two centuries they had led a double life. Publicly they professed Catholicism, attended services and received the sacraments, while in the privacy of their own homes they tried to observe the essentials of Judaism, abstaining from eating pork and managing to observe the sabbath and the festivals of Purim and Yom Kippur, without drawing attention to themselves. The *chuetas* took all kinds of precaution, especially that of marrying among themselves. The Old Christians suspected something was afoot, as did the inquisitors, but they turned a blind eye, no doubt because they did not realise that the *marranism* of the *chuetas* was so extreme. In 1672, the Council of the Inquisition, the *Suprema*, called the Palma court to order, for it seemed hardly active at all. The local inquisitors then opened a routine inquiry that resulted in the arrests of a number of Judaisers. These confessed to the most undeniable and most anodine facts, pleading ignorance, protested their good faith and promised to mend their ways. The Inquisition believed in their sincerity. The five autos da fé held in 1679 produced not a single death sentence. The *chuetas* had saved their skins, but they were ruined by confiscations and fines. They were consumed by anxiety: further charges against them would be fatal, as they would be considered to have relapsed. They would have liked to live like anyone else, with nothing to hide, and so considered becoming sincere Christians. One actually took that step. He married a Christian woman. But his friends forthwith rejected him, calling him a renegade. Eventually he could bear it no longer. He sought out a Jesuit and told him what went on in the homes of the *chuetas*. On the basis of his information, the Inquisition pressed new charges. Between 1688 and 1691, the Holy Office made 150 arrests. In 1690, thirty-seven of those arrested were sentenced to death.[8]

The Moriscos

In medieval Spain, a second religious minority was to be found alongside the Jews: the Muslims, known as Mudejars, who likewise enjoyed a status that guaranteed them the freedom to practise their own cult. Between 1502 and 1526, these Mudejars were forced to convert to Catholicism; they were now known as Moriscos. The expulsion of the Jews had taken place at an early date and *conversos* had very soon become the victims of the Inquisition. But where the Moriscos were concerned, Spain for a long while hesitated and the Inquisition acted less harshly. That was because the Moriscos lived on the margins of Christian society rather than intermingled with it, as the Jews did. They posed a problem that was more social than religious.

When Granada was captured, the Catholic sovereigns had not sought to convert the Muslims. They hoped they would eventually become Christian, but had no plans to force them to do so. They were counting on the evangelisation of the first archbishop, Friar Hernando de Talavera, and were anxious not to act hastily and meanwhile to resort only to peaceful methods. But perhaps it was felt that the hoped-for conversions were too long in coming. In 1499, Cardinal Cisneros was ordered to speed things up. The Muslims felt that the promises they had been given were being broken, and revolted. This, in 1502, provided the sovereigns with a pretext to oblige all Muslims in the kingdom of Castile to convert. In 1520–22, the Muslims were caught up in the revolt of the Germanías in Valencia, when the Old Christian populace attacked them as allies of the feudal lords, forcing baptism upon them. In consequence their status was altered. In conformity with canon law, this conversion was declared valid: even when administered by force, baptism created an irreversible situation; there could be no going back. The Muslims of Valencia were condemned to remain Christian whether they liked it or not. The next step was taken in 1526, when it was decided to force conversion upon the Muslims of the kingdom of Aragon. Thereafter, officially there were no Muslims in Spain. The reality was otherwise, however, and nobody was fooled. The Moriscos remained what they had always been: Muslims. As for the Catholic sovereigns, they realised that the newly converted Moriscos would never be Christians, but hoped that their children and grandchildren would be. To hasten that assimilation, the Moriscos were required to give up their festivals, their traditional clothing and their use of the Arabic language; but no coercive measures were taken. The Inquisition, established in Granada in 1526, was ordered to act benevolently. Likewise, in Valencia: in 1524, a circular from the grand inquisitor recommended that the Moriscos be left alone unless their manifestations of Islam became too blatant.

In the second half of the sixteenth century, the Holy Office acted with greater severity, but far fewer Moriscos than *conversos* were sentenced. The death sentence was seldom passed. Between 1550 and 1580, in Granada, only fourteen were sent to the stake, and six of those were condemned for having taken part in the 1569 rebellion. The most frequently imposed penalty was 'reconciliation', accompanied by the confiscation of property. Between 1530 and 1609, in Valencia, over 5,000 individuals were charged, most of them Moriscos. But few received the death sentence. They were accused of conspiring with the pirates of Algiers or of having preached of

Islam. Political conspiracy and religious proselytism were regarded as the most serious crimes that Moriscos could commit.

The problem posed by the Moriscos was more acute in some places than in others. It all depended upon their density within the local population; and that, in turn, depended upon the vicissitudes of the Reconquest. For the most part, the Reconquest had been accompanied or followed by the emigration or expulsion of the Muslims. In the Niebla region, reconquered in 1262, for example, no Muslims at all remained. The documents record no conversions, so it must be concluded that the original Muslim population had been obliged to leave. A similar situation recurred a century later, at the time of the Reconquest of the Guadalquivir valley: almost all the Muslim inhabitants were expelled. In Andalusia, now Christian again, the Mudejars represented barely 0.5 per cent of the population. In the sixteenth century Moriscos were few in number generally, scattered among small urban communities where they were gradually being assimilated. Externally, there was nothing to distinguish them from the Old Christians, except in three zones: Aragon, Valencia and Granada. In the first two, the earliest to be reconquered, they led a precarious existence, without leaders to guide or advise them. In Granada, on the other hand, where the Reconquest was much more recent, the Moriscos preserved their religious and social elites. Everywhere, they were placed under the domination of local lords who exploited them but also protected them against harassment from the administration, insofar as they represented a workforce that was hardworking, docile and efficient. This explains how it was that Islam was able to survive in sixteenth-century Spain. Of course, the religious practices of the Muslims were confined to a few simple expressions: they refrained from eating pork and from drinking wine, recited the prayers of the Koran, and observed Ramadan and the major religious festivals. Meanwhile Arabic books continued to circulate, despite the vigilance of the Inquisition. Officially the Moriscos were Christians, but in reality they were Muslims.

Few efforts were made to integrate the Moriscos. In 1559, in Granada, Archbishop Pedro Guerrero entrusted the Jesuits with the running of an elementary school set up in the heart of the Moorish quarter, the Albaicín. Here, the children were taught to read and write and to say a few prayers. In 1568, this establishment catered for 300 pupils, but only one third of them were Moriscos, for Morisco parents would withdraw their children as soon as they were old enough to work, that is to say at the age of eight or nine. Juan de Albotodo, a Morisco turned Jesuit, devoted himself to the evangelisation of his brothers. A few other Jesuits tried to preach in Arabic but were soon discouraged by the passivity of their audiences. The Jesuits also carried out missionary work in two other Morisco zones, Aragon and Valencia. In the latter region, the efforts of the Duke of Gandia, Francisco de Borja, were particularly noteworthy. He opened a college intended to receive young Moriscos. When the duke entered the Jesuit order, he passed his college over to the Society of Jesus, but the results proved disappointing: in 1554–5 all twelve places reserved for Moriscos were vacant. Saint Tomás de Villanueva, archbishop of Valencia from 1544 to 1555, was less ambitious. In anticipation of Pascal's *'abêtissez-vous'* (be mindless), he suggested that if the Moriscos were obliged to follow the outward practices of Christianity, the rest would follow naturally. His successor Juan de Ribera was more demanding. He held everything Arabic in horror, so forbade his clergy to learn Arabic. But many Moriscos understood no Spanish. It should be added that, in regions inhabited by Moriscos, the parishes were even more neglected than those of the Christian countryside: parish priests were few and far between, for the most part uneducated, and the churches were left to disintegrate. Hapsburg Spain has often been criticised for making no effort to evangelise and thereby assimilate the Moriscos, but the Old Christians who dwelt in Christian zones were hardly better treated. Most received no religious instruction. However, they were nevertheless considered good Christians, whereas the Moriscos were set apart from the rest of the population by everything: their language, their daily customs, their culinary practices (they cooked with oil, not lard), and so on. In the eyes of the Old Christians all these peculiarities could be put down to the Muslim religion, all being manifestations of Mohammedanism. In truth, what opposed the Old Christians and the Moriscos was not religion, but their respective civilisations and lifestyles.

In 1556, the Council of Castile decided to apply the measures of the 1526 edict, which had until then remained a dead letter. Moriscos were now forbidden to speak Arabic, to celebrate their traditional festivals, to use public baths, and to wear specified garments. The women were no longer allowed to be veiled. The Moriscos appointed a representative to negotiate with the authorities. Francisco Núñez Muley argued that clothing had nothing to do with religion; every region in Spain had its own traditional costumes; why not consider those of the Moriscos simply as peculiar to the province of Granada? But Philip II would not hear of it. The decisions of the Council must be applied without delay. This could not have come at a worse time. For several years the authorities had been harassing the Moriscos in more and more ways: charges were laid against petty felons who believed they had been amnestied, and these now took to the maquis and swelled the ranks of the outlaw bands that roamed the mountains; peasants were ordered to produce title-deeds for the land that they farmed, but many were unable to and found themselves expropriated; the taxation on silk-producers was increased and at the same time, around 1566, the price of silk slumped. In these circumstances, the measures decided by the Council of Castile were the last straw. On Christmas Day 1568, agitators tried to stir up the Albaicín, the Moorish quarter of Granada. The marquis of Mondéjar, viceroy of Granada, managed to put down this uprising, but the revolt spread to rural zones and the Alpujarras mountains. The rebels were said to intend to reconstitute the emirate of Granada and appeal to the Turks for help. Philip II charged his half-brother Don Juan of Austria with crushing the revolt by any means possible. After three years of campaigning, the army finally defeated the last remaining fighters. To avoid another insurrection and to facilitate assimilation, Philip II ordered the Moriscos to be deported and scattered throughout Castile.

The Old Christian masses saw the Moriscos as competition on the labour market, people who were responsible for lowering rents and wages and, on top of that, they accused them of being bad Christians. Many Moriscos spoke no Spanish, which further marginalised them. The rift between the Old Christians and the Moriscos deepened daily. In the 1580s, the State authorities tended to regard the Moriscos as a kind of fifth column, enemies within, ready to ally themselves with the Turks or the Protestants of Béarn. How could the problem be resolved? The most extreme solutions were envisaged: castration, deportation to the New World and so on. The idea of expulsion gained ground, but Philip II was still against it. It was his weak successor Philip III who, upon advice from the duke of Lerma, took this decision, despite the objections of many theologians. These pointed out that theoretically the Moriscos were Christians, so to expel them would be tantamount to forcing them into apostasy – a point of view that the authorities of the Holy Office also adopted. In 1492, it had been the grand inquisitor, Torquemada, who had recommended expelling the Jews. But in 1609, the Inquisition was hostile to applying such a measure to the Moriscos whom it persisted in regarding as Christians since they had been baptised. The archbishop of Valencia, Juan de Ribera, did not agree: they should be called not Moriscos, but authentic Moors. Lerma too was determined to have done with the matter. The truce that Spain had just signed with the Dutch rebels afforded him a certain respite at this point and presented him with the means to act. The expulsion decree was signed on 9 April 1609, but the decision was not made public until 20 August. Unlike the Jews in 1492, the Moriscos were allowed to take with them all the possessions that they could carry. It is hard to say how many Moriscos were expelled. The most credible estimates mention 300,000 departures, that is to say less than 5 per cent of the total population of Spain. The regions most affected were Valencia (at least 120,000 departures) and Aragon (just over 60,000). Some went to France, where they met with a more or less hostile reception. Forty thousand went to Morocco, where they were also badly received, on the grounds that they were Christians! Those who fared best were the Valencians who settled in Tunisia – maybe 50,000 to 80,000 of them.

Spain's Semitic heritage

The manifestations of the Spaniards' attitude to the Jews and the Muslims and their more or less sincerely converted descendants differed. But they were all part of a movement that affected the Christian elite groups as well as the masses. It involved the rejection of all reminders of the long presence of Semites in the Iberian peninsula and a desire to efface all traces of their influence. Today, our contemporaries are sensitive to the brilliance of the Arab civilisation in Spain, the flowering of the arts, the wide intellectual and scientific influence of the Caliphate of Cordova – in short the great wealth that this cultural cross-fertilisation could bring to those who were in contact with the Muslims, that is to say both the Christians and the Jews. In the Middle Ages and even still in the Modern Age, Christian Europe saw things differently: the Saracens and their co-religionaries, the Moors of Spain, were implacable enemies, infidels who had seized the Holy Places, North Africa and, most recently, Constantinople. They were also despots who tolerated no intermediate body between the Grand Turk and subjects who were no more than slaves; they were barbarians and said to be cruel and depraved. Nor did the Jews deserve any more consideration: they were responsible for the death of Christ and were accused of oppressing the poor. In the eyes of Europeans, Spain was thus suspect since, for 700 years, Muslims and Jews – all of them Semites – had lived there alongside

Christians and must have perverted them to some degree, infecting them with their doctrines and customs.

Fifteenth-century German travellers, noting the large numbers of Jews, *marranos* and Moors in Spain, and all that was of oriental origin in the customs, music and so on, were astonished and scandalised. In his *Table Talk*, Luther presents the Spaniards as faithless Jews and baptised Moors. Erasmus, the prince of Humanists, was equally hostile. '*Non placet Hispania*,' he wrote to Thomas More around 10 July 1517, after being invited by Cardinal Cisneros to collaborate on a polyglot edition of the Bible: why should he go to a country where it was hard to find a proper Christian?[9] In Italy, perhaps because a Spanish presence was solidly established there, the reputation of the Iberian peninsula was even worse. Italians vituperated against the eastern influences among the Spaniards: for example, their guttural way of speaking, their clothes, their games, their riding style, their cooking. When, in 1527, an imperial army, for the most part composed of German foot-soldiers and Italian mercenaries, sacked the city of Rome, it was the army's Spanish *marranos* that the Italians blamed for this outrage. Pope Paul IV, elected in May 1555, poured abuse upon the Spaniards, calling them nothing but heretics, schismatics accursed by God, the spawn of Jews and Moors, the very dregs of the world, and he deplored the plight of Italy, reduced to serving such an abject nation. At the height of the Flanders War, William of Orange echoed such sentiments in his *Apologia*: 'I should not be surprised if the general belief is true, namely that the majority of Spaniards, in particular those who consider themselves aristocrats, belong to the race of Moors and Jews.' In the seventeenth century, in France, de Thou, speaking of the 1569 Alpujarras War, accused the Spaniards of having sodomised those whom they conquered, such behaviour being explained by the fact that they had themselves been infected by their long contact with the Moors.

Today, many people think of Spain as a nation so attached to Catholicism that it did not hesitate to punish those who strayed from the true faith with the utmost severity. But in the sixteenth century, Europeans held quite the contrary view: the reason why it had seemed necessary to create such a terrible inquisition was the need to convince the Spaniards to remain faithful to Catholicism. That is certainly the view expressed by Quirini in 1506 and repeated by Guiciardini in 1513: Spain was so full of Jews and heretics that, unless care was taken, it would soon cease to be a Catholic nation. In Italy, people spoke ironically of the *peccadiglio di Spagna*, when referring to those who rejected the dogma of the Holy Trinity, thereby espousing the views of Semites – Muslims and Jews – all of whom were anti-Trinitarians. In this connection, it is perhaps worth noting the Iberian origins of Miguel Servet, the author of a little book on *The Errors of the Trinity* (he was a native of Aragon). The feeling that the peninsula was deeply steeped in eastern values was, paradoxically, reinforced by the precautions that it was felt necessary to take in order to get rid of them. Grand Inquisitor Cardinal Niño de Guevara testified to this in the early seventeenth century. On the strength of his experience as a former ambassador of the Holy See, he was in favour of doing away with the discrimination that afflicted the descendants of Jews and Moors. Such measures greatly harmed Spain's reputation abroad. All Christian nations included faithful who were of Jewish origin, but they were careful not to draw attention to this, whereas Spain's excessive zeal simply rebounded against it. Because it believed itself obliged to take such precautions, it was regarded throughout Europe as a country infected by Judaism.

This argument deserves further consideration. Among the reasons that persuaded the Catholic sovereigns, as soon as the Reconquest was accomplished, to take action against the Judaisers and to expel the Jews and then take similar measures against the Muslims and their descendants, must have been the unease of a Spain that had long remained on the margins of Christianity and that now desired to be fully integrated as soon as possible. Of course, this involved eliminating all Semitic influences in the domain of religion, but it was felt that the elimination should also apply to cultural, and even daily life. What was needed was to close the parenthesis opened by the Arab invasion and return to the point where history had been interrupted in 711. Descent from the Goths was enough to stamp a gentleman with all the marks of nobility. To have originated in Asturias, the mountains of Santander or the Basque provinces, that is to say regions that had not been occupied by the Moors or that had soon ejected them, was no less honourable. But anything that recalled the Muslim period was stamped with discredit, and this feeling was particularly strong in Andalusia. The chroniclers of the sixteenth and seventeenth centuries (Juan de la Cueva, Juan de Mal Lara, Luis de Peraza and so on) portrayed Seville, the most famous town in Spain, as the *caput Hispaniae*, but also as the town founded either by Heracles or by Julius Caesar which was, consequently, unsullied by all Muslim influence. The glorious present could in this way link up with the ancient past. From this point of view, the construction of an avenue, the Alameda, inaugurated in 1574, is significant. It was bordered with poplar and orange trees and adorned with two columns topped, respectively, with statues of Heracles and Julius Caesar that had been salvaged from the Roman ruins of the Street of Marbles. It was the modern town's way of connecting to a glorious past and the old Hispalis.

The desire to return to classicism and ancient Rome was affirmed in architecture. When, in 1487, Cardinal Mendoza had the idea of building the College of Santa Cruz in Valladolid, his nephew, Iñigo López de Mendoza, recently back from Rome, immediately suggested adopting a Renaissance style, a style *a lo romano*. 'Do not introduce anything that comes from France, Germany, or the Moors; everything must be Roman,' he advised. The success of Vitruvius's *De Architectura* confirmed this return to the style of antiquity. In 1526, Diego de Sagredo translated it into Spanish (*Medidas del Romano*). The aesthetics of the Escorial, imposed by Philip II, represent the peak of this tendency. The Escorial was built in reaction against the excesses of the 'Mudejar' and 'Plateresque' style, and also testified to a profound disgust with medieval barbarism. No sooner does one cross the threshold, the chronicler Siguenza tells us, than one has an impression of majesty and grandeur, things that are rare in the monuments of Spain which for so many centuries was subjected to the barbarity and crudeness of the Arabs. Those invaders did little to accustom the people to the beauties of architecture.

In the face of such a hostile attitude to Spain's Muslim past, what was known as 'maurophilia' now focused exclusively upon an aristocratic mode of Moorish civilisation. The epic and chivalric atmosphere of the last years of Muslim Granada were idealised. A passion for a mixture of history and legend was long to delight cultivated Europe, right down to the Romantics and even beyond, as is testified by Chateaubriand (*The Last of the Abencerrajes*) and, closer to our own times, Aragon's *Le Fou d'Elsa*. However, such Romanticism should not mislead us. Those passionately moved by reading such stories were full of scorn for the descendants of the Moors, the Moriscos, and for everything that they represented.

The Jews of Andalusia were said to have a bad smell – *hediondos judíos* – as the chronicler Bernáldez put it at the end of the fifteenth century. He thought that it was olive oil that tainted their breath. The Old Christians, who originated from the central Meseta and had repopulated the Guadalquivir valley in the thirteenth century after most of the Muslims had been ejected, cooked with lard and detested olive oil, the use of which did not become general until very late, possibly the eighteenth century, in this region. To be considered good Christians, the *conversos* and the Moriscos would have had to give up not only their religions but also the eating and other habits that they had acquired in their earliest childhoods. And it is easier to change religious – or political – opinions than tastes and lifestyle. Bernáldez was well aware of this: to require a person to give up ancestral customs is, in a way, to deal him a death blow (*mudar costumbre es a par de muerte*). He, along with most Old Christians, nevertheless continued to confuse faith and cultural practices that were foreign to him.

𝔅lood purity

In truth, in the Spain of the Ancien Régime, the distinction between Old and New Christians was not so much religious as sociological, as can be seen from the development of what came to be called blood purity.

Blood purity was what attested a family's Catholic orthodoxy: a heretical ancestry implied tainted blood. In sixteenth-century Spain, a distinction was drawn between two kinds of faithful: on the one hand, those who had been born into a family that had always been Christian; on the other, all the rest, the descendants of converts, whether Jewish or Muslim. In concrete terms, the insistence on blood purity took the form of rules written into the statutes of a number of fraternities, associations, religious orders, military orders and diocesan chapters. Every postulant had to submit to a preliminary inquiry designed to prove that none of his ancestors, however far back, had belonged to an infamous 'race'.

But those statutes were not as widespread as is sometimes claimed. They were a feature of most of the *colegios mayores* (prestigious schools that functioned alongside the universities), of military and religious orders (the Jesuits resisted them for a long time, but eventually gave in), and of many, though not all, diocesan chapters. Domínguez Ortiz believes it fair to say that only one third of the diocesan chapters of Spain possessed statutes relating to blood purity.[10] Even where such statutes did exist, they were not applied systematically. Practice was a far cry from theory. In order to prove blood purity, all you had to do was choose your witnesses carefully, then solicit and maybe even bribe them.

Right from the start, the principle of blood purity had been denounced by numerous theologians, and as time passed this hostile trend became increasingly widespread. The theological criticisms (no distinctions ought to be made between those who had been baptised) were amplified by others based on common sense: how could anyone believe that the descendants of Jews who had converted in the fifteenth century still preserved traces of Judaism three, four or five generations on? Between 1580 and the downfall of the count-duke of Olivares in 1643, considerations such as these persuaded the highest State authorities to envisage not suppressing the Statutes (prejudice was too strong for that), but at least limiting their abuse and effects by banning genealogical investigations more than 100 years into the past, that is to say beyond three generations. The 1600 Cortes addressed the problem. A majority of deputies sought to reform the statutes on blood purity, but without success. However, the opponents of the statutes did not give up. In the 1618 Cortes, one deputy returned to the offensive, crying that it was a shocking thing to have the honour of a family depend on the allegations of three or four witnesses who had heard rumours that so and so, on his grandfather's or grandmother's side, was more or less strongly suspected of having Jewish origins. And he went on to observe that in these days, in Spain, to be regarded as of noble or pure blood, you needed either to have no enemies or to be rich enough to buy false witnesses, or else to be of such obscure origin that no one knew where you had come from; if you were completely unknown, you could pass for an Old Christian. All in vain, however. Blood purity continued to be a prerequisite for access to distinctions of many kinds.

The fact is that blood purity was not primarily a religious concept. The notion was of a sociological nature. The first thing to note is that discrimination seldom affected professional activities that presupposed particular skills in some domain or other. That is why sovereigns, administrative bodies, universities, guilds and religious orders – even those with statutes – had no qualms at all about recruiting New Christians and availing themselves of their services. But it was quite a different matter when it came to honorific positions that conferred social prestige upon their incumbents, even when those positions offered no financial or material advantages. In those cases, blood purity operated as an extra filter against the increasing numbers of individuals who aspired to honours and social consideration. The most significant example is provided by the military orders: to become a knight of Santiago was the dream of many sons of good family. They would put themselves forward on the strength of the services that they or their parents had rendered the State. However, competition was stiff. The insistence on blood purity was a means of disqualifying certain candidates and reserving honorific distinctions for a minority of privileged individuals.

In late sixteenth-century Spain, blood purity functioned as a weapon wielded by the mass of Old Christians, a weapon all the more powerful given that no tangible proof was necessary to discredit a candidate; mere insinuation sufficed. Blood purity meant revenge for petty men, nobility for those who had no other claim to it. Anyone can buy a title, they would say; it is harder to buy ancestors. Millions of peasants and artisans communed together in the exaltation of blood purity, a demagogic sentiment that inevitably led to a levelling down. It was also, as we shall see, a logic dear to the Inquisition, which relied on the egalitarian sentiments of the Old Christian populace to encourage it to denounce all talk, attitudes and behaviour of a non-conformist nature.

2   Defending the faith

The Inquisition was created to punish converted Jews who reverted to their former religion. The repression of the years 1480 to 1500 seems to have achieved its objective. By the beginning of the sixteenth century, fewer and fewer Judaisers were to be found. In those circumstances, was it really necessary to prolong the existence of the Holy Office and turn it into a permanent court? A number of indications suggest that its initiators had had in mind an inquisition that would not be permanent and was intended to fight not heresy in general, but one particular form of it, the heresy of Judaisers. As we have seen, even that was something that shocked men such as Talavera and Pulgar. At the very point when the above question arose, more and more people were criticising the methods and abuses of the inquisitors. The opponents of the Inquisition were to exploit this situation and try to persuade the political authorities to suppress a jurisdiction that appeared to have had its day and was now attracting disapproval from part of the population.

The Lucero affair

The Lucero affair burst upon the scene at a time when the throne of Castile was trying to cope with a difficult political situation, following the death of Queen Isabella (1504) and the clash between her husband, Ferdinand of Aragon, and her children, in particular her daughter Joanna, who was married to Philip the Handsome. Diego Rodríguez Lucero had been appointed inquisitor of Cordova on 7 September 1499. He arrived in a town racked by millenarian tendencies fomented by the rantings of a member of the municipality, Juan of Cordova, who was at the centre of judaising activities. Convinced that the end of the world was nigh, *conversos* were apparently not only continuing to judaise, but going so far as to profane communion hosts and crucifixes. There was talk of clandestine synagogues where prominent members of society would congregate. Lucero arrested many leading figures in Cordovan society. The arrests were followed by death sentences – probably as many as 120 between December 1504 and May 1506, then another 100 in June 1506. Lucero did not hesitate to pass prison sentences on the sister and nephews of the archbishop of Granada, Hernando de Talavera, who had been one of Queen Isabella's confidants and also her confessor. Even Talavera himself was under threat.

The death of Philip the Handsome, in September 1506, encouraged the malcontents to make a move. The marquis of Priego launched his armed forces against the Inquisition's prison, liberated the prisoners, and arrested the procurator. Lucero managed to flee. The canons, the municipality and the nobility – the marquis of Priego and the count of Cabra – all denounced the excesses, corruption and abuses of the inquisitor. The king of Aragon, who in 1507 turned his attention to the affair, declared Grand Inquisitor Deza responsible for the situation. He forced him to resign and, on 5 June 1507, appointed Cardinal Cisneros in his place. The latter ordered the arrest of Lucero (May 1508) and convened a general congregation to investigate and shed light on the whole affair.

The Inquisition confirmed

The scandal produced by the Lucero affair might well have led to the Inquisition being called into question. Some of its opponents hoped that Philip the Handsome's consent to this could be obtained – or bought. But with Philip's death and the return of the king of Aragon who, from 1507 onward, resumed the government of Castile in the name of his daughter, the queen – Joanna the Mad – that possibility disappeared. Ferdinand was far too attached to the institution that, despite all criticisms, he had imposed. At his death in January 1516, the enemies of the Holy Office pinned their hopes on the new king, the future Charles V, trusting that he would do away with the more questionable aspects of the inquisitorial court, for example the secrecy of its procedures. The Cortes of Valladolid (1518) went further. They demanded that the pursuit of heretics be entrusted to civil authorities: this was tantamount to suppression of the Inquisition. The chancellor, 'Wild John', seemed well disposed to the idea. He apparently prepared a pragmatic plan that reiterated the principal demands: inquisitors should be required to consult the civil authorities before making any arrest; they should in future receive a fixed salary instead of being remunerated from confiscations, a practice that encouraged them to multiply their arrests; the accused should have the right to challenge certain judges and freely to choose their own lawyers; the whole procedure should be made public; and those found guilty should be allowed to appeal to the Royal Council or the Holy See.

'Wild John' died on 7 June 1518, before winning approval for his proposal. But the Inquisition's opponents still did not lose heart. A group of *conversos* offered Charles V 400,000 ducats to reinstate his chancellor's plan. They also approached Pope Leo X who, in a brief issued on 20 May 1520, expressed his disquiet at the excesses drawn to his attention: the inquisitors who multiplied verdicts of guilt in order to seize the confiscated possessions of their victims; others who abused the wives and daughters of detainees; yet others who, to strike at personal enemies, charged them with offences that had nothing to do with heresy. However, Cardinal Adrian who, in the absence of Charles V, was soon to take over the government of Castile, was firmly opposed to any reform, partly out of personal conviction and partly because Cardinal Cisneros, before his death, had warned him against the *conversos*. The religious revolution that broke out in Germany at this time also alarmed those in charge. It provided a new justification for the Inquisition. People now looked to it to prevent Luther's heresy from spreading to Spain. This change of policy was not made lightly. Up until 1524 the Inquisition was concerned only with Judaisers. But in that year, it took action for the first time against Illuminists, Erasmists and Lutherans.

Lutheranism and Erasmism in Spain

As early as 12 April 1521, the authorities suspected that certain parties were trying to disseminate Luther's ideas in Spain, using translations of his work that they attempted to smuggle in. Spanish *conversos* who had taken refuge in the Netherlands were believed to have amassed funds for the printing of Luther's works and for sending them to the Iberian peninsula. In 1524, a German merchant by the name of Blay was found guilty in Valencia of importing suspect literature. Bookshops and printing works were now kept under close surveillance. In that same year, a Flemish vessel bound for Valencia was diverted to San Sebastian. In the hold, two barrels stuffed full of Lutheran books were discovered and were there and then sent up in flames, on the beach. In the following year, Venetian ships were discovered attempting to land similar literature on the coasts of the kingdom of Granada. When informed of this, the *corregidor* arrested the crews and seized the cargoes. In 1531 a pedlar was brought to trial for distributing Lutheran books. An Augustine monk from Toulouse, on a pilgrimage to Santiago de Compostela and Guadalupe, purchased one out of curiosity but then, seized by remorse, burnt it. He was nevertheless arrested by the Inquisition and sentenced to recite the seven Penitential Psalms seven times and to attend a mass in honour of the Virgin Mary. In 1542, the inquisitors of Calahorra reported an attempt to import between three and four hundred copies of a book published in Antwerp, entitled *The Institution of the Christian Religion*, by Francisco de Encinas, one of the rare Spanish Protestants (to whom we shall return presently).

Was Lutheran propaganda finding echoes in Spain? In August 1523, a certain Gonzalo de Mejía was denounced to the Inquisition for having agreed with a theory of Luther's that favoured communal property – a thesis that would, in fact, be hard to find in the works of the reformer – but it is true that the same man also approved of the praises that were lavished on the Grand Turk. He was clearly not really a Lutheran. Also in 1523, a painter from the Albacete region was reported to have been arrested in Palma de Majorca, condemned to death, and executed as a Lutheran by the town's inquisitorial court. If the facts are correct, this was Protestantism's first Spanish victim; but Lea expresses doubts about this. It is unlikely that 'Luther's errors' could already have found disciples in the Balearic Islands at this early date and likewise that the local inquisitors could have had any clear understanding of those errors.

Actually, almost all the Lutherans – or those claimed to be Lutheran – charged by the Inquisition in the first half of the sixteenth century were foreigners: for instance, English traders and sailors who put in to San Sebastian in 1539 and were denounced to the Navarre Inquisition for making suspect declarations in the course of a brawl in the harbour. A Spaniard had apparently said that all the English were Lutherans and the English had retorted that their country's religion was better than that practised in Spain: you did not have to fast in order to win salvation, nor did you have to confess your sins to any man, be he priest or monk, but only to God. Six of these Englishmen were put on trial for Lutheranism; some were sentenced to pay small fines or to recant publicly. Only one received a prison sentence. He managed to escape, was recaptured, recanted, and then, on 21 May 1539, was burnt at the stake in Bilbao. But this was probably a case of anti-papism rather than Lutheranism.[1] According to J.-P. Dedieu, nearly all the Lutherans charged in the district of the Toledo Inquisition were foreigners such as a certain Jean of Châlons, a French clockmaker who worked at the court of the marquis of Villena, at Escalona. He was arrested around 1535 because he was criticising monks, indulgences and the papal bull on the crusade, and had expressed doubts as to the existence of hell. The sentences passed on such Lutherans were severe; at least one was condemned to death.

There were rare exceptions, however. A few Spaniards, too, were arrested and tried for Lutheranism. The best-known case is that of Francisco de San Román, who had converted to Lutheranism after a business trip to Antwerp. He was sentenced to death in 1542 and was soon regarded as a martyr to the faith. Most Spaniards who were attracted to Lutheranism at this time judged it prudent to leave the country to escape the Inquisition. This was the course adopted by Miguel Servet, born in Aragon in 1511. He started his studies in Saragossa, continued them in Toulouse, then travelled to Italy and visited a number of towns in Germany, where he met several of the reformers: Melanchthon, Bucer, Oecolampadius, among others. In 1531, he published a little book on *The Errors of the Trinity*, in which he rejected official doctrine. The treatise shocked many – Protestants as well as Catholics – including Calvin himself. On 24 May 1532, the Inquisition ordered his arrest, but as he was living abroad it was not possible to apprehend him. Eventually, on 26 October 1553, Servet was burnt at the stake in Geneva by Calvinists.

The first authentic Spanish Lutheran seems to have been Francisco de Encinas (1518–52), from Burgos. He belonged to a family of merchants with connections all over Europe, a fact that enabled him to travel and to study first in Louvain, then in Wittenberg, where he was attracted by the personality of Melanchthon. In 1540–41, Antwerp saw the publication of his *Una breve y compendiosa institución de la religión cristiana* under the pseudonym Francisco de Elao (*elao* being the Hebrew for *encina* (oak)). This was a translation of Calvin's *Catechism* and Luther's *Treatise on Christian Liberty*. In 1543, still in Antwerp, his translation of the New Testament from the Greek version produced by Erasmus was published – the first complete Spanish translation to appear. At this point he must still have believed in the possibility of a Spain that would tolerate evangelism, since he dedicated his translation to the emperor, but he was soon forced to acknowledge that he was mistaken. He was one of the rare Spaniards to adhere to the Augsburg confession. He died without ever returning to the land of his birth.

In truth, in the first half of the sixteenth century it was not so much Lutheranism, but rather Illuminism or Erasmism that preoccupied the inquisitors. We shall be examining Illuminism presently. For the moment let us concentrate on Erasmus. By 1515 his prestige was already considerable. Cardinal Cisneros had even invited him to the university of Alcala, to work on a multilingual Bible under preparation there. We have already noted Erasmus's reasons for declining. In 1520, numerous Spaniards accompanied the young Charles V to Germany, where he was crowned king of the Romans. Among them were Juan de Vergara and Alfonso de Valdés. The former was professor of philosophy at Alcala. He had collaborated in the publication of the Complutense Bible, for which he translated the Book of Wisdom. While canon of Toledo, he had served as Cardinal Cisnero's secretary. Alfonso de Valdés was a high-ranking official, soon to occupy a very important post as the secretary for Latin correspondence, working for the chancellor, Gattinara. In the Netherlands, these two men met up with a compatriot, Luis Vives, a Valencian who, since 1519, had been a professor at the University of Louvain.[2] Vives was an admirer of Erasmus. From their contact with him, the Spaniards from Charles V's entourage discovered how highly the Humanist from Rotterdam was regarded in northern Europe. When they returned to Spain in 1522, they were to encourage the vogue for Erasmism in the Iberian peninsula.

Marcel Bataillon's great book devoted to this matter, published in 1937, enables us to gain a better understanding of the reasons for the success of Erasmism.[3] The evangelism of Erasmus found a favourable welcome in areas previously prepared by Cardinal Cisneros, who brought to bear on a reform of the clergy and spirituality all the authority conferred upon him by his roles (confessor to Isabella the Catholic queen, archbishop of Toledo, grand inquisitor and twice regent for the kingdom of Castile). Erasmus's reputation as a Humanist won him the respect of university circles, but it was his religious ideas that fascinated the intellectual elite. They were attractive by reason of their measured tone, a far cry from both the intransigence of Rome and the excesses of Luther. In opposition to Rome, Erasmus emphasised the need, indeed the urgency, of a reform of the Church and its religion, which needed to be purged of its dogmatist and formalist aspects: too many theological speculations and routine practices that bordered on superstition. He recommended a return to the Gospel, a more spiritual religion, and an internal cult. In opposition to Luther, he defended free will and endeavoured to preserve the unity of the Christian world. For him, the ideal would have been irenic reconciliation, with neither side the victor or the vanquished – reconciliation that would ensure necessary Church reform but at the same time avoid schism.

His *Enchiridion*, a handbook on a spiritual Christianity, was translated into Spanish as early as 1525. This work delighted some elite groups but its audacity alarmed the regular clergy, for Erasmus spared neither institutions nor doctrines, and called the very status of the religious orders into question. However, at Court, Erasmus had many fervent and unconditional admirers, such as Chancellor Gattinara and his secretary, Alfonso de Valdés. The grand inquisitor, Alfonso Manrique, archbishop of Seville, who was likewise sympathetic to Erasmus's ideas, thought of a way to parry and end the malicious attacks. In the spring of 1527, he convened a commission in Valladolid. It was composed of theologians and representatives of the religious orders and its task was to decide whether or not Erasmus's works constituted a danger to the faith. The commission broke up without adopting any clear position but, though there was no formal approval, Erasmus at least obtained an official letter from the emperor, who guaranteed his orthodoxy. So many translations of his works appeared between 1527 and 1532 that Marcel Bataillon speaks of a veritable 'Erasmian invasion'. Erasmus's influence was proceeding from strength to strength and Spain seemed on the point of adopting him as its master of thought and its guide.

Illuminism

However, Erasmus's opponents had not laid down their arms. They took advantage of the 1525 campaign launched against Illuminist tendencies, to compromise a number of well-known Erasmists and get them condemned by the Inquisition. The fact was that Erasmism was but one of the aspects that religious unease took on in Spain. Here, as in the rest of Europe, ever since the fifteenth century an aspiration towards an inner life of the spirit had been detectable. In its own way, Erasmism reflected that aspiration which, however, had appeared some time earlier and had originally owed Erasmism nothing at all. Nor should this yearning for an inner life be attributed principally to the *conversos*, whom Marcel Bataillon describes as 'people uprooted from Judaism', although it is true that the massive conversions of the fifteenth century and the expulsion decree of 1492 had produced many *conversos* who were seeking to break with the formalism and ritualism characteristic of Judaism. This movement towards a more internal life of the spirit sometimes took forms not at all compatible with traditional Catholic orthodoxy. One form was Illuminism, for the *alumbrados* claimed to abandon themselves to divine inspiration without any controls, and to interpret the Gospel texts altogether freely. They declared that they were moved solely by the love of God, from whom their inspiration stemmed directly. They no longer had any will of their own, for God dictated their conduct, and consequently they could never sin. The *alumbrados* rejected the authority of the Church, its hierarchy and its dogmas, along with all traditional forms of piety in which they perceived constraints (*ataduras*): religious practices (devoutness, charitable good works, etc.), the sacraments and so on. From 1525 on, the Inquisition moved energetically against all such tendencies. The Toledo auto da fé of 1529 checked the first wave of Illuminism in Spain, without, however, passing any death sentnces.

What the *alumbrados* and the Erasmists shared was their rejection of scholasticism and forms of piety that bordered on superstition. But that apart, the two groups had nothing in common. The Erasmists were Humanists schooled in university disciplines and with a developed critical spirit. Inevitably, they were shocked by the excesses of some *alumbrados*, mostly simple folk with no more than an elementary education (*idiotas*, that is to say uneducated or self-taught people). The Erasmists were very different from the *alumbrados* who rejected free will and all personal responsibility and abandoned themselves to free divine inspiration – all notions utterly foreign to Erasmus and his Spanish disciples, who certainly desired an inner religion but an enlightened one, controlled by reason. However, some Erasmists were imprudent and compromised themselves with *alumbrados*. The most typical cases were those of Canon Vergara, his half-brother Bernardino de Tovar, and the brothers Juan and Alfonso de Valdés. Conversely, certain *alumbrados*, when arrested by the Inquisition, declared themselves to be Erasmists – in most cases quite implausibly. What is the explanation for such behaviour, which ended up confusing the issue and misleading not only inquisitors but historians too? The fact is that in the 1520s Erasmus had been the object of no official condemnation in Spain; on the contrary, he enjoyed the protection of the highest State authorities, whereas, from 1525 on, *alumbrados* were being hunted down. It was therefore less dangerous to claim to be a follower of Erasmus than to pass for an *alumbrado*. José C. Nieto calls this 'a screening Erasmism' or 'a masking Erasmism': Erasmus would be invoked so as to avoid far graver accusations and being found guilty of professing Illuminist or – worse still – Lutheran ideas.[4]

This was the line of defence adopted by Juan de Valdés when harassed on account of his *Diálogo de doctrina cristiana* (1529). He owed much to Illuminism, but claiming to be influenced by Erasmus, who was then much in vogue in Alcala, seemed an elegant and clever way to parry the most dangerous attacks against himself. The manoeuvre was successful, and Juan de Valdés got off lightly. He was able to move to Italy where, far from the Inquisition, he proceeded to elaborate religious ideas that would have cost him dear had he remained in Spain. By assuming the mask of Erasmism, Valdés fooled the vigilance of the Inquisition, which did not clearly perceive his links with Illuminism or even suspect how much he owed to Luther. Now, however, all that is quite clear: in his *Diálogo de doctrina cristiana*, Valdés freely adapts passages from Luther, some of which he translates almost word for word.[5]

Vergara and his half-brother Bernardino Tovar were denounced as Illuminists and arrested in 1533. On 21 December 1535, Vergara was sentenced to spend one year in seclusion in a monastery and was fined 1,500 ducats. The Inquisition dismissed the accusation of Lutheranism which, if retained, would have been punished far more severely. Erasmism remained suspect in the eyes of the inquisitors, but was treated relatively leniently up until the death of Fonseca, the archbishop of Toledo, in 1534, and that of Grand Inquisitor Manrique in 1538. It was Manrique who, as archbishop of Seville, recruited for his diocese a number of successful preachers in tune with the new spirituality. One was Doctor Gil, who was considered a fine representative of Christian Humanism. Gil's liberated tone shocked traditionalists. In the pulpit, he frequently commented with irony on the religious practices of the masses and on Church structures; he criticised certain forms of asceticism, and recommended relying in all things upon Jesus Christ. There was, at least at first sight, nothing fundamentally Lutheran in all this, but his cast of mind did disturb the inquisitors. In 1549, Doctor Gil was arrested and in 1552 he appeared in a small auto da fé, where he received a minor sentence. He died in 1555.

The Protestants of Valladolid and Seville

During the first half of the sixteenth century, the Inquisition had encountered Illuminist sects, pseudo-mystics and Erasmists, but not authentic Lutherans (or so it thought), and this explains the moderation of the sentences that it passed. The situation changed abruptly in 1558. In that year, Lutheran groups were discovered in two of Spain's largest towns – Valladolid and Seville. In Seville, precise accusations were brought against members of the clergy – canons, monks and nuns – and against nobles and other members of social elites. Files that had been shelved were reopened. The trial of Doctor Gil, who had died in 1555,[6] was resumed. Canon Constantino de la Fuente, who had succeeded him, was arrested. In Valladolid, those implicated included Agustín Cazalla, the canon of Salamanca and chaplain and preacher to Charles V, along with other members of his family, monks, aristocrats and highly placed officials such as the Italian Carlos de Seso, the *corregidor* of Toro, who was arrested just as he was about to cross into France. A blast of hysteria struck Castile. Suspects filled the prisons, where there was soon no room for newcomers. Nor were there enough inquisitors to conduct the trials. Others had to be brought in from Cuenca and Murcia. There were even plans to draft in magistrates from the Royal Council and the Chancellery. It proved necessary to provide special protection for the detainees, to prevent them being lynched by the infuriated populace. In his retreat in Yuste, Charles V was horrified. He pressed the regent queen, his daughter Joanna (Philip was still in the Netherlands) to act with the utmost rigour: the arrested must be treated, not as heretics, but as rebels who threatened the security of the State.

The first auto da fé took place on 21 May 1559, in Valladolid.

Fourteen of the accused were condemned to death. They included Agustín Cazalla, his brother Francisco de Vivero, a parish priest in the diocese of Zamora, and his sister Beatriz de Vivero. Even the mother of the Cazalla brothers, Leonor de Vivero, who was dead, did not escape dishonour: her corpse was exhumed and burnt in effigy. All the condemned were strangled before being taken to the stake, except for one, Antonio Herreruelo, a qualified lawyer from Toro, who refused to acknowledge his errors and paid in this this way for his obstinacy. On 24 September, over 100 individuals were sentenced in Seville; twenty-one received the death penalty. Among them was a son of the count of Bailén, first cousin to the duke of Arcos. Here too, one man was burnt alive for having remained true to his convictions to the end. On 8 October, Philip II presided over the second auto da fé of Valladolid in the course of which fourteen individuals were sentenced to death, among them Carlos de Seso, who was burnt alive for persisting in his errors. Then, on 22 December 1560, another auto da fé took place in Seville: seventeen of the accused were sent to the stake, three of them in effigy, one of whom was Doctor Constantino Ponce de la Fuente, who had died in prison (possibly a suicide). Two years later, in 1562, the remains of Dr Gil were exhumed and burnt.

Were these people really Protestants? In the mid twentieth century some historians wondered whether they were not rather clerics and laymen who had been won over by Erasmus's writings to the cause of spiritual Christianity and whom inquisitors, insensitive to such nuances, wrongly identified as Lutherans. But today, no doubt remains: the victims of the autos da fé of 1559–60 were indeed Lutherans. At the time of these events, sympathisers with the Reformation made no mistake about it.[7] It was after the autos da fé of Valladolid and Seville that the campaigns against the Spanish Inquisition started. The thousands of Judaisers executed at the end of the fifteenth century had not been enough to move an intellectual Europe inclined to anti-semitism. But the few dozen Lutherans burnt at the stake in 1559 gave rise to a movement of sympathy and solidarity among their brothers in religion. Pamphlets attacking the Spanish Inquisition now appeared in northern Europe, many of them signed by Spanish Protestants who had fled their country.[8] The arrest and trial of Doctor Gil in Seville, in 1549–52, had alarmed a number of his fellows there, who had judged it prudent to flee, first to Paris, then on to the Netherlands. In 1555, others had fled to Geneva. In 1557, twelve Hieronymite monks from Seville, assiduous readers of Luther and Melanchthon, had also settled in Geneva. They included figures such as Antonio del Corro, Cipriano de Valera, and Casiodoro de Reina. Almost all of them were burnt in effigy in 1562. The most representative was probably Casiodoro de Reina who, when in exile, always signed himself 'the Sevillian *Hispalensis*'. He died on 15 March 1594.

Without a doubt, the victims of the Inquisition in 1559–60 were Lutherans. That wave of persecution put paid definitively to Protestantism in the Iberian peninsula. After 1560, Protestant books, mostly Calvinist, continued to be smuggled into Spain, but the few Protestants to appear before the Inquisition were foreigners – French, English, German and so on – who had either settled in Spain or, more frequently, were traders or sailors passing through. For political reasons, the Inquisition had been ordered to turn a blind eye. In 1597, a decree reassured merchants from the Hanseatic League whose business brought them to Spanish ports: the Inquisition would not bother them. All that was required of suspects was not to provoke a scandal. That 'tolerance' was later extended to English traders, and then to the Dutch.

If the grafting of Protestantism never succeeded in Spain, it was not solely due to the control exercised by the Inquisition. Repression has never prevented ideologies from flourishing, provided their roots are deep enough. We need to seek other explanations. Spain was a long way from the epicentre of the religious revolution; the reforms that had already been introduced into ecclesiastical discipline and the religious orders in the early sixteenth century, although limited, had helped to correct a number of abuses; and finally, here, religious disquiet had taken a form peculiar to the Iberian peninsula. The strongest temptation came from Illuminism rather than Lutheranism and Calvinism, as the inquisitors realised. The persecution of 1558–9 marked a clear anti-mystical turning point and was directed against Illuminism more than Lutheranism, as is clearly indicated by the 1559 Index and the Carranza affair.

The anti-mystical turning point of 1559

The Index that Grand Inquisitor Valdés published contained 701 items, including, among others, works of Erasmus, translations of the Holy Scriptures, Catechisms and Books of Hours. Particularly notable is the inclusion of treatises on spirituality written in the vernacular (among them the *Book of Prayer*, the *Guide for Sinners*, the *Handbook of Various Prayers* by Luis de Granada, and the *Audi filia* by Juan de Avila), and entire editions of the Bible devoid of any commentaries setting out the interpretation favoured by the Church. This Index targeted all forms of the spirituality that was affecting both elites and the masses and that left room for free inspiration, internal religious feeling and heartfelt effusions of sentiment.

At the same time, the Inquisition attacked Bartolomé Carranza, archbishop of Toledo and primate of Spain, a brilliant theologian and one of the luminaries of the Dominican order, who had represented Spain at the early sessions of the Council of Trent. What was the Inquisition's quarrel with him? In the first place he had not denounced Lutherans who had confided in him and who were later among those found guilty in 1559; and secondly, he had published a *Catechism* that needed revision on a number of counts.

Upon interrogating the first suspects arrested in Valladolid, the inquisitors discovered that some had been in contact with Carranza, in particular the *corregidor* of Toro, Carlos de Seso, who stated that he had spoken at length with the archbishop of Toledo about purgatory and the benefits bestowed by Christ. Carranza, he said, had advised him to stick to the teaching of the Church and had seen fit to add that their conversations should remain secret, urging him to mention them to nobody. By omitting to report those conversations to the Inquisition, Carranza had committed an offence. As we shall see, in the eyes of the inquisitors, heresy was not only a sin, but also a crime. A confessor could absolve a sin, but had a duty to denounce a crime.

The *Catechism* that Carranza had recently, in 1558, published in Antwerp aggravated his position. The Inquisition, alerted by malevolent rumours, seized the few copies (perhaps a couple of dozen) that the author had sent to theologians, prelates and grandees. This work was not a catechism in the usual sense of the term, but an account of Catholic doctrine for the use of clerics with pastoral duties and for the educated faithful in general. Carranza tackled the subjects of prayer, faith, good works and many other controversial matters, explaining, discussing and qualifying. His aim was to provide his readers with knowledge that would enable them to resist bad pastoral advice. That was his error: this was not a moment for dialogue, but a time for assertions and excommunications. Since 1558, the Inquisition had imagined Lutherans at every turn. Even the most anodine of words became compromising if they were penned by heretics. Carranza, for his part, was seeking to understand, to explain and to convince at a time when an admission of the slightest nuance already seemed like a concession to the enemy. A sermon that he preached in the summer of 1558 aggravated his position. In the sermon, it was precisely this collective phobia that Carranza deplored: out of fear of being taken for a Lutheran or an *alumbrado*, one no longer dared to speak of certain things. Just because mental prayer was advocated by the *alumbrados*, there was no reason to reject it and rule out all but vocal prayer.

Carranza challenged the procedure of the Inquisition: since he was an archbishop, only the pope held the power to judge him. Pius IV shared that opinion. He demanded that Carranza be transferred to Rome, to be judged. The Carranza case now took on the proportion of a State affair. Philip II declared that, as a matter of principle, the pope should not interfere in the kingdom's internal affairs; Spaniards should be judged by Spaniards; affairs of heresy, in particular, fell within the competence solely of the Spanish Inquisition. However, in 1567, when Pius V threatened to excommunicate the entire kingdom, Philip was forced to give way. Carranza was transferred to Rome, where he was subjected to another trial, which dragged on into the pontificate of Gregory XIII. The final judgement was pronounced in 1576: the archbishop of Toledo was told to amend his linguistic imprudences and abjure the errors of interpretation to which his writings lent themselves. After seventeen years of incarceration, Carranza was set free; a few weeks later he died.

With the Carranza affair, Lutheranism seemed to become a matter of secondary importance. What the Inquisition was out to combat was, once again, pseudo-mystical tendencies, if not mysticism itself. One man, in particular, played an essential role in the orientation that Spanish Catholicism now adopted. This was Melchor Cano (1509–60), a theologian who, while remaining faithful to the teaching of Saint Thomas Aquinas, had also managed to assimilate the lessons of Humanism. Cano applied great rigour to his examination of the major problems posed by the spirituality of his day. What bothered him was the tendency of the faithful to embrace forms of spiritual life that left plenty of room for free inspiration, internal religiosity and effusions of the heart and that were available to the elite and the masses alike. Was it prudent to place practices such as mental prayer and meditation within the reach of one and all? Melchor Cano attacked Carranza, Luis de Granada and all supporters of spiritual religiosity on the following issues: the acceptance of the principle that anyone can accede to contemplation and perfection, and the dissemination, among the Christian masses and in the vernacular, of notions that could only ever concern an elite group of believers. According to him, prudence recommended that understanding of things to do with God and the spiritual life be reserved for a clerical elite; the faithful masses should stick to routine practices. Cano was convinced of this. If women had an insatiable appetite for the Holy Scriptures, in his opinion they should be forbidden those scriptures: a blade of fire needed to be interposed between the Bible and the populace!

These were the criteria that inspired the Index of 1559. It was designed to ward off the temptation of Illuminism that had been detectable ever since the beginning of the sixteenth century. Illuminism did not constitute a homogeneous body of doctrine. It developed within a variety of sects that all aspired to a more authentic and liberated religious life, freed from the dogmatic and ceremonial requirements of official Catholicism. Small groups would come together to read the Bible, to comment on it, and to discuss means of becoming directly united with God. An internal spirituality thus began to develop, with no need of images, intellectual mediations or an external cult. Religious practices (vocal prayer, attendance at mass, the sacraments) were seen as so many obstacles, a formalism that prevented the love of God from spreading freely. Instead you should try to abandon yourself to God; and once you believed you had reached that stage, you no longer needed to worry whether what you did was good or bad, since now you lived in the love of God and this inspired all your actions. It was impossible to sin, for you were beyond it. The Inquisition denounced Illuminism as a deviant perversion that should be energetically opposed. In 1559, it was not so much Lutheranism and the sequels to Erasmism that the Inquisition targeted, but Illuminism. It was thought to have been eliminated in the campaign waged against it in the kingdom of Toledo in 1525. But at the turn of the century it had resurfaced. In the Iberian peninsula, it was now to be found in circles surrounding certain *beatas* (pious women), particularly in a number of provinces such as southern Andalusia and Extremadura.

Beatas was the name given to pious women who lived withdrawn from the world, either alone or in small communities, some of which were attached to a Franciscan or Dominican third order. They were frequently surrounded by an aura of holiness and enjoyed great prestige in popular circles. Up until 1550, the Inquisition made no move against the *beatas*. Certain great figures, such as Grand Inquisitors Cisneros and Manrique, even took some of them under their protection. In the early years of the sixteenth century, Sister Maria of Saint Dominic, known as the *beata de Piedrahita*, received many admirers and followers in her cell. She also ventured out into society. For example, she sometimes graced the salons of the duke of Alba, where she would watch his guests playing chess and draughts; the moves of the chessmen and counters interested her, reminding her of man's progress, through penitence, to God. In 1507, the prior of the Dominicans asked her to go and reform the convents of Toledo, and in that same year the king of Aragon invited her to his Court. In January 1516, she sent him a message, telling him that he would not die until he he had conquered Jerusalem! But the prophetess was out of luck: only a few days later, the king died. Her raptures and revelations were widely admired: when she took communion, she saw Jesus in the host; she had visions of herself with a ring on her finger, betokening her mystical marriage with Jesus. Her behaviour was sometimes disconcerting: she would frequently receive visitors at night, when in bed. They would sit on the bed or else close beside it. There was talk of mystical dances and disturbing behaviour: kisses, embraces and caresses with those who visited her when she was in a state of ecstasy. Yet the Inquisition made no move. It was the ecclesiastical courts, alerted by the Dominicans, that passed judgement on her on 23 March 1510, paying her homage and pronouncing her person, her life and her holiness to be most worthy and her teaching most admirable. The papal nuncio and Cisneros themselves testified in her favour.

Sister Magdalena de la Cruz was less fortunate. She was the abbess of the convent of Saint Isabella of Cordova and said she had been sanctified while still in her mother's womb. She claimed that her only form of nourishment was eucharistic bread and would frequently fall into a trance of ecstasy. She had prophetic gifts, had foreseen the imperial army's victory at Pavia in 1526, and the captivity of Francis I. Pilgrims would come to see her; Grand Inquisitor Manrique himself had made the journey. Empress Isabella sent her her portrait, and at the birth of the future Philip II, in 1527, clothing that Sister Magdalena had worn was placed on the cradle. But on 1 January 1544, the Inquisition arrested the *beata* and, when subjected to close interrogation, she confessed that she had always been a fraud. On 3 May 1546, she was ordered to abjure *de vehementi* (in other words, she was judged to be a heretic) and was condemned to end her days in a convent in Andujar.

During the reign of Philip II, one of the most famous *beatas* was Sister Maria of the Visitation, known as the Lisbon nun and renowned on account of her stigmata (five bleeding wounds in her side, in the form of a cross), her ecstatic trances and her visions. Venerable religious figures such as Fray Luis de Granada and Archbishop Ribera of Valencia admired her and testified to her orthodoxy. However, when her 'visions' led her to criticise in increasingly vehement terms the incorporation of Portugal into Philip II's monarchy, the governor of Lisbon asked the Inquisition to look into her case more closely. It was then noticed that the stigmata were the result of pin-pricks and the halo sometimes seen surrounding her was produced by manipulating candles and mirrors. Sister Maria was condemned as a fraud in 1588, and ended her days in Brazil.

In some areas such as Andalusia and Extremadura, there were literally hundreds of *beatas*. In these regions, from which so many young men emigrated to America or enlisted in the royal armies, sometimes the only men available were priests. The *beatas* would confide what they believed to be their spiritual problems to these priests. As Melchor Cano noticed, this could easily lead to an equivocal situation. Women inclined to prayer would be tempted to seek out a master, for advice. In the interests of discretion, their consultations would occur, not in a public place or a church, but in some remote spot or even a closed room, where, as can be imagined, temptation would be strong. In 1525, such behaviour was already a feature in the lives of the *alumbrados* of the kingdom of Toledo, and was even more prevalent among the *alumbrados* of both sexes of southern Andalusia and Extremadura. Records relating to the *alumbrados* of Llerena show that the leaders of the sect there (eight priests) were, in truth, not particularly interested in the subtleties of prayer. They would move from village to village, seeking contact with the younger women, for preference, since – they claimed – after a certain age it was no longer possible to make spiritual progress! In 1563, one of these priests, Hernando Alvarez, was arrested. He had allowed himself all kinds of liberties with the girls who brought their confessions to him, telling them that this was no sin. Another, Cristóbal Chamizo, who was charged in 1574, had apparently seduced thirty-four *beatas*. The auto da fé of 1579 put an end to the affair, but no death sentence was passed on any of the nineteen accused.

The foremost culprit in Jaen was a parish priest by the name of Gaspar Lucas, who was a great success with the *beatas*. In 1585, one of them denounced him to the Inquisition. Although his bedside reading was found to be Ruysbroek, the great master of northern mysticism, he was accused not so much of doctrinal deviance, but rather of moral depravity. Gaspar Lucas used to check out his penitents personally, to see if they were virgins. He led them to believe that one could not be responsible for certain actions performed under the influence of diabolical possession. When he slept with a *beata* he would persuade her that this was the best way to accede to sanctity, for God granted that favour to the souls that he loved, in order to test their chastity! On 21 January 1590, Lucas was sentenced to ten years' seclusion in a monastery.

The Inquisition and witches

The Inquisition was relatively lenient to witches. In Spain, we find nothing like the phobia that gripped the rest of Europe in the sixteenth and seventeenth centuries and as a result of which hundreds or even thousands of poor women were burnt at the stake. The Holy Office seldom passed the death sentence on witches. It regarded them as victims rather than criminals – at least it did until the eighteenth century.

The tone was set as early as 1530 by a treatise written by Pedro Ciruelo that was to run to several editions.[9] In it, the author sought natural explanations for the extraordinary tales that were told. He accepted that certain practices did stem from the supernatural and implied a pact with the devil, but he urged magistrates to treat popular superstitions with indulgence. The inquisitors seem to have adopted this maxim as their rule of conduct. It was not a foregone conclusion that the Inquisition should be made responsible for repressing sorcery. After all, it was the Council of Navarre – that is to say ordinary jurisdiction – that organised the inquiry into the events of January 1525 in the Roncesvalles region. Here, sorcerers were accused of causing the deaths of children, poisoning people by serving them a 'green soup' made from toads and children's hearts, and smearing their own bodies with an ointment before attending nocturnal meetings in the course of which they would kiss a black cat. The magistrate in charge ordered dozens of arrests. To identify the sorcerers, he employed the services of a female 'expert' who examined the left eyes of the suspects, as it was supposedly there that the devil left his mark.

This episode does not appear to have led to any death sentences, but its consequences were to prove decisive for the handling of cases of sorcery. By May 1525, the Council of Navarre was in dispute with the local inquisitors, the latter claiming that they alone were competent in matters concerning witchcraft. To worship the devil and call upon his intervention was, without a doubt, an affront to the faith;

and the defence of the faith was a task that fell solely to the Inquisition. To resolve the conflict, Grand Inquisitor Manrique convened a mixed commission in Granada, to decide upon the correct way to deal with cases of witchcraft. Among the points on the agenda were two that raised fundamental issues:

- who was responsible in such matters: the ordinary secular jurisdiction or the Inquisition?
- did the witches' sabbath really take place or was it a figment of the imagination of those who claimed to take part in it?

An initial decision was reached in 1526: the Council of Navarre was divested of such responsibilities, in favour of the Inquisition. But in other parts of the realm the situation remained confused. In general, from 1530 on, the Inquisition alone was deemed competent to deal with matters involving witchcraft in the domains of the kingdom of Castile; but in the territories of the kingdom of Aragon, matters were less clear-cut, as regional institutions tried to limit the Inquisition's interventions solely to manifest crimes of heresy. This did not appear to cover witchcraft, so ordinary judges had the power to apply an emergency procedure (*judício sumarísimo*) against which there could be no appeal. This was the position upheld by the Cortes first in 1593, then again in 1626. The inquisitors challenged this. The disagreement was a source of rivalry and many cases seem to have involved a kind of race between the inquisitors and the magistrates. By the time the inquisitors took action, it was too late: the witches had already been tried and the sentence executed in accordance with the emergency procedure.

With regard to the second point on the agenda, the matter of the witches' sabbath, the Granada commission was divided. By and large, the theologians were convinced that the devil did indeed possess the power to bring about all that the witches described. Doctor Luis Coronel, a man of Erasmist inclinations, belonged to this group. The jurists, who included the future grand inquisitor, Fernando de Valdés, took the opposite view. They did not believe in the reality of the sabbath. According to them, it was a total figment of the imagination. In the fifteenth century, already, this had been the position adopted by Lope de Barrientos, the bishop of Cuenca. He had appealed to common sense to show that the tales told by witches were improbable: bodies were, after all, three dimensional, so to pass from one place to another they needed adequate space. How, then, could witches leave a house through a crack, a hole in the wall or a chimney, as they claimed? In Granada, the theologians won a majority (six to four), but still the jurists did not give up. They continued to reckon that the stories about the sabbath originated in the minds of people who were deranged or as the result of the absorption of hallucinogenic substances. This raised the question of the ointment with which witches smeared themselves and which, they said, conferred extraordinary powers upon them. It had long been known that certain substances plunged those who absorbed them into a deep sleep and could provoke either nightmares or delicious dreams.[10] The Inquisition accordingly recommended a very precise interrogation of suspects: what was the ointment used? Who made it, using what components? It advised that, whenever possible, the ointment should be seized and examined by doctors and pharmacists.

Theologians and jurists continued to argue about the facts relating to witchcraft, but the latter were gaining ground. In 1537, the Supreme Council of the Inquisition (the *Suprema*) issued precise instructions to the regional courts. Before bringing charges of witchcraft, they should ascertain that the facts were well established: had there been disappearances or deaths? Had harvests been destroyed? If so, the causes (disease or otherwise) should be investigated. The rule to follow was that laid down in 1527 by the inquisitor Martín de Castañega: regard as extraordinary only facts for which no natural explanation can be found;[11] mistrust denunciations and pay no heed to any confessions made by those presumed guilty (for weak women could be made to say anything); avoid sending simple-minded people to prison; and if, despite all such precautions, it was still thought necessary to bring charges, at least show the greatest indulgence;[12] when the facts seemed to justify a death sentence, send the whole file to the *Suprema*, which would decide the matter. In 1547, the appointment of the jurist Fernando de Valdés to the post of grand inquisitor strengthened the trend towards scepticism. In 1550, the inquisitor Sarmiento, of Barcelona, was dismissed for having sentenced six witches to death without proof. In 1555–6, the Supreme Council ruled that witches in Guipuzcoa had been condemned with insufficient proof, and the verdict was revoked.[13]

It would seem that most inquisitors considered that witchcraft could be explained by ignorance. In some valleys in the Basque country and in Navarre, the inhabitants had never received any religious instruction. Rather than blame unfortunate women, the common people should be educated and the remnants of paganism should be wiped out. Missionaries speaking the local language should be sent to such regions. The witches were really more to be pitied – or treated – than blamed. In 1554, Valdés went even further. He expressed his conviction that episodes of witchcraft stemmed from imposture, for the witches could be made to confess to anything. In most cases, the best thing to do was send them home.

In the light of recommendations such as these, it is not hard to see how it was that Spain became involved in witch-hunts far less than the rest of Europe. In cases that fell within the jurisdiction of the inquisitors of Cuenca and Toledo, torture was seldom used on witches and, in the 307 known trials of this kind that took place no death sentence was ever passed. Of the 2,203 cases that came before the Santiago court in Galicia between 1560 and 1700, 140 related to witchcraft. In all but two the accused were released after a simple abjuration. In Jaen, between 1526 and 1834 only five out of 113 trials related to witchcraft and pacts with the devil. In the district of

Cordova, the demonic aspect of witchcraft was seldom mentioned. Here, it was female magicians, rather, who were brought to court for claiming the power to influence love intrigues or effect cures or discover secrets. Seventy-nine individuals were detained for this type of offence – five men and seventy-four women. The women were generally young; they operated as magicians between the ages of twenty-five and thirty-five.

On 8 December 1572, Leonor Rodríguez, the famous *Camacha* of Montilla mentioned by Cervantes in *El Coloquio de los perros*, was paraded in an auto da fé. This woman, who was forty years of age at the time, was accused of entering into a pact with the devil and of 'bringing hearts together or tearing them asunder'. Although she was accused of Satanism, her sentence was light: abjuration, 200 lashes and a heavy fine (for she charged highly for her services!). Also in Cordova, in June 1664, four women were sentenced to a public whipping, as magicians. They were paraded, riding on mules, naked to the waist and wearing caps of infamy; and the spectators pelted them with onions. In Catalonia, where cases of witchcraft were eventually removed from the Inquisition's jurisdiction, the penalties were much harsher. In 1618–20, in Vich, civil justice passed several death sentences, prompting a protest from the bishop of the diocese, in whose opinion all the tales told about witchcraft were nothing but stuff and nonsense. In Valencia, where witchcraft also fell within the province of civil justice, 337 trials of this nature took place between 1540 and 1700. They did not relate to the sabbath. Instead, those detained were accused of predicting the future, practising various superstitions and, above all, procuring beverages designed to favour illegitimate love affairs or to cure the sick.

The trial that took place in Logroño in 1609–10 was very different. It complacently referred to classic sabbath scenes: the seeking-out of a newly fledged sorcerer, whose hands, face, chest, private parts and soles were rubbed with a stinking green liquid and who then was made to fly to the spot where the sabbath was celebrated.

Here, the devil presided, seated on a kind of throne. His appearance was that of a black man with shining horns that illuminated the scene. The newcomer renounced the Christian faith, recognised the devil as his god and lord, and worshipped him, kissing his left hand, his mouth, his chest and his private parts. The devil then turned round and presented his backside, which the sorcerer also had to kiss. The account continues with a description of black masses and acts of sorcery. The sentences passed were very severe: of the twenty-nine accused, six were burnt alive, six died in prison and seventeen were absolved. Compared to the hundreds of executions recorded at this time in French territory, on the other side of the Pyrenees, such verdicts might have seemed clement. In Spain, however, they appeared scandalous. Despite the scepticism of the *Suprema*, two of the three local inquisitors believed in phenomena said to indicate witchcraft. The *Suprema* asked the third inquisitor, Salazar, to send in a full report. This presented Salazar with an opportunity to review the whole question. His conclusions were those to be expected from a jurist: namely, that the phenomena of witchcraft were unfounded and were nothing but unbelievable and ridiculous stories. Salazar added a perceptive comment: as soon as episodes of supposed witchcraft were mentioned in books or sermons, a spate of denunciations tended to follow. So it would be best to give them no publicity. Witchcraft would disappear of its own accord if no one spoke of it.

The contrast between Spain and the rest of Europe in the treatment of witchcraft has intrigued a number of historians. Could it be explained by the difference between, on the one hand, the point of view of the Catholic world, which was more indulgent towards popular superstitions and, on the other, the Protestant world, determined to combat paganism and Satanism? H.R. Trevor-Roper prefers to draw attention to social pressures and collective phobias. Society sought scapegoats for the misfortunes of the time – wars, plagues, famines and so on. In Spain, the Jews were blamed for such things, and this accounts for the Inquisition's moderation towards sorcerers. In Germany, it was the other way round. But either way, non-conformists were hounded.[14] However, that is not a convincing explanation: there was nothing to stop the Spanish Inquisition from pursuing both Judaisers and witches at the same time. In my view, there are other reasons for the specificity of the Spanish situation. Once witchcraft was regarded as a kind of heresy, the Inquisition was justified in claiming expertise, since its acknowledged mission was to defend the faith. Civil jurisdiction was sensitive to anything that affected public order and was therefore attentive to the pressures of a society that regarded witches as criminals and Satanic fiends; while the Inquisition, for its part, was interested only in offences against the faith. Superstition bothered it less than Protestantism did. Furthermore, the Inquisition took the time necessary for a thorough examination of the cases set before it; and therein lay its strength. It drew on the advice of authorities, and seldom acted in haste. Faced with fragile evidence, inconsistent accusations and old wives' tales, the Inquisition inevitably manifested indulgence – at least the Inquisition of the Golden Age did. In the eighteenth century, affairs involving witchcraft seem to have taken on greater importance, in fact they seem to have constituted the essential part of the Holy Office's activities. It is true that its penalties remained for the most part moderate, but there were some exceptions: the last death sentence ever passed by the Inquisition, in 1781, was upon a witch who was first garrotted, then burnt, in Seville. She was an old madwoman, known in the town as the Blind Zealot (*la Beata Ciega*), who had confessed to seducing young clerics and performing acts of magic.

Faith and behaviour

The Inquisition was concerned with what people believed, not what they did; with faith, not behaviour. However, some kinds of behaviour indicated that the subject was either ignorant of dogma or deliberately flouting it. In such cases, the Inquisition intervened, not to punish a sin, but to draw attention to an article of faith and to inculcate understanding. It reached this position gradually and not without hesitation. In the instructions that he drew up in 1500, Grand Inquisitor Deza recommended that blasphemers and heretics should not be confused; there was no reason to arrest the former.[15] However, from the mid sixteenth century onward, the Holy See did begin to pursue Old Christians who blasphemed or did not respect the Ten Commandments of God, and even those who did not know what a sacrament was. The fact was that Judaisers were becoming increasingly rare and, to justify their existence, inquisitors needed to keep busy. Moreover, at around this time, the Council of Trent was recommending that greater attention be paid to the religious instruction of the faithful: the fear of punishment could be brought to bear here, although the penalties for offences of this kind were quite light.

Many trials concerned what the Holy Office called 'unseemly talk' (*palabras deshonestas*), that is to say blasphemy, scandalous remarks, dubious jokes about the faith, its rituals and its ministers and so on. According to J.-P. Dedieu, who devoted his thesis to the charges brought against Old Christians in the district of Toledo, the Inquisition did not regard such offences as very serious. It would run through the trials swiftly, rounding them off with a spiritual penance such as the recitation of a few 'Paters' and 'Aves', occasionally accompanied by a fine, never very heavy.

Such talk could lead to severe penalties if it appeared to indicate that the speaker doubted the immortality of the soul and the resurrection of the dead, and professed materialism. But if it was accidental, the speaker would be let off lightly. For example, Catalina Zapata, the 33 year-old wife of Juan de Moya, a tailor in Alcalá, deliberately denounced herself to the inquisitor on 29 September 1564, having remembered that twelve or thirteen years previously, without realising what she was saying, she had twice exclaimed: 'You don't see me in misery in this world, nor will you find me suffering in the next.'

Upon hearing the edict on faith, she realised that she had sinned against the faith and the immortality of the soul. The inquisitorial court simply reprimanded her and ordered her to fast on two Fridays and to recite the rosary four times in the coming week.

In other cases, incriminating talk was judged to be blasphemous and was punished as such, as Francisco Martínez Berralo, of Ocaña, discovered. He had exclaimed that if so-and-so went to paradise, his own donkey would go there too, harness and all. He found himself summoned to appear at the 1555 auto da fé, in Toledo. Almost a century later, a similar misadventure befell a Frenchman, one Pedro Baurès, aged twenty-two or three, who was arrested on 3 May 1640 in Madrid. He had been bragging, declaring that God was not all-powerful, as his own stick could prove, for God could not stop him burning it, nor could he prevent it having two ends! Six months later, on 19 September 1640, he received a serious warning.

These examples, and others too suggest that, in Spain, Lucien Febvre's classic thesis is not borne out.[16] Here, incredulity was not excused; unbelievers were miscreants and atheists. At the end of the sixteenth century, Pedro de León, a Jesuit attached to the Seville prisons, described the detainees as godless, irreligious pagans. And Sarabia de la Calle, a keen observer of the economic life of Seville, drew attention to its usurers: they would stop at nothing, he said, because they believed in nothing, neither God nor eternal life. Another well-known case was that of Admiral Sancho de Cardona, of Aragon, a great Valencian lord who was arrested by the Inquisition in 1568. He had been to neither confession nor communion for more than twenty years. He spent Holy Week in the Morisco villages of his domains, in which he had authorised the construction of mosques. At the end of the fifteenth century, a *converso* was recorded as exclaiming 'The only God for me is Zocodover Square!' (Zocodover Square was the marketplace and business centre of Toledo).

The most significant formulation of the expression of materialism was 'Men are born and die. Full stop, that's it' (*No hay sino nacer y morir*). It crops up dozens of times in inquisitorial trials from the fifteenth century onward, sometimes as above, sometimes followed by the word 'just like beasts' (*como bestias*). Even Old Christians, when upset, sometimes used the expression in moments of disarray. For example, it is recorded that in 1521, a certain Alonso de Peralta, carried away by emotion caused by the execution of a *comunero* leader, Juan de Padilla, cried: 'If God allows such a thing, it must be that He does not exist; all there is to believe is that one is born and one dies.' In the great majority of cases, however, the use of those particular words was believed to indicate the Jewish ancestry of whoever had pronounced them.[17] Ever since the late fourteenth century, Averroist and rationalist tendencies had attracted followers among the Jews and the *conversos*. Among elites, some tended to ascribe a merely allegorical interpretation to the Torah; they preferred the morality of Aristotle to the precepts of Jewish Law; and many no longer believed in either providence or the immortality of the soul. It was at this point that the formula 'Man is an animal like the rest: he is born, then dies and, after death, returns to nothingness' began to spread. Tugged this way and that by Christianity and Judaism, many educated *conversos* eventually became indifferent to matters of religion; they no longer believed in anything. This was the intellectual climate in which *La Celestina*, an unsettling work by a *converso*, was produced. It was clearly not a Christian work, but nor did it appear to purvey a covert version of Jewish thought and morality. Its characters seemed to move in a world that was neither Christian nor Jewish, but secularised. This was the atmosphere in which Spinoza was raised; and it helps us to understand certain aspects of his *oeuvre*.[18] In the inquisitors's view the use of that particular formulation of words unmistakably signalled that the speaker came from a family of Judaisers and was professing his materialism.

Humble folk interpreted the sixth commandment very freely. They knew it was wrong to covet a neighbour's wife, but did not consider fornication pure and simple to be forbidden. Many people joked about the matter: surely it could not be a sin to create souls to go to Heaven? In 1582, a shepherd from Ronda was arrested. His crime? To have told a friend the following story: one day Christ caught Saint Peter making love with a female innkeeper. 'What are you doing there?' he asked. To which Saint Peter replied, 'I am reproducing the species.' 'Right,' said Christ. 'But be quick about it.' Many honest people thought that to sleep with an unmarried woman or a prostitute could not be a sin, for if it were, neither the pope nor the king would allow brothels. In 1573, the Inquisition decided that it was heretical to maintain that to indulge in sexual relations outside wedlock was not a mortal sin and, in the following year, this offence figured in an edict of faith. The faithful were encouraged to denounce any such case that came to their notice. However, those who expressed such views had long been targeted by the Inquisition. As we have seen, the Holy Office punished this kind of offence with minor penalties. In 1585, an inquisitor in Galicia justified such indulgence: most country-dwellers had received no religous instruction. They did not make heretical declarations intentionally; they simply did not know what they were saying.[19]

Remarriage in the lifetime of one's spouse was an offence punishable by law. How did people become bigamous? In some cases, more or less unintentionally. A man and a woman who had lived together for some time became subject to social pressure. They were urged either to regularise the situation or to separate. One of them was already married, but this was not known and he/she was perhaps not keen that it should come to light. When exhorted no longer to live in concubinage, a man or woman was pressured into committing an even more serious offence, the sin of bigamy. In many other cases, it was a matter of a person who had been separated from their original spouse for many years: a man who had been obliged to leave his village for one reason or another, a woman whose husband had left and never returned. They would remarry, hoping that the previous marriage would never come to light. Ever since the Middle

Ages, the law had prescribed penalties for bigamists, such as bans on domicile. In the sixteenth century, as the practice was tending to become increasingly common, more stringent steps were advocated. In 1544, for instance, the town of Guadalajara instructed its deputies in the Valladolid Cortes to insist on more severe sanctions, such as the branding of bigamists. Petition 105 of the Cortes of Valladolid (1548) made similar recommendations, and the king gave them his approval. Bigamists could now be sentenced to hard labour. This became the penalty generally imposed under Philip II.

But bigamy was also a sin and, in that it flouted the indissoluble nature of the sacrament of marriage, a form of heresy. That is why the Inquisition turned its attention to bigamy when the virtual disappearance of crypto-Judaism obliged it to seek new *raisons d'être*. The Council of Trent manifested similar preoccupations on the part of the Church. The *Instructions* that Grand Inquisitor Valdés published in 1561 included bigamy among the offences of heresy. From this date on, in Castile at least, the Holy Office was *de facto* the only institution that dealt with crimes of bigamy. This situation remained unchanged until the eighteenth century, when Charles III transferred competence to the royal courts of justice, except in cases where the Inquisition could produce proof that those accused were deliberately behaving as heretics.[20] The Inquisition sentenced most bigamists to three years' hard labour, which was a severe penalty. No other offence, except heresy in the strict sense, was punished so harshly.

It was for similar reasons (that is, in order to extend its competence to offences not obviously linked with faith) that the Inquisition took over cases of solicitation. In the case of a priest, solicitation meant exploiting the privacy required for the hearing of confession to indulge in dishonourable propositions or caresses, or (even worse) encroachments on the persons of his penitents. This was a long-standing and widespread evil. The Council of Trent recommended the setting up of confessionals in order to thwart temptation, but it was some time before their use became general. For a long time, such offences had fallen under episcopal jurisdiction but in 1559, the arch-bishop of Granada suggested that their repression be entrusted to the Holy Office. Solicitation certainly did imply scorn for the sacrament of penitence; and the sacraments were fundamental to dogma. To profane them was therefore to commit an offence against the faith, and this could be assimilated to heresy. Grand Inquisitor Valdés accepted this and, in 1561, solicitation was assumed into the domain of the Holy Office's activities. In a papal brief issued by Gregory XV on 30 August 1622, the papacy finally accepted this point of view: from then on solicitation was the province of the Holy Office, rather than ordinary civil justice. Inquisitorial courts showed great indulgence to priests accused of solicitation, for they did not wish to attract publicity to this kind of offence.

The behaviour described above might, at a pinch, be considered to reflect attitudes that undermined a healthy interpretation of faith and dogma, although it may certainly be argued that the connection was extremely tenuous. But what of sodomy, the repression of which was likewise entrusted to the Inquisition? For the Christianity of the Ancien Régime, the word 'sodomy' 'covered many kinds of practices that were not exclusively homosexual [...] Sodomy covered the huge domain of sexual acts that were not for the purpose of procreation, which the Church denounced with more or less virulence, depending on places and times: *coitus interruptus*, masturbation, fellatio, anal coitus, whether heterosexual or homosexual, *coitus inter femora* [between the thighs] ...'[21] Hieronymus Münzer, who visited the Iberian peninsula in 1494–5, reported that, in Spain, those accused of sodomy were strung up by the feet with their severed testicles draped round their necks. A little later a Pragmatic Sanction dated 22 August 1497 assimilated sodomy to the crime of heresy or treason and specified as penalties death at the stake and the confiscation of all the culprit's possessions. It was in the early sixteenth century that the Inquisition began to manifest an interest in what, in Spain, was called *el pecado nefando*, literally 'the sin without a name'. However, in December 1504, the town of Cartagena protested vigorously: this vice was no business of the inquisitors; the common law could punish it perfectly well. The king ordered the Holy Office not to meddle with the problem. The following year, the Inquisition requested the support of the municipality of Murcia in an inquiry that it was pursuing into clerical and lay sodomites who were said to be gathering in a church in the town, where they indulged in debauchery. The municipal magistrates reckoned that it was none of the Inquisition's business. In general, the civil authorities, the Cortes for example, judged that the Inquisition should limit itself solely to heretical offences and not seek to extend its jurisdiction beyond that. Where sodomy was concerned, this view eventually prevailed in the domains of the kingdom of Castile. Ordinary justice, either civil or ecclesiastical, was ruled to be competent here, despite an attempt by Philip II, in 1596, to entrust such affairs to the Inquisition, which the pope refused to countenance. In the kingdom of Aragon – Aragon, Catalonia and Valencia – on the other hand, the Holy Office obtained full powers.

Of the matters that we have examined in this chapter, strictly speaking only those that concerned the Protestants and the Illuminist sects related to the defence of the faith. How the rest related to Catholic orthodoxy is more questionable. Motivated by its desire to perpetuate itself, the Inquisition nevertheless did extend its competence to those doubtful areas. Between 1500 and 1510, the Holy Office appeared to have completed the mission entrusted to it in 1480: it had dealt with the problem of crypto-Judaism, which was not to resurface until the end of the sixteenth century, with the arrival of the Portuguese *marranos* in Spain. To justify its existence, the Inquisition was therefore seeking new fields of activity. The Spanish Protestants, in fact, constituted too small a group to represent a threat to Catholic orthodoxy. Nor were the Illuminists sufficiently numerous to provide full-time occupation for a personnel that had expanded considerably since the early days of the Inquisition. By turning its attention to the mass of Old Christians and by, in many cases, quibbling over the meaning of words – sorcery, superstition, improper talk, deviant behaviour – while continuing to pursue Judaisers and Protestants if any still came to their notice, the Inquisition found a way to survive right up to the early nineteenth century.

The end of the Inquisition

By about 1750 the Inquisition had lost its *raison d'être*. It had been created to eradicate all traces of Semitism in Spain. The Jews and the Moriscos had long since been expelled and two and a half centuries of persecution had eventually eliminated the Judaisers. Yet the statutes on blood purity still did not disappear; in fact, in the course of the eighteenth century they tended to multiply, although to what extent they were effective remains doubtful. They no longer constituted any serious obstacle to a career in the Church, the official administration, or civic society. Inquiries on this score were now so much a matter of pure form that at the highest State levels it was thought that the time had come to do away with all measures of discrimination against *conversos*. The very expression 'New Christians' no longer made any sense.[22] Just as it had eliminated the Judaisers, the Inquisition had managed to stifle all tendencies that might have called orthodox Catholicism into question. There simply were no longer any Protestants, non-conformists or Illuminist sects in Spain.

However, we should not conclude that the Holy Office no longer constituted a threat to individuals. It continued to pursue charlatans and witches. It also kept the behaviour of clerics and monks under surveillance, more strictly than that of laymen. Above all, for the State authorities, it had become an instrument of control used for the repression of all ideological and political opposition. In this respect, it could still prove to be terrifyingly effective, as we shall see in relation to the Macanaz affair and the Olavide trial. By the end of the eighteenth century, essentially the Inquisition was operating as a political policing force devoted to opposing the introduction of revolutionary and liberal ideas. It is true that it seemed to have softened its attitude. It no longer published edicts of faith encouraging the faithful spontaneously to denounce their neighbours and their relatives.[23] Nor did it any longer torture its prisoners. Nor did it kill them – or rather, to be more precise, capital executions were now extremely rare:[24] the autos da fé of the past, which had attracted thousands of spectators, were replaced by discreet, almost secret ceremonies.

Most historians reckon that the reign of Charles III (1759–88) marked the peak of the Enlightenment in Spain. However, the king and his enlightened ministers certainly appear to have accommodated the Inquisition. In 1768, Campomanes and Floridablanca regarded the inquisitorial court as 'the most fanatical State body', but they did not envisage suppressing it. The Inquisition could still be a useful instrument for the State and render it valuable services. We shall presently see how Floridablanca used it to prevent the propagation of French revolutionary ideas in Spain. It was important to ensure that the Inquisition was in a position to carry out the tasks that the State entrusted to it. To that end, it made sense to improve the education of its staff and to define more clearly the missions assigned to the institution.

At the end of the Ancien Régime, a growing contrast was evident between, on the one hand, the upper echelons of the Holy Office, who were close to the State authorities and inclined to collaborate in reforms, and, on the other, its ignorant and retrograde lower levels. One of the most brilliant representatives of the former category was Juan Antonio Llorente. Llorente was a Holy Office commissioner attached to the Logroño court when, in 1788, Grand Inquisitor Rubín de Cevellos summoned him to Court to be the secretary of the Supreme Council. Five years later, in 1793, the new grand inquisitor, Manuel Abad y la Sierra, asked him to report on a possible reform of the Inquisition. In 1798, Llorente completed his report, *Discursos sobre el orden de proceder en los tribunales de la Inquisición* (Discourse on the procedures of the courts of the Holy Office), but it did not see publication until 1995. Llorente had protectors, in particular Godoy, Charles IV's all-powerful minister, but he had also made enemies in the inquisitorial court itself. These accused him of having abused his functions and consulted, then divulged documents that should have remained secret. In 1801, Llorente lost his post as secretary to the *Suprema* and was sentenced to a fine and a month to be spent in seclusion in a monastery. In 1805 he was restored to his post. In 1808 he, like other high-ranking officials, was summoned to Bayonne, where Napoleon forced Charles IV and his son Ferdinand VII to hand over the Spanish throne. Llorente now entered the service of Joseph Napoleon, who appointed him director of the national assets. Using the notes that he had taken when working for the *Suprema*, Llorente produced a memorandum on the Inquisition and national opinion in Spain (*Memoria histórica sobre cuál ha sido la opinión nacional de España acerca del tribunal de la Inquisición*). It was published in 1812. The fall of Joseph Bonaparte forced Llorente into exile in France. He took with him, in his luggage, thousands of documents from the archives of the Holy Office, some of which he sold to the Paris Bibliothèque royale. Thanks to these documents, in 1817–18, while in Paris, he was able to publish the work that made him famous, *L'Histoire critique de l'Inquisition espagnole.*

Llorente unquestionably belonged to the enlightened elite which, in the last third of the eighteenth century and in the early nineteenth, was still dreaming of the regeneration of Spain. It is thanks to Llorente that we know what those reformers thought of the Inquisition. His 1798 report recommended not the suppression of the Holy Office, but the introduction of reforms to guarantee the right of defence. In line with what is sometimes called Jansenism but should more correctly be termed regalism, he advocated reducing the autonomy of the Inquisition and placing it under the control of ordinary civil justice. At this point Llorente was not yet thinking of drawing attention to the inhumanity of the inquisitors and the huge number of their

victims. What shocked him most were not the pyres lit by Torquemada, but the fact that the Holy Office showed so little respect for
royal prerogatives and had usurped the jurisdictional powers of the
bishops. In the early eighteenth century, Macanaz had expressed
the very same criticisms. Jovellanos, a friend of Llorente, shared his
views: the bishops ought to recover their responsibilities and powers
where heresy was involved, since in that domain they were far better
qualified than ignorant monks. Llorente, like Jovellanos, moreover
reckoned that the censorship of books that the inquisitors exercised
was stupid: not only did it contribute to sullying Spain's prestige
abroad, but it furthermore maintained 'a slavery of the mind, to the
great detriment of humanity'.

However, we should not be misled by all these indictments. The
reason why Llorente wished to strengthen the role of the bishops was
that they, unlike the monks, were appointed by the political authorities and so were more amenable to the instructions that they received
from the royal Court. Like most Spanish reformers (whom it would
be mistaken to assume to be *philosophes* or *encyclopédistes* in the French
manner), Llorente was not out 'to crush the Beast', as Voltaire put
it. He simply wished to rid religion of its more questionable aspects
– the devotional acts, the pilgrimages, and so on – which could be
compared to manifestations of superstition and fanaticism. For the
Inquisition, as it was operating at the end of the Ancien Régime,
seemed to the reformers to be encouraging the very worst tendencies
of popular religion. One example was provided by the eighteenth-
century inquisitors' behaviour in affairs of witchcraft. When they
hounded poor women accused of casting evil spells of various kinds,
they not only demonstrated their own ignorance but at the same time
encouraged popular superstitions, whereas their sixteenth- and seventeenth-century predecessors had wisely refused to associate themselves with the witch-hunts then so common in the rest of Europe.
Because of its present inquisitors, Spain had become the laughing-
stock of Europe and was generally considered a country of fanaticism

and obscurantism. The enlightened elite of the day seemed obsessed with the subject of witchcraft, an anachronistic resurgence right in the middle of the Age of Enlightenment. Attempting to understand the phenomenon, Jovellanos procured a copy of the old fifteenth-century handbook, *Malleaus Maleficarum*, Moratín republished the account of the 1610 Logroño auto da fé,[25] and Goya included the theme of witchcraft in his series of Dreams and Caprices and composed a number of paintings depicting such subjects. Goya was a friend of both Moratín and Llorente (and painted a portrait of the latter). In the face of such excesses, Llorente, along with a number of other reformers, reckoned that a reformed and more closely controlled Inquisition would offer the State advantages that it would be misguided to reject.

This was typical of the Enlightenment in Spain. People wanted reforms but no upsets. The attitude of enlightened minds sensitive to what was happening in France from 1789 on was quite different. Some did not hesitate to emigrate and place themselves at the service of, first, the French Revolution, then Joseph Bonaparte. Among these was Marchena. He detested everything that encouraged despotism, fanaticism and obscurantism in Spain. He considered the Inquisition particularly odious, calling it 'a court of darkness that dishonours even despotism'. In a *Manifesto to the Spanish People*, dated 1793, Marchena pretended to be a Frenchman who had never visited Spain but had acquired a great deal of information about it. He reminded his readers of the persecution that had claimed, among so many others, Carranza, Fray Luis de León and Olavide as its victims, and exclaimed with indignation, 'Can even the Bastille, so loathed by all of us, and rightly so, be compared to your odious and abominable court?' The answer was certainly 'no': the Bastille was a State prison in which despots had incarcerated their opponents. There, the latter endured a taxing captivity, but no attempt was made to dishonour either the prisoners or their families. They could always retain the hope of getting some minister to relent. On the other hand, had there ever been an inquisitor who relented?

The idea of suppressing the Inquisition came not from the Spanish reformers, but from Napoleon.[26] Taken by surprise by the riot of 2 May 1808 and the resistance of the Spanish people, Joseph Bonaparte had been obliged to leave Madrid in July 1808, soon after the capitulation of Dupont's army at Bailen. At this point, Napoleon decided to take the situation in hand. He himself took command of the *Grande Armée* that now invaded Spain. By 4 December 1808, he was at the gates of Madrid. But before entering the capital and restoring his brother to the throne there, the emperor signed a number of decrees in Chamartín, thereby abolishing the Ancien Régime in Spain in the space of a few minutes. The Inquisition figured large among the institutions that were suppressed. Such radical measures took the Spanish elites by surprise, for they had never dared to hope to carry things so far. Many, including Llorente, rallied; many others, out of patriotism, rejected the reforms imposed by an army of occupation and an intruder king. They were certainly eager for the regeneration of Spain, but were also fighting for national independence.

When the Cadiz assembly drew up a liberal Constitution, the question of the Inquisition inevitably arose. Had the Cortes really suppressed the Holy Office? That was what all the newspapers declared. Yet the decree of 22 February 1813 was full of ambiguities. It asserted that the Catholic, apostolic and Roman religion would enjoy the protection of the Constitution and the laws (article 1), that, because the inquisitorial court was 'incompatible with the Constitution' (art. 2), it was necessary to revert to medieval legislation (the *Partidas*) and restore jurisdiction on matters of faith to the bishops, in conformity with canon law. Likewise in conformity with medieval legislation and canon law, secular justice was now empowered to impose on heretics the penalties prescribed by law (art. 3). Article 4 laid down that 'every Spaniard may denounce the offence of heresy to the ecclesiastical court'. Chapter 2 of the same decree reaffirmed the need to prevent books that were prohibited or contrary to religion from entering the country. Permission from a bishop was required before a book on a religious subject could be published and civil magistrates were made responsible for the seizure of all the works that the bishops had banned. Were the Cadiz liberals really determined to suppress the Inquisition? The institution was declared illegal but heresy was still a crime and was still punishable by law. Likewise, the censorship of books was maintained. The only difference was that it was now the bishops who held the powers previously assigned to the inquisitors. There can be no denying that the Chamartín decree had been far more forthright.[27]

Despite all those precautions, the edict on the Inquisition received no more than ninety votes in the Cortes. Sixty deputies who were averse to change in any form voted against it.[28] The Cortes had also ruled that the decree abolishing the Inquisition should be read out in every church on three consecutive Sundays. Most of the clergy refused to comply with the order and the regency (that is to say the provisional government) did not intervene. Once back on the throne, Ferdinand VII's first priority was to restore the Ancien Régime, so the Inquisition was, of course, reinstated among the State institutions. On 21 July 1814, the king announced, 'The Inquisition constitutes the most effective means to spare my subjects internal divisions and to afford them peace and tranquillity. In the present circumstances, I have therefore judged it most opportune to restore jurisdiction to the Holy Office.' The court that Ferdinand VII re-established concentrated almost exclusively on freemasonry, and it still devoted its attention to drawing up lists of banned works, first and foremost the 1812 Constitution. Judaisers were no longer a concern. All the same, Borrow, the Englishman who, between 1835 and 1840, travelled extensively in the Iberian peninsula selling Bibles, claimed that he had encountered an old inquisitor who reckoned there were two kinds of Judaism: the black kind, that is to say Judaism in the strict sense, and the white kind, which included Lutheranism and freemasonry. Six years later, in 1820, the liberals restored the Constitution and again suppressed the Inquisition. The masses rose up and attacked the Inquisition's Madrid prison, situated in the street named after the Catholic monarch Isabella, only to discover that it now contained only one detainee, a certain L. Duclos, a French legitimist emigré who had written a number of treatises on spirituality that had attracted the attention of the ecclesiastic authorities.

Once the duc d'Angoulême's French army (the Hundred Thousand Sons of Saint Louis) had put an end to the constitutional regime, Ferdinand VII did not dare to resuscitate the Inquisition yet again, at least not under that name. In its place, he created 'Faith Commissions' (*Juntas da fé*), one for each diocese. The local bishop presided over each one. These commissions were not recognised legally but were nevertheless tolerated by the civil authorities, who agreed to implement their decisions. In 1826 one of them, over which Bishop Simon López presided, condemned to death Cayetano Ripoll, a schoolteacher in Ruzafa, in the Valencian region. This unfortunate man had been so imprudent as to declare that Jesus was not the son of God. He was accused of deism, condemned to death, and hanged. Not until after the death of Ferdinand VII was the Holy Office definitively abolished by a decree passed by the regent, Maria-Cristina (15 July 1834). In 1838, Larra composed its epitaph: 'Here lies the Inquisition, the daughter of faith and fanaticism. She died of old age.' The words were apposite enough.

3 The administrative apparatus of the Holy Office

The Spanish Inquisition was an ecclesiastical court placed under the authority of the State. This is what distinguished it from the Inquisition created in the thirteenth century to operate against the Waldesians and the Cathars. That medieval Inquisition removed from the ordinary jurisdiction of the bishops the responsibility for defending the faith and repressing heresy and, instead, entrusted this mission solely to the pope. In the case of the Spanish Inquisition, the pope renounced that prerogative in favour of the civil authorities. This was established by the foundational papal bull, *Exigit sincerae devotionis*, dated 1 November 1478. Sixtus IV authorised Ferdinand of Aragon and Isabella of Castile to appoint inquisitors charged with the task of investigating converts who judaised and bringing them and their accomplices to justice. It was also clearly stated that, to defend the faith, these inquisitors would take over the jurisdiction, powers and authority that had previously belonged to the bishops. On the strength of this foundational bull, on 27 September 1480, the sovereigns announced the names of the first inquisitors for the kingdom of Castile. As we have seen, Ferdinand eventually obtained the same privilege for the kingdom of Aragon. Three years later, a new procedure was introduced: acting upon the sovereigns' proposal, the pope made Torquemada grand inquisitor, with the responsibility of appointing delegated inquisitors. In 1488, Innocent VIII agreed that, when the time came, the sovereigns of Spain should nominate Torquemada's successor. This was the procedure that remained in place until the abolition of the Inquisition: the pope appointed as grand inquisitor the person nominated by the king of Spain and charged him to battle against heresy; the grand inquisitor then sub-delegated his powers to district inquisitors. In this way, the Spanish Holy office depended entirely upon the grand inquisitor, or rather the State, which had nominated him.

The grand inquisitor

Torquemada had been appointed grand inquisitor for the kingdom of Castile and shortly after was also appointed grand inquisitor for the kingdom of Aragon. On 11 February 1486, Innocent VIII reworded those measures, making Torquemada grand inquisitor for all the territories placed under the authority of Ferdinand and Isabella. That decision should be seen as an attempt to introduce the beginnings of centralisation in Spain. From 1479 until the end of the seventeenth century, the Hispanic monarchy included in effect territories with a variety of statuses: seigneuries, principalities and kingdoms, some with crowns of their own (Castile, Aragon and, from 1580 to 1640, Portugal), each of which preserved its own autonomy, its own institutions, its own law, economy, currency and, in some cases, language. The Inquisition was the only institution common to the entire monarchy and, as we have seen, no *fueros* could obstruct it. In 1507, however, Ferdinand appeared to back-pedal. He appointed two grand inquisitors, Cardinal Cisneros for the kingdom of Castile, and Juan de Enguerra, followed by Luis Mercader, for the kingdom of Aragon. The prevailing circumstances provided the explanation for this division of powers. Since the death of his wife Isabella, Ferdinand had been king only of Aragon; in Castile, he governed in the name of his daughter, Joanna the Mad. He was afraid that Castile and Aragon might again be separated, as they had been before 1479.

The appointment of two grand inquisitors at least guaranteed that, whatever happened in the future, Ferdinand would retain his control over the Inquisition of Aragon. Ten years later, the situation had changed and the risk of the realm splitting up had receded. The future Charles V waited until Cisneros died, then reunited the Holy Office. In 1517, Cardinal Adrian was appointed grand inquisitor for the whole of the realm.

As we have seen, the grand inquisitor was appointed by the pope, following a proposal made by the ruler of Spain. This was a point upon which the latter always insisted. Formally, the grand inquisitor received his powers from the pope, but the pope was obliged to appoint the Spanish monarch's nominee. In 1522, when Adrian VI was elected pope, he ruled that initially the privilege of nominating the grand inquisitor had been granted to the king of Aragon personally; so now that he had passed on, all prerogatives reverted to the pope. Charles V held a different view. In a letter from Brussels dated 29 March 1522, he expressed vehement objections. Adrian VI backed down. The appointments of grand inquisitors always took the form of a *motu proprio* in which no reference was made to any nomination on the part of the king of Spain. However, that subtlety fooled nobody: it was certainly the king who nominated grand inquisitors and who, in consequence, indirectly controlled the Inquisition. This raised a potential problem: if the king, *de facto*, appointed the grand inquisitor, could he also dismiss him? In principle, no; but he could certainly marginalise him or exert pressure to force him to resign. Alonso Manrique provides the only example of a case in which the solution of marginalisation was adopted. In December 1529, he incurred the wrath of Isabella, then, in 1534, that of Charles V.[1] The Inquisition Council, the *Suprema*, seized the opportunity to replace the grand inquisitor's authority with its own. It was an abuse of power, but nobody protested.

On the other hand, cases of enforced resignation were more frequent. We know of at least five. In 1507, Deza, who was compromised by the Lucero affair; in 1599, Portocarrero, edged out by Philip III; in 1602, Niño de Guevara, also a victim of Philip III's hostility; in 1621, Aliaga Martínez, whom Olivares judged to be corrupt; and in 1643, Sotomayor, who was too old to carry out his obligations. Given that the grand inquisitor acted by virtue of pontifical delegation, his powers should, strictly speaking, have ceased at the death of the pope who had appointed him. However, it was understood from the start that the next pope would confirm the grand inquisitor in his post. Throughout its long history, the Spanish Inquisition always retained this mixed character of jurisdiction that was religious by virtue of its (at least theoretical) objectives, and political by reason of its close links with the State. What would have happened if a pope had refused to appoint a grand inquisitor? The Spanish Holy Office would have disappeared on the spot. But no pope ever did dare to risk conflict with the kings of Spain over this issue. The Inquisition lasted for as long as the political authorities wished it to, and the pope never did anything to oppose this.

There were forty-five grand inquisitors between 1480 and 1820. Because this was a political post, the sovereigns were particularly vigilant in their choice of nominees. The first grand inquisitors, Torquemada and Cisneros, were of moderately humble origins. When Manrique, appointed in 1523, took over, the Holy Office found itself headed by a representative of the highest nobility, but this was an exception. In the sixteenth century, the sovereigns preferred to appoint prelates who were already archbishops of either Seville or Toledo or who had been members or presidents of the Castile Council. Most had pursued studies in one of the top three universities – Salamanca, Valladolid, or Alcala. From the seventeenth century on, a greater diversity was introduced: now many grand inquisitors were products of the *colegios mayores* of Santa Cruz (Valladolid) or San Ildefonso (Alcala).

Tomás de Torquemada was the nephew of the theologian Juan de Torquemada and, like him, was a Dominican monk. He was the prior of the monastery of Santa Cruz in Segovia, and confessor to the Spanish sovereigns. His reputation for intransigence and rigour is well justified. Spurred on by him, the Inquisition proved appallingly severe and murderous. It was during this inauguration period that the greatest number of sentences were passed, most of them death sentences. It was Torquemada who persuaded the sovereigns to expel the Jews in order to deprive the *conversos* of all links with the judaism of their ancestors.[2] Torquemada's successors did not resemble him in this respect and cannot be described as fanatics. Deza can be reproached for lacking lucidity and firmness in the Lucero affair. Cisneros's personality was much more complex. In 1499, before he had become grand inquisitor, Cisneros reckoned that the evangelical methods of Talavera were not very effective: there were few Muslim converts in Granada. So he decided to speed things up. On his own initiative, he forcibly baptised hundreds of infidels and burned all Arab books, except works of medicine. Yet almost concurrently, he manifested remarkable open-mindedness when he founded a new university in Alcala de Henares where, for instance, he left the students free to choose their preferred philosophical system: Thomism or Nominalism. He encouraged the study of ancient languages and saw no reason why well-known *conversos*, such as the brothers Juan and Francisco de Vergara, should not be recruited as professors. The polyglot Bible that he commissioned proved to be one of the finest expressions of Spanish Evangelism and Humanism. As mentioned above, it was Erasmus's loss that he failed to associate himself with that work and declined Cisneros's invitation to collaborate on it.

Manrique probably did not deserve the reputation of Humanist or even Erasmist with which he was credited. After all, it was he who, as bishop of Cordova from 1516 to 1523, allowed part of the mosque to be destroyed to make room for a cathedral.[3] Moreover he proved unable to prevent the persecution of his own Erasmist and spiritual friends. Juan de Avila, Vergara and others too were arrested and convicted by the Holy Office, without any effective interventions from him. Admittedly though, for the greater part of his mandate (from 1529 to his death in 1538) Manrique, who was disgraced, exercised no real authority over the body that he was supposed to control.

Fernando de Valdés came closer to one's idea of an intransigent and rigorous inquisitor. He was born in 1483 and was admitted to the Council of the Inquisition in 1524, remaining there until 1535, when he took over the presidency of the Valladolid chancellery; so he was certainly familiar with the internal workings of the Holy Office. From 1539 to 1546, Valdés presided over the Royal Council, the monarchy's most eminent institution. In 1547, he was appointed both archbishop of Seville and grand inquisitor. Was this a tactful way of removing him from the Royal Council? There are serious indications to suggest as much; in the first place the somewhat hostile judgements expressed by Charles V. In 1556, Valdés's career seemed to be under threat. The monarchy was going through a difficult period. It was at war with France, and the new king, Philip II, strapped for money, was turning to the bishops of Spain and requesting voluntary contributions to finance his foreign policy. All the prelates but one responded with generosity. The exception was Valdés, the archbishop of Seville, one of the richest, most lucrative livings in Spain! Charles V, in Yuste, was indignant; so was Philip II, who considered confining Valdés to his own diocese, which would prevent him from exercising his mandate as grand inquisitor. Fortunately for Valdés, he was saved by the internal situation. It was at this point that the existence of Protestant circles in Valladolid and Seville was discovered. Did Valdés exaggerate the number of suspects? Possibly. At any rate, he remained in his post. It was unthinkable to change the grand inquisitor at such a time.

In 1559 Valdés associated himself with the antimystical trend. Was he solely responsible for what took place? No, even without him the situation would no doubt have evolved in much the same way. Throughout Spain, and beyond too, the religious situation was hardening. The opposition between Catholics and Protestants was becoming increasingly clear-cut. The force of circumstances, more than human wilfulness or the rise of a new generation, can account for the changes that now took place. However, Valdés was undoubtedly instrumental in imparting a deliberately aggressive twist to this turning point of 1559. It was also he who was responsible for sending the archbishop of Toledo to prison. For years, he had been jealous of Carranza's prestige and success. Now that he had a chance to get back at him, he seized it. He was so hostile to Carranza that the latter had no difficulty in getting Valdés rejected as his judge, although that did not prevent the trial from taking its course. In all fairness, however, it must be admitted that Valdés was at the same time a first-rate organiser. As we shall see, it was he who was responsible for publishing an up-to-date account of inquisitorial procedure. Valdés's successors were more moderate. They were also extremely attentive to the political questions of the day. Quiroga, for example, whose mandate lasted from 1573 to 1594, never disguised the friendship that linked him with Secretary Antonio Pérez, who was accused of treason. Apparently, Philip never held this against him. It was Quiroga who, in 1576, insisted that Fray Luis de Leon be acquitted of the charges brought against him. This was a most unusual occurrence, given the habitual behaviour of the Inquisition. The difference from Manrique, who had proved powerless to secure justice for the Erasmists, is obvious.

In the seventeenth century and most of the eighteenth, the grand inquisitors were not, strictly speaking, mediocre men, but they lacked personality. They were, however, upright enough officials, as is suggested by the title of a famous book by Julio Caro Baroja, *El señor inquisidor*. Not until the last years of the eighteenth century do we find, in Cardinal Lorenzana, a grand inquisitor who returned to the great cultural tradition of men such as Cisneros. Lorenzana was the very epitome of the kind of enlightened prelate much beloved in the time of Charles III. He began his career as archbishop of Mexico, in which capacity he was extremely active not only in encouraging religious teaching but also in promoting interest in scientific knowledge. In 1770, for example, he published a richly documented and illustrated history of New Spain. In 1772, Charles III appointed him archbishop of Toledo. Lorenzana placed the huge income from this living at the service of the poor and of culture in general. He funded libraries, took an interest in regional antiquities, published a variety of works on Gothic and Mozarabic rituals, and financed the publication of the works of Saint Isidore of Seville. Lorenzana could hardly be branded a narrow-minded and fanatical inquisitor. It was not so much the men of the Inquisition who were to be feared, but the institution itself.

The Council of the Inquisition

The first reference to the Council of the Inquisition, the *Consejo de la Suprema y General Inquisición*, known as the *Suprema*, for short, was created in 1488, at the wish of Ferdinand of Aragon. At first it consisted of a few members of the royal Council, who were required to follow the affairs of the Holy Office and advise the grand inquisitor, who presided over it. As has been mentioned above, in 1507 Ferdinand had seen fit to appoint two grand inquisitors. As a result, two supreme councils were formed, one for Castile, the other for Aragon. When Cardinal Adrian became once again the single grand inquisitor for both kingdoms, in 1518, the Council too was reunified, or rather the Council of Aragon disappeared. The *Suprema* was composed of four councillors (six by the end of the sixteenth century) and two secretaries, one for Castile, the other for Aragon, plus two representatives from the Council of Castile. Its members were appointed by the king on the recommendations of the grand inquisitor, who drew up a list of three names (*la terna*) for each post to be filled. The Council was thus wholly dependent upon the civil authorities. It constituted one of the elements of the polysynody that was characteristic of the Hapsburgs. By decision of Philip II, it occupied the third official position in the hierarchy of the monarchy's councils, just below the councils of Castile and Aragon.

The areas of competence of the *Suprema* were never clearly defined. In principle, it held no power of decision in matters of heresy. That rested entirely with the grand inquisitor, to whom alone it had been delegated by the sovereign pontiff. The role of the Council expanded in periods when the grand inquisitor was absorbed in other functions, as when Cisneros, on two separate occasions, was required to govern Castile, as regent, or when the grand inquisitor had lost the confidence of the sovereign, as happened to Manrique from 1529 to 1538. In his *Grand Memorandum* of 1624, Olivares, who was well versed in the institutions of the monarchy, represents the *Suprema* as essentially required to examine appeals against judgements given by provincial courts.[4] From the mid sixteenth century on, the Council also prepared clarificatory statements on controversial questions – matters to do with witchcraft, for instance – and communicated these to the courts in the form of circulars (*cartas acordadas*), with a view to coordinating their actions and enlightening them as to the course to adopt in this or that domain.

The inquisitorial districts

The first inquisitors, appointed to Seville in 1480, were soon overwhelmed by the number of Judaisers in southern Andalusia so, by 1482, Torquemada had created a new permanent court in Cordova as well as two others, which he set up in Valencia and in Saragossa, in the kingdom of Aragon. In the following year, two more districts were created, Jaen and Ciudad Real, the latter holding jurisdiction over the greater part of New Castile, La Mancha and even Extremadura. In truth, Ciudad Real had been chosen because Archbishop Carrillo refused to allow the creation of an Inquisition in Toledo. At Carrillo's death, in 1485, his successor Cardinal Mendoza, for his part, made no objections, so the inquisitors transferred from Ciudad Real to

Toledo. The entire southern half of the peninsula thus found itself under the surveillance of the Holy Office and this chequering of the terrain was further strengthened by the creation of the districts of Llerena (1485), Cuenca (1489), and Siguenza and Jerez (1491). Meanwhile an inquisitorial court was also established in Murcia, in 1488. In 1486, to deal with a concrete situation, the discovery of crypto-Judaism within the Hieronymite order, a special court had been set up in Guadalupe, which continued to operate until 1491. Up until 1526 there was no court in Granada. The first archbishop there, Talavera, whose influence over Queen Isabella was strong, had been opposed to it, although this had not stopped inquisitors from Cordova from investigating *conversos* in the town. According to Navagero, the papal nuncio to Charles V, at the time of Granada's capitulation King Ferdinand had promised that no inquisitorial court would be created in the town, and as a result suspects from all over Spain took refuge there. In 1485, the Inquisition made its appearance to the north of the Guadarrama, when a court was created in Medina del Campo (this was transferred to Salamanca in 1488), followed by courts in Segovia and Lerida (1486), Valladolid (1488) (transferred to Palencia in 1493), and Leon (1492). During this same period, a court was also established in the Balearics (1488).

Between 1480 and 1495, a whole succession of courts appeared (twenty-three by 1493), forming a network that covered the entire peninsula with the exception of Galicia and Navarre, which was independent at this time. This proliferation had proved so costly that efforts were now made to economise by regrouping the districts. Thus, in 1502, the districts of Burgos, Leon, Salamanca, Avila, Segovia and Valladolid merged, with a court located in Valladolid. In 1503, Seville absorbed Jerez, and Cuenca, Siguenza and Calahorra came together to form a single district. The situation then began to stabilise. In 1513, when Navarre had been reattached to Castile, it was decided to create a court in Pamplona; in 1516 this was transferred to Tudela, then to Calahorra (1521) and finally, in 1570, to

Logrono. The last inquisitorial court to be established was that of Santiago de Compostela (1574). Up until then, Galicia had been part of the district of Valladolid. The objective of the establishment of an autonomous court at Santiago was to combat the Lutheran propaganda that was finding its way into Spain through the ports of the Cantabrian coast. To this end, the inquisitors of Galicia were given the right to inspect foreign ships, seize prohibited books, and even arrest the Lutheran sailors who put in there. Under Philip II, when Madrid became the seat of the royal Court, it was felt necessary also to set up a new structure there. However, its official existence was not recognised until the mid eighteenth century and, in the meantime, officially the court of Toledo operated for Madrid.

The Inquisition was also installed in the Canaries (on a permanent basis in 1568) and in America. In 1569, Philip II created the districts of Lima and Mexico; and a third court was created in 1610 in Cartagena. It is worth noting that the native American Indians were not placed under the jurisdiction of the Holy Office; they were assimilated, in theory at least, to Old Christians. In 1571, Philip II also received papal authorisation to create a special, itinerant, maritime court with jurisdiction over the army and the fleet commanded by Don Juan of Austria, which was soon to distinguish itself in the Battle of Lepanto. The first maritime inquisitor was Jerónimo Manrique (an illegitimate son of Grand Inquisitor Alonso Manrique) and it was he who celebrated a solemn auto da fé in Messina, in 1572, after the naval victory. Subsequently this court ran foul of the military and naval authorities and, in consequence, although never officially abolished, it ceased all activity.

As can be seen, the inquisitorial districts did not always coincide with the map of the dioceses nor with the political divisions of the realm. For instance, Orihuela, part of the kingdom of Valencia, was dependent upon not the inquisition of Valencia, but that of Murcia, a town situated in the kingdom of Castile. Such apparent incoherences were deliberate. The districts were organised in as rational a fashion as possible, sometimes ignoring ecclesiastical and political divisions, since the overriding consideration was the efficiency of the institution. From this point of view, the Inquisition introduced an improvement that would eventually lead to political centralisation. It was certainly not by chance that Ferdinand imposed it upon his subjects in the kingdom of Aragon, despite the local *fueros*.

The administration of the Spanish Inquisition acquired its definitive form in the seventeenth century, when the districts were regrouped into two sectors, corresponding to the two principal kingdoms of the realm, Castile and Aragon. Each sector had its own secretariat. The courts of Toledo, Seville, Valladolid, Granada, Cordova, Murcia, Llerena, Cuenca, Santiago de Compostela and the Canaries were all administered by the secretariat of Castile. The administrative authority of the secretariat of Aragon extended to the courts of Logrono, Saragossa, Valencia, Barcelona, Palermo, Mexico, Lima (then known as Ciudad de los Reyes), the Caribbean Cartagena, Majorca and Sardinia. By and large, this arrangement respected the political divisions of the realm, but there were some inexplicable anomalies: Logrono, Mexico, Lima and Cartagena should have depended on the secretariat of Castile, since Rioja and the West Indies belonged to the crown of Castile. Perhaps the intention was to apportion the administrative tasks of the two secretariats more or less equitably, regardless of political divisions. At any rate, this example shows that the affairs of the Inquisition took precedence over the concerns of the various territories that made up the realm.

The inquisitors

In general, two inquisitors were assigned to each court (although there seem to have been three in Valencia). They were aided by two secretaries, a public prosecutor (*fiscal*), a police officer (*alguacil*), a receiver, a nuncio, a porter, a magistrate responsible for administering the property that was sequestered and confiscated and a doctor. The

grand inquisitor was responsible for appointing all these, without consultation with the Supreme Council. That was logical enough, since
the grand inquisitor acted by delegation from the sovereign pontiff.
He alone could subdelegate his powers to others. At his death, the
staff that he had appointed in the districts lost their posts. Actually,
though, according to a custom that quickly became established, the
new grand inquisitor would then renew the powers delegated by his
predecessor, so there were no problems of continuity.

Of all the agents who formed the permanent staff of the inquisitorial court, the inquisitors themselves were the most important. It was
they who decided upon arrests, prepared the cases for judgement and
delivered the verdicts. In 1478, in a foundational bull, Sixtus IV had
authorised Ferdinand and Isabella to appoint three inquisitors who
were to be 'bishops or others with dignified official positions, regular
or secular priests, aged forty or over, who believed in God, possessed good characters and were from honourable families, and were
masters or bachelors of theology or possessors of degrees in canon
law'. For reasons unknown, in the *Instructions* that he published on
6 December 1484, Torquemada made substantial alterations to this
text. All that he now stipulated was that inquisitors be university
graduates (*letrados*) of good reputation, but not necessarily ecclesiastics. Neither did Alexander VI any longer specify that inquisitors
must be ecclesiatics when he renewed the powers of Grand Inquisitor
Deza, on 24 November 1498 and then again on 1 September 1499.
It was indeed common enough for inquisitors never to have taken
holy orders. All that was required was that they be celibate and resign
their posts if they married. King Ferdinand is known to have written
to Cisneros, on 28 June 1515, to say that he had just learned that
the university graduate Nebrada, an inquisitor in Seville, was about
to marry. As he had served the crown well, the king asked that he
quickly be found another good post.

At the end of Philip II's reign, the *Suprema* debated this point.
It had been pointed out that some inquisitors had received only

minor orders. Some were even known to have been married yet then obtained further employment. The *Suprema* wished to have done with such irregularities. It decided that all inquisitors should now be required to be priests. In the *Instructions* that he passed to Grand Inquisitor Manrique de Lara in 1595, Philip II ruled that inquisitors and procurators should in future be ordained men. However, in the *Instructions* that he issued in 1608, Philip III did not specify this. Not until 1632 did the *Suprema* rule definitively on the matter: inquisitors who were not ordained had to resign their posts. This whole affair shows the extent of the real authority that the sovereigns of Spain exercised over the Inquisition. It was certainly they, not the pope, who decided on important matters such as these.

There were similar hesitations over the age of inquisitors. The foundational papal bull specified forty years of age at least, but on 3 February 1485, when Innocent VIII confirmed Torquemada's powers, he lowered the minimum age to thirty, and Alexander VI maintained that ruling in the texts in which he granted Deza apostolic delegation to exercise the functions of grand inquisitor (24 November 1498 and 1 September 1499). The years passed. Philip II would have preferred more mature inquisitors, aged at least thirty-five. It was possibly to please him that, in 1596, when appointing Portocarrero to head the Holy Office, Clement VIII reintroduced the initial regulation: the lower age limit would now revert to forty. However, Portocarrero raised objections: it was not always possible to find enough candidates. So Clement VIII revised his decision. From then on, until the institution was abolished, the papal documents and internal regulations omitted to specify the minimum age required for an inquisitor. They simply expressed the wish that they be recognised to be 'prudent, competent men, of good reputation, of healthy mind, and filled with zeal for the Catholic faith'.

Contrary to common belief, monks in general and Dominicans in particular were always a minority among the personnel of the Holy Office. It would indeed have been astonishing had this not been the case. Unlike the medieval Inquisition, the Spanish Inquisition was placed under the authority of the State. The sovereigns preferred to deal with secular clergy as they were more docile than regulars, who were dependent upon their superiors and the pope. Out of a total of forty-five grand inquisitors, only six were Dominicans (Torquemada, Deza, García de Loaysa, Luis de Aliaga, Antonio de Sotomayor and Juan Tomás de Rocabertí); Cisneros was a Franciscan; all the rest belonged to the secular clergy. The situation was similar in the provincial courts. In Toledo, for example, out of the fifty-seven inquisitors recorded between 1482 and 1598, only one was a Dominican. In Valencia, out of the twenty inquisitors employed prior to 1530, five were Dominicans, but most of those appointed between 1530 and 1609 were from the secular clergy. In the seventeenth century, this trend was confirmed: without exception, all the inquisitors of Spain, as well as all the public prosecutors, were secular priests rather than from the religious orders.

How were inquisitors trained? Where it was a matter of magistrates whose task was to pronounce on the orthodoxy of this or that statement, it would be natural to expect men with a solid grounding in theology to have been preferred. However, that was not the case. Most inquisitors were jurists who specialised in canon law. In 1545 the legal expert Diego de Simancas declared categorically that jurists were of more use to the Inquisition than theologians. Grand Inquisitor Fernando de Valdés, himself a jurist, openly favoured canonists, maintaining that they were better qualified to clarify questions of procedure for, when all was said and done, it was a matter of judging people and therefore of knowing the law. In 1558, there was a shortage of personnel to deal with the numerous suspects recently arrested for Lutheranism, and extra collaborators were needed. Four members of the *Suprema* were still available, but one was a theologian who, Valdés reckoned, would be of little use in the existing situation.

This preference for jurists produced a set of contrary consequences. On the one hand, it prolonged the trials. The concern to verify everything and overlook no procedural rule resulted in considerably protracting procedures, most unfortunately for the wretched suspects on remand. Carranza's trial dragged on for seventeen years; and Fray Luis de León languished in prison for four years, and, after all that time, the former was eventually sentenced only to a minor penalty, while the latter was acquitted. On the other hand, the advantage of jurists was that they assessed the evidence and proofs more rigorously. This could be to the advantage of the accused, particularly in affairs involving witchcraft, as Julio Caro Baroja has shown. Canonists tended to dismiss as valueless most testimony offered by minors and more or less to disregard statements made by the elderly, by women, and by witnesses who were obviously partial and seeking by every means to harm the accused. In this respect, the choice of jurists rather than theologians was favourable to those accused of witchcraft.[5]

In general, the post of inquisitor was regarded as a step up in an official's career. Considerations of ability and zeal were not always the determining factors in the selection of inquisitors. In the seventeenth century, it was not so much the merits of an ecclesiastical career that counted for a would-be inquisitor, but rather the advantage of having held a post in the service of the king. That was, obviously, hardly surprising. After all, the Holy Office was a State institution. At the beginning of the seventeenth century, for example, inquisitors in Seville proved themselves worthy of office, both before and after their recruitment, by scoring highly in the collection of taxes: the Holy Office was feared, and people paid up with greater alacrity when the tax collector was also an inquisitor. So it is not surprising to find the king or Olivares recommending the appointment of this or that inquisitor on the basis of reasons that had nothing at all to do with the defence of the faith. Such considerations are bound to temper the image usually formed of inquisitors. In the last analysis, they included fewer fanatical and bloodthirsty figures than is sometimes believed. On the other hand, mediocre men were common in their ranks, as were individuls who abused their power: Jaime Contreras draws our attention to a Muñoz Cuesta, a womaniser (even among nuns!), and a certain Ochoa who openly lived with a married woman who was his concubine and whom he allowed to preside over court sessions.[6] It is worth repeating that it was not the men of the Inquisition but the institution itself that was so daunting.

The public prosecutor

The public prosecutor (*fiscal*), along with the inquisitors, was central to inquisitorial procedure. It was he who, having examined the recorded denunciations, decided whether there were grounds for laying charges against a suspect. He drew up the charges, investigated and interrogated the witnesses, and brought them into confrontation with the accused whom he was seeking to convict of heresy and whom he pressured with a view to obtaining a full confession. The *fiscal* took no part in the deliberations that led up to the verdict: that was the job solely of the inquisitors. That being said, however, his connivance with the inquisitors was total, so much so that the two careers eventually came to be confused: after a few years' service, a *fiscal* could expect to be promoted to the post of inquisitor.

Subordinate personnel

It was also the grand inquisitor who appointed the junior staff of the inquisitorial courts. The secretaries were present at all interrogations and kept a legal record of the entire procedure: the declarations of witnesses, the statements of the accused, the torture sessions, the subsequent deliberations and the sentences. They alone, apart from the inquisitors and the public prosecutor, had access to the court's archives. Their functions made them the most important of all the district agents, even more important than the inquisitors themselves, for the latter could be removed whereas the secretaries, barring exceptional circumstances, were permanent, embodying, as they did, the written memory of the Holy Office.

The *alguacil*'s job was to make arrests and take possession of the impounded goods of the accused. He handed the prisoner over to jailers, who were responsible for keeping him isolated from the outside world for the whole duration of the inquisitorial procedure. In some important seventeenth-century courts, Seville and Cordova for example, an *alguacil mayor* was to be found. This was an honorific title that was conferred upon nobles whose forebears had served the Inquisition by, for instance, placing at its disposal more or less prestigious premises (castles, palaces and so on). In 1655, the *alguacil mayor* of the court of Cordova was none other than Luis Méndez de Haro, heir to the count-duke of Olivares. A receiver (*juez de bienes confiscados*) administered whatever possessions had been seized or confiscated. The agent who diffused and publicised the court's announcements was known as a *nuncio*. He also acted as a messenger and courier. In a town such as Valencia, the Inquisition's doctors (whose presence was required at all torture sessions) were drawn from among the most brilliant university professors.

Agents appointed by the Holy Office tended to pass on their jobs to their children or other relatives, and the *Suprema* made no objections. In 1595, Philip II had forbidden the transfer of jobs to brothers or children, except in exceptional circumstances. However, his successor Philip III revoked that order. In 1695, Charles II tried to introduce an amendment: responsibilities could only be handed on from father to son or brother, and even then only if the new incumbent was qualified for the job. However, eventually he too agreed to revert to the rule laid down by Philip III: at the death of an agent, priority should be given to one of his children, as his replacement.

Voluntary personnel

Strictly speaking, the above-mentioned agents constituted the staff of the Holy Office, which paid their wages. But the Inquisition also used other, unpaid, categories of personnel that were indispensable to its regular functioning: 'qualifiers', consultants, representatives of ordinary civil jurisdiction, commissioners and 'familiars'.

As we have noted above, inquisitors were for the most part recruited from amongst jurists who specialised in canon law. They had to determine whether such or such an accusation deserved to be described as heresy or an offence against the faith; and this presupposed theological qualifications that they did not always possess. In the most delicate cases, they took the advice of reputable theologians, or 'qualifiers'. As the word suggests, the role of the latter was to qualify whatever offences the suspects were accused of and pronounce upon whether or not they amounted to heresy. For such clarification, the Inquisition appealed to monks – Dominicans, Franciscans, Jesuits (many of whom were university professors) – taking good care to maintain a balance between those various religious orders. It was important to avoid granting to any one of them a kind of monopoly over matters of faith. When it was thought that enough charges against an individual had been amassed, the whole file (known as a *sumaria)* was passed to the qualifiers, who were required to pick out anything in the actions, speech or writings of the accused that implied that this individual was a heretic or strongly suspected of being one. The qualifiers were also frequently asked to pronounce on books of a doubtful nature from the theological point of view.

In some cases, the inquisitors could appeal to consultants, that is to say to jurists belonging to some other institution, such as a Council or another court of justice. They would ask those consultants for their opinion on the juridical aspects of a case and the penalties that would be appropriate. The consultants would contribute to the final phase of a trial and the wording of the verdict, but only in a consultative capacity and without any deciding vote. They received no remuneration for their work; nor did the representative of ordinary jurisdiction, an ecclesiastic appointed by the local bishop. However, this representative did take part in the final decision and was entitled to a vote, just as the inquisitors were.

The administrative apparatus of the Holy Office was completed by two other categories, commissioners and 'familiars', who ensured that the entire territory of the monarchy was covered by inquisitorial surveillance.

The medieval Inquisition had likewise relied on commissioners. Nicolas Eymerich, who had been grand inquisitor for the kingdom of Aragon in the fourteenth century and whose handbook *Directorium inquisitorum* (1376) continued to be consulted in the sixteenth century, recommended the appointment of a team of commissioners in every diocese: they were authorised to receive denunciations, to summon suspects and witnesses, to arrest and interrogate, and even to torture, when they judged this to be necessary – in short, to act in every respect as inquisitors. They were, in effect, delegated inquisitors. In the Spanish Inquisition, the powers of the commissioners were less extensive. Initially, there were no commissioners. They began to appear only between 1537 and 1548. But in the second half of the sixteenth century, they were to be found all over the place. District inquisitors could not be everywhere at once and so fell into the habit of appointing ecclesiastics as commissioners (seldom parish priests, but usually men who received some kind of a stipend) and assigning them to missions, at first of a temporary nature but which then became permanent, in ports, frontier-posts or towns and regions distant from the location of inquisitorial courts. In principle, the commissioners did not have the power either to lay charges or to pass judgements. All they were supposed to do was receive denunciations, collect the testimony of witnesses, and send the lot to the *Suprema*. But in fact they frequently exceeded their powers. They received no salary from the Holy Office, but their services earned them by no means negligible rewards. These took the form of material advantages as well as certain privileges (as described below). For instance, commissioners were frequently required to investigate the blood purity of men seeking honorific posts, say, in an order of chivalry. In such cases, it was up to the candidate to reward the investigator. The number of commissioners was never very high. In the seventeenth century, in Galicia, it rose to several hundred as a result of the desire to deter Lutheran propaganda. But in the eighteenth century, the force was much reduced. By then, there were fewer than a dozen commissioners in Catalonia, for example.

In the Middle Ages, whenever inquisitors moved from one place to another, they were accompanied by men-at-arms, to ensure their protection and to carry out their orders. These were said to be part of the inquisitor's entourage or family. Hence the name by which they were known: familiars of the Holy Office. In the early days of the Spanish Inquisition, an armed troop of 250 familiars followed Torquemada wherever he went. Later, the role of the familiars changed. The Inquisition regarded them as agents whom it did not have to pay, particularly in rural zones, where they were assigned the task of keeping the population under surveillance, denouncing unrest and suspect talk, encouraging denunciations, and providing the inquisitors with a strong arm for the arrest of heretics. At the end of the sixteenth century, the historian Mariana declared that the Inquisition 'has deprived us of the freedom to talk among ourselves; in every town, village, and hamlet, it has individuals ready to inform it of everything that goes on'. The familiars constituted a supplementary police force in the service of the Inquisition.

The role of the familiars rapidly evolved. Their social origins improved and their number greatly increased. At first they had been recruited from popular circles in the world of small-scale artisans and shopkeepers, But as time passed, particularly in the kingdom of Castile, more and more men from elite groups volunteered. Soon gentlemen were in the majority. In Jaen, in the mid seventeenth century, all nine familiars came from the aristocracy; one was a knight of Santiago; practically all were municipal officers. Even members of the nobility claimed the honour of becoming familiars. At the auto da fé celebrated in Madrid on 4 July 1632, the standard of the Holy Office was carried by the admiral of Castile, who was flanked by the supreme commander and the duke of Medina de las Torres; all three were familiars and were from the highest ranks of the realm's nobility. The fashion became so pronounced that the king, seeking to profit from it, took to putting familiar titles on sale.[7] In 1642, no fewer than 300 of these titles were offered to the public.

In the kingdom of Aragon, however, familiars continued to be recruited from the popular or middle strata, and this was seen as a means of social advancement and of acquiring respect from one's compatriots. In Valencia, for example, the proportion of aristocrats, ecclesiastics and rich wholesalers among the familiars was very low (5.6 per cent, 2.5 per cent and 6.5 per cent respectively), whereas labourers (*labradores*, that is to say well-to-do peasants) represented 44.2 per cent, and artisans 31 per cent of the total. They even included a scattering of Moriscos.[8] In 1593, the situation worried Philip II, who remarked, 'It has come to my notice that, in the kingdom of Valencia, familiars are recruited from the lower social classes and among shopkeepers, who see this as a way of improving their trade.'[9]

The success of the familiars eventually caused the authorities concern. The familiars assumed that their status allowed them to do anything they wished and they tended to abuse their position. As a matter of urgency, their numbers had to be limited. In the kingdom of Castile, it was the future Philip II who, acting as regent in the absence of his father, on 10 March 1553 decided to take action in Seville, Toledo and Granada, in each of which there were thenceforward to be no more than fifty familiars. In Valladolid, Cuenca and Cordova, their numbers were reduced to forty; in Llerena and Calahorra, to twenty-five; in the rest of the kingdom, ten familiars were allowed to villages of over 3,000 households, six to those of 1,000 households, four to those of fewer than 500, and even then only if the inquisitors deemed them necessary. The inquisitors were required to provide a list of their local familiars for the *corregidores*, in order for these to check that the numbers conformed with the regulations.

It would seem that the edict of 1553 was somewhat disregarded, as were similar regulations that the regional authorities imposed in the kingdom of Aragon. As early as 1512, the Cortes of Monzon had expressed reservations over the question of familiars. In Catalonia, their number was not supposed to exceed thirty-four, but a census taken in 1567 revealed the presence of 785, one for every forty-three households: seventy-nine for the town of Barcelona alone, eighteen in Perpignan, twenty-four in Gerona, nineteen in Tarragona ... but in the countryside the situation remained by and large unchanged. By 11 March 1554, the Council of the Inquisition and the Council of Aragon had reached agreement on the kingdom of Valencia where, at that time, there was one familiar for every forty-two households: a high figure.[10] It was decided that there should be no more than 180, maximum, in the town of Valencia, eight in the villages of more than 1,000 households, six in those of between 500 and 1,000 households, no more than four in hamlets of between 200 and 500 households, and only one or two in all others. However, these proposals were not approved until 1599, forty-five years later! At this point, the Holy Office ruled that the approval of the pope himself was also indispensable. Apparently, no one remembered to make the necessary approaches to the Holy See, so the agreements remained a dead letter.

How many familiars altogether were there in the Iberian peninsula? It is hard to say with accuracy: between 10–12,000 from 1570 to 1620, probably more, perhaps 20,000, in the mid seventeenth century, at the height of the craze.

Holy Office privileges

The reason why the body of familiars was so successful lay in the advantages that membership procured, in particular the right to bear arms, and, above all, the jurisdictional privilege from which all members of the Holy Office benefited. They eluded ordinary civil and even ecclesiastical justice, and could be tried only in an inquisitorial court. In theory, this privilege was justified: nothing must obstruct inquisitors in the accomplishment of their mission. To hamper it constituted an offence liable to the same penalties as those for heresy. To subject agents of the Inquisition to ordinary civil justice would have been to expose them to pressures, perhaps to prevent them from exercising their functions. Only the pope, in specific circumstances, could excommunicate an inquisitor or punish him. This exorbitant privilege was soon extended beyond inquisitors, to all agents of the Holy Office, including subordinate personnel such as caretakers, familiars and so on, and to their relatives and servants too, even when they had committed actions defined as offences and crimes in common law, such as theft, armed assault, murder and so on. In such cases, only the courts of the Holy Office were competent and only the Supreme Council could, where necessary, act as a court of appeal.

The Holy Office consistently took care to protect its personnel and servants and even to guarantee them a kind of immunity. Systematically, it covered up for even their most reprehensible actions and refrained from passing severe sentences. In most cases, culprits got off with a few words of blame and remonstrance. Occasionally they were temporarily suspended for a year or two; even more rarely they might be retired early, but were still allowed to claim half their salary, just as agents who were too old or sick did. In justification of this leniency, the Holy Office maintained that a scandal would be graver than any crime, in that it would harm the Inquisition's reputation. This attitude became manifest as early as the beginning of the sixteenth century. On 17 May 1511, the king of Aragon made this clear to an inquisitor who had tabled serious complaints against one of his subordinates and was intending to sack him. The king explained that when an agent of the Holy Office committed an offence, he should be reprimanded. If he persisted, he should be criticised in the presence of his colleagues, in order to shame him. If even this did not suffice, the matter should be re-examined in the presence of the whole inquisitorial staff, but further steps should be taken only with the greatest circumspection. At all costs, the dismissal of a member of the Inquisition was to be avoided, for it would provide ammunition for the enemies of the faith. In 1553, Prince Philip, as regent, reminded the courts of justice of the kingdom of Castile that they should not intervene in affairs in which members of the Inquisition were implicated, even if they were of the opinion that the delinquents had not been punished as they deserved and felt that injustices had been committed. Those who felt wronged by the inquisitors could appeal before the *Suprema*. This body would examine litigations and, if necessary, would overrule any ecclesiastical prohibitions and convictions mistakenly pronounced. The Inquisition from then on sheltered behind this document, for such recommendations in effect guaranteed immunity to all agents of the Holy Office, whatever their crimes.

This jurisdictional privilege was the most spectacular of the advantages enjoyed by the personnel of the Inquisition. But there were others too, such as exemption from certain taxes and dispensation from the obligation to billet soldiers in transit and to provide draught animals for military and other equipment; and meanwhile the Holy Office insisted that when its own agents were obliged to move from one place to another, they should be lodged at the expense of local inhabitants.

Finally, we should not underestimate the importance of matters of precedence in Ancien Régime societies. By reason of its sacred nature and the apostolic delegation that it had received from the Holy See, in all ceremonies and protocol the Inquisition claimed precedence for itself and its agents. It asserted its right to take precedence over both members of the clergy and representatives of the State, however highly placed. In ceremonies and demonstrations, members of the Inquisition paraded behind their standard, a green cross on a black background with an olive branch to the right and a sword to the left. To assert its pre-eminence, the Holy Office never hesitated to brandish its canonical weapons: prohibitions and excommunications. In 1598, in Seville, the ceremonies organised to mark the death of Philip II gave rise to a notorious scandal. Dissatisfied with the position allotted to them in the cathedral, the inquisitors withdrew, after excommunicating all the personnel of the Court of Justice (*Audiencia*) and ordered the religious service to be halted. This was going too far, and the new king, Philip III, insisted on an apology. There were no doubt many such incidents in the history of the Holy Office.

All these exemptions and privileges and this kind of pre-eminence made the Inquisition an institution to be feared, all-powerful, and able to resist even the greatest State institutions, right up to the end of its existence. It is true, though, that in the second half of the eighteenth century it lost much of its prestige. A report dated 1746 represents it as a refuge for ecclesiastics who lived at the expense of the collectivity. The number of consultants was definitely in decline, a clear sign that the defence of the faith was no longer in fashion. 'Qualifiers' now spent most of their time censoring books and periodicals; there were no more jailers because there was no longer anybody to imprison; and as for receivers of confiscated goods, they had completely disappeared except in the Balearic Islands: nowhere else was there anything for them to do.[11] The Holy Office nevertheless survived for another fifty or so years.

The finances of the Holy Office

At a very early date rumours were already drawing attention to the cupidity of the kings and the inquisitors, who were accused of laying charges against wealthy *conversos* and declaring them heretics the better to fleece them. In 1520, the town of Burgos urged its representatives to the Cortes to recommend that the king desist from confiscations so as to discourage such rumours. In truth, from an economic point of view, the Holy Office was never a successful business except during the first twenty years of its existence, when the many convictions brought in huge returns. It was partly in order to boost declining revenues, when Judaisers became hard to find, that in 1520 the Inquisition set about seeking out other categories of heretics: Illuminists, Protestants and Old Christians who made unseemly remarks or married several times over. It was not until around the mid sixteenth century that the Holy Office found a virtually definitive solution to its financial problems.

From the point of view of the Inquisition's finances, the date 1559 marked an upturn in its history, for this was the point at which the Holy Office secured a budgetary autonomy that enabled it to meet most of its obligations. Up until 1559, the Inquisition had been totally dependent on the political authorities. Courts could pass sentences that resulted in the confiscation of property and could impose fines, sometimes heavy ones, on those found guilty, but the crown was the sole beneficiary of this income and could dispose of it as it saw fit. According to canon law, a condemnation for heresy, even just a 'reconciliation', automatically entailed the confiscation of property, to the profit of the prince or the local temporal lord; and that confiscation dated from the time of the offence, not the day of judgement. Even when inquisitors showed clemency towards heretics who repented, that made no difference to the fate of their possessions: those belonged to the crown. The Inquisition was not free to dispose of them. When the heretic was an ecclesiastic, the situation was rather different: the Church became the proprietor of all the confiscated property and could return it to the Inquisition. Even then, though, King Ferdinand claimed a tax amounting to one third of the value of the confiscated goods. In 1559, for example, two thirds of the goods belonging to Doctor Cazalla (condemned to death for being a Lutheran) were assigned to the bishop of Palencia, who was willing to present them as a gift to the Inquisition. But the last third went to the crown and the king could do as he wished with it. In 1509, Ferdinand passed on to the duke of Alba one third of the possessions confiscated from heretics living in his States. Other nobles too benefited from similar favours – a fact that confirms a remark made above, in Chapter 2: the reason why the king felt obliged to grant such compensations to the aristocracy was that the latter felt it had been injured by the institution of the Holy Office. It was therefore most unlikely to have encouraged its creation. That being said, the king did return most of the confiscated property to the Inquisition, which then auctioned it off and used the proceeds to pay its agents and finance its courts. In other words, without trials there was no money; and that was a fact that fuelled unsympathetic rumours. A tract posted up in Toledo Cathedral in November 1538 denounced the situation in no uncertain terms: 'Inquisitors must be paid by means other than confiscations. The existing state of affairs is scandalous: without deaths at the stake, no victuals on the table; without convictions, the inquisitors die of hunger.'

Confiscations did not constitute the sole source of revenue for the Inquisition. So-called 'composition fines' also generated a large fiscal income, at least until around 1515. It should be remembered that a conviction of heresy involved not only the confiscation of the victim's property but also his ineligibility for certain public posts, ecclesiastical livings and some professions. This inelegibility affected not only the directly interested parties but also their immediate descendants. Conviction also included the obligation to wear a tunic of shame (*sambenito*). Such inelegibilities and the *sambenito* were felt to be particularly severe penalties: the inelegibilities prevented those convicted and their descendants from occupying lucrative posts; and the *sambenito* placed them beyond the pale of society and consigned them to dishonour. The sovereigns early on accepted the principle of those affected being allowed to buy back their honour and be reintegrated into the social body and relieved of their inelegibilities in exchange for the payment of a flat fee (usually a high one). This was known as a composition fine.

We know that in certain towns such composition fines were accepted at an early date: in 1482 in Valencia and 1487 in Cordova. But it was from 1494 onward that the practice spread. Miguel Angel Ladero Quesada discovered a list of 1,750 Sevillian *conversos* who were rehabilitated in late 1494 and early 1495.[12] We also know of 1,641 *conversos* of Toledo who benefited from similar measures in 1495 and close on 2,000 who did so in 1497. These operations channelled huge sums into the royal treasury: some 15 million *maravedís* in Seville, 14 million in Toledo. In Toledo a new composition fine was exacted in 1498, involving 20 million *maravedís*. On 18 December 1508, the heirs of Judaisers convicted in the dioceses of Seville and Cadiz were allowed, in return for 20,000 ducats (7.5 million *maravedís*), to buy back the possessions confiscated from their parents from the time of the creation of the Holy Office up to 30 November 1508, with the exception of the property that had belonged to individuals who had appeared at the auto da fé of 29 October. In Seville, on 22 September 1509, a composition was decided by the royal authorities, who fixed upon the overall sum to be paid. Each of the potential beneficiaries was then ordered to pay his share. Those who declined to take advantage of this measure and to pay their contribution could be forced to do so by the others. In other words, the richer victims were encouraged to strip the poorer ones. On 10 October 1509, the Judaisers condemned at Ayamonte and La Redondela, in Andalusia, were authorised to emigrate to America upon the payment of 40,000 ducats. Finally, another composition was ratified in Seville on 15 June 1511. It involved a fine of 80,000 ducats. Subsequent years saw further amnesties of this kind, but far fewer of them and involving much smaller sums. However, at the end of the sixteenth century, the royal authorities revived this practice, which they now applied to Judaisers of Portuguese origin.

The royal treasury made money from the confiscations and fines, including the composition fines, and could use it as it wished. However, it did reserve the greater part for the running of the

Holy Office. In the Inquisition's budget, as in the budgets of any institution, a distinction was made between ordinary expenses and extraordinary ones. The former category included the payment of the personnel (which in itself probably accounted for three quarters of the budget) and running costs: furnishing, upkeep and heating of premises, office supplies, correspondence and staff gifts (when major festivals were celebrated, inquisitors had a right to three *arrobas* of sugar – about thirty kilos – notaries to one and a half, junior staff to one). Among the extraordinary expenses were the costs of feeding destitute detainees, the repair of premises, and the costs occasioned by particular events such as the funerals of sovereigns or princes of the blood, when all personnel received money to buy themselves mourning apparel. The heaviest costs arose from the organisation of autos da fé, always the responsibility of the court, except when the local municipality agreed to make a contribution, which was by no means always the case.

The great persecutions of the Inquisition's early days, between 1480 and 1500, had provided it with huge financial resources. Yet even in this period, the Holy Office did not enjoy great opulence, to judge from the many documents that record complaints from the staff, whose wages were almost always late. A note written in 1504 shows that the Inquisition's outlay tended to exceed its income. Once most of the Judaisers had been sentenced, the Holy Office entered upon leaner times. Ricardo García Cárcel describes the court of Valencia, in the first half of the sixteenth century, as a ruinous establishment, smothered under the weight of an overstaffed, inefficient bureaucracy. Jean-Pierre Dedieu, for his part, refers (no doubt somewhat exaggerating) to 'the great poverty' of the court of Toledo between 1540 and 1558. In 1543, there was apparently not even enough money to organise an auto da fé, and the abolition of the court was contemplated. In 1551, the authorities decided to desist from passing prison sentences: the costs of upkeep had to be cut back. According to Dedieu, it was this precarious situation that drove the court to adopt a new course: in the absence of Judaisers, it would now concentrate on witches, the superstitious and Old Christians who made impious remarks and considered it no sin to sleep with a married woman. Almost twenty years later, in 1569, when civil war was raging in the Alpujarras mountain range, the inquisitors of Granada were sorely bewailing the state of affairs: prices were constantly on the rise; their domains were being ruined by the fighting; and they could no longer collect their customary dues because the Moriscos had all been expelled.

It was Grand Inquisitor Valdés who found a quasi-definitive solution to these administrative problems. He skilfully exploited the disarray caused by the discovery of hotbeds of Lutheranism in Valladolid and Seville. At his request, Philip II approached Pope Paul IV and got him to agree that, in all the monarchy's cathedrals and collegial churches one dignity of canon should henceforth be reserved for the Holy Office, with corresponding revenues. Such a step had already been envisaged by Charles V in the testament that he drew up in Brussels on 6 June 1554. In this way, the Inquisition acquired a relative autonomy. It no longer depended exclusively upon the temporal power and confiscations to finance it. Of course, this measure was not at all popular with many would-be canons, for it was a living lost to them. The chapter of Granada pointed out that the income of the diocese was too low for it to comply, as it was such a recent creation, and Philip II conceded the point; but everywhere else, he was intractable and rigorously applied the pope's decision. Valdés also obtained other advantages for the Inquisition, in particular the right to an agreed annual levy from the Morisco communities of Spain; in return, he promised not to confiscate the possessions of Moriscos who were convicted. Subsequently, the Inquisition managed to acquire yet further sources of revenue: rents and mortgages and what was known as consignations, that is to say contributions that the better-off courts had to pay to those that were struggling. Such was the basis upon which the Inquisition functioned to the very end. But it should not be assumed that all its difficulties had disappeared. The crisis of the seventeenth century struck a serious blow to its finances, In the Toledo district, two thirds of its resources came from ecclesiastical livings (canonries) and hence from tithes; the decline in agricultural production inevitably resulted in decreasing revenues; nor did the situation improve in the eighteenth century – quite the contrary, for now that there were no major trials, likewise there were no more confiscations and no more fines either.

4   The trial

The Inquisition took its name from the procedure elaborated to fight heretics. In Latin, *inquiro* means 'I seek out', *inquisition*, 'a search'. In matters of faith, what the judges sought to establish was whether an accusation was true. In this, the Inquisition was innovative, for it diverged from Roman law and what was known as the accusatory process, according to which the party that considered itself wronged had to prove what it asserted. The other party produced arguments to the contrary, and the judge decided in favour of either the one or the other. Medieval justice also applied the *lex talionis*: if the accuser could not prove his allegations, he could be sentenced to the very penalty threatening the person he was accusing. It was a way of deterring rash accusations. In contrast, the inquisitorial procedure allowed a judge to operate even without an accuser initiating legal action: public rumour on its own was reason enough. A judge could also act upon denunciations laid before him. In such cases, the *lex talionis* was not applied to a denouncer unable to provide proof to support his accusation. The very most that he risked was the penalties for slander if a preliminary inquiry showed that he was motivated by malevolence. Finally, an inquisitor was not simply a judge. He received depositions, interrogated witnesses and the accused, then eventually delivered his verdict.

He personally thus combined policing and judicial powers but, according to canon law, he did not act as a prosecutor since he sought only to establish the truth with impartiality and not to get the better of an adversary. In the fifteenth century, when the bishops took up the struggle against heresy, diocesan courts started employing a public prosecutor, a *promotor fiscal*. So it looked, on the face of it, as though the trial proceeded following the ordinary accusatory course, with the public prosecutor acting as plaintiff, the accused defending himself, and the bishop (or his representative) acting as judge. The Spanish Inquisition carried on in this way, portraying itself as a trial that opposed a prosecutor to an accused; but that was no more than an outward appearance. In reality, the inquisitor was at once judge and counsel for the prosecution. Admittedly, a *fiscal* was present, but his only role was to maintain the fiction of a trial of opposed parties. Contemporary commentators openly acknowledged that the whole operation was a fiction. One, Diego de Simancas, declared in the sixteenth century that, even when the accused confessed, the *fiscal* still had to present a formal accusation so that a trial could take place in the presence of a prosecutor, an accused and a judge. In reality, the *fiscal* was an inquisitor like the rest, except that he did not take part in the vote on the sentence.

The Spanish procedural rules for inquisitorial trials essentially took over those earlier elaborated by the medieval Inquisition, as set out, in particular, in Bernardo Gui's *Practica inquisitionis*,[1] of 1324, and Nicolas Eymerich's *Directorium inquisitorum*,[2] produced in about 1376. Were the earliest Spanish inquisitors familiar with those procedural rules? Probably not.[3] At any rate, their behaviour was strongly criticised in Rome, where they were censured (in a papal bull dated 2 February 1482) for acting *inconsulte et nullo iuris ordine servato*, that is to say in an ill-considered manner, outside the law. This is what may have prompted the creation of the post of grand inquisitor, which Torquemada was the first to hold. His official mission was to review procedure and implement the proper rules. In Seville, he convened 'a general *junta* composed of the inquisitors of the four courts that he had set up in Seville, Cordova, Jaen and Ciudad Real, his two assessors, and a number of royal counsellors; and on 29 October 1484 he published 'the first laws of the Spanish establishment, to be known as "instructions"': *Compilación de las instrucciones del Oficio de la Santa Inquisición*.[4] He later completed these documents with the so-called 'Valladolid instructions' (1488) and 'Avila instructions' (1498). Grand Inquisitors Deza and Cisneros later added a few minor complementary instructions and the whole collection was published in 1536 on the orders of Alonso Manrique.[5] In 1561, Valdés decreed new rules that modified some of the existing ones.[6] After 1561, no further changes were made to procedure or to the instructions, but from 1572, circulars issued by the Supreme Council (*cartas acordadas*) clarified details whenever it was felt necessary to do so.

The edict of faith

Every inquisitorial campaign began with a solemn invitation to all, to denounce themselves if they feared they had been heretical, and also to denounce all those whom they had reason to believe to be heretics. This was the objective of what was known as the edict of faith, or sometimes the edict of grace, because it allowed heretics thirty to forty days' grace in which to denounce themselves. In the early days, *conversos* who reckoned that they were bound to be arrested hoped to save their skins by confessing. They did not know that, even if they did so, inquisitors were forbidden to give them absolution in secret. Everything had to be public. Heresy was a crime as well as a sin. Where it was only a matter of an ordinary sin, any priest could give absolution without any need to inflict upon the sinner the humiliation of a public trial. But because heresy was also a crime, the inquisitors considered that a public trial was indispensable and that it was not up to confessors to absolve heretics. One stipulation in the edict of faith underlined this point: confessors must refer to the inquisitors any penitents who came forward to denounce themselves for sins against the faith. All that a suspect who denounced himself could avoid was the usual penalty for heretics: death. He could not elude other penalties – the infamy, the confiscation of property and so on. There was something terrifying about this rule. It delivered up to the shame of a public auto da fé even those who confessed their offence of their own free will. Huge numbers of Old Christians appealed to the pope, offering to make a sincere confession of their past behaviour and promising in future to be faithful to their obligations as Christians, if they were allowed to confess in secret. Sixtus IV was not unmoved by these arguments. The papal bull of 18 April 1482 agreed to make allowances for suspects who confessed their sins spontaneously; they could receive absolution and be condemned to private penitence, without being forced to abjure in public. However, Ferdinand of Aragon reacted immediately, in a letter dated 13 May, without even waiting for the bull's publication, and by 9 November the pope was back-tracking.[7]

Self-denunciation was not enough. You also had to denounce your accomplices, that is to say all those – relations, friends, and acquaintances – who had taken part, along with the suspect, in reprehensible practices and, with him, had attended ceremonies or meetings in the course of which Jewish prayers were recited. The obligation to denounce all those whom one suspected of being heretics extended to all the faithful, on pain of excommunication. In 1559, one of the grievances held against Archbishop Carranza, on the basis of which he was arrested and pronounced guilty was, precisely, that he had concealed facts known to him: when Carlos de Seso, later condemned as a Lutheran, had told him of his doubts concerning certain articles of faith, Carranza had advised him to say nothing on the subject, despite the fact that it was his duty to denounce Seso to the Inquisition. Where heresy was concerned, there was no way out. Even the death of a suspect did not halt the application of inquisitorial justice. When it could be proved that the deceased had been a Judaiser or had committed some other form of heresy in his lifetime, his remains were exhumed and burnt, and his possessions were confiscated. The edict of faith spelled out all these rules. In the early days of the Inquisition, this document would be read out whenever the inquisitors arrived in a town. Later, when the Holy Office had become a permanent institution, inquisitors were required periodically to leave their headquarters and set themselves up as itinerant courts, holding a series of sessions as they moved from place to place throughout their district. In theory, they were supposed to make one such tour (*visita*) each year; but in practice two years would sometimes elapse between *visitas*. A *visita* had to last at least four months. First, an edict of faith would be published in all the localities to be covered. Many minor offences would be tried at this point. In some cases, though, judgement would be deferred until the inquisitors returned to their district headquarters. It was customary to read out the edict of faith slowly and in a loud voice once every year, on a Sunday in Lent, at the moment of the offertory. After this, the officiating priest would remind his congregation of the duty of all the faithful to denounce themselves and those who seemed suspect, even if they were family and even if those presumed guilty were already dead.

The edict of faith was essentially a detailed inventory of all the remarks and attitudes likely to indicate heterodox opinions. In short, it set out to explain to the faithful how they could recognise heretics. The edict of faith acquired its definitive form in the seventeenth century. From 1630 on, the same text was read out throughout Spain.

Crypto-Judaism occupied a prominent place in this document and constituted its foremost and most discussed subject. The edict listed all the remarks and practices typical of Judaisers: avoiding reciting certain words (the *Gloria Patri* at the end of a psalm, for instance), slaughtering animals in a particular way, abstaining from eating certain foods and from working on a Saturday and fasting on particular days at particular times of the year. Edicts of faith also pronounced at length on funerary practices. When a dying person was turned to face the wall, when the deceased's body was washed in hot water, when its beard and armpits were shaved, when it was wrapped in a new winding-sheet and the head was propped up by a cushion filled with virgin earth, or a coin or a pearl was placed in the mouth, and when water was sprinkled everywhere in the house where a death had occurred – then in all probability one was in the presence of Jewish practices.[8]

Then came five paragraphs devoted to the 'sect of Mahomet', the 'sect of Luther', the 'sect of Illuminists', various other heresies and, finally, the books that it was forbidden to possess or read.

As signs indicating Moriscos who continued to practise Islam, the edict cited the customs of celebrating particular days and particular festivals, of fasting during Ramadan, of slaughtering animals in a particular way, of performing ritual ablutions (washing arms, hands, elbows, the face, the mouth, the nose, ears, legs and private parts) and abstaining from the consumption of wine and pork, not to mention funerary rites quite similar to those to be found among Judaisers: washing the dead, enveloping them in a clean shroud, burying them lying on their side, placing a stone close to the head, along with honey, milk and other food for the soul of the deceased.

In relation to Lutheranism, the edict drew the attention of the faithful to a number of particular declarations: claims that all that was necessary was to confess one's sins to God, that neither the pope nor priests possessed the power to absolve sins, that the consecrated host was not really the body of our Lord, that it was pointless to devote a cult to the saints and to hang their images in churches, that purgatory did not exist, so praying for the dead was a waste of time, that good works were not indispensable (for faith and baptism sufficed to procure salvation), and that priests, monks and nuns had the right to marry.

It was reasonable to suspect Illuminism when one heard someone recommending mental prayer and disparaging the recitation of prayers out loud, or maintaining that marriage is not a sacrament and that one should be guided by the inspiration of the Holy Spirit.

Other types of heresy listed in the edict included assertions of a materialistic nature (denials of the existence of paradise and hell, and of the immortality of the soul), blasphemy, remarks that cast doubt upon the virginity of Mary, superstitions and practices similar to those of magic and witchcraft, solicitation in the confessional, bigamy and the belief that ordinary fornication was not a sin.

It was, of course, forbidden to possess or read the works of Luther and his disciples, the Koran and other books of the 'sect of Mahomet', the Bible written in the vernacular, and all books that appeared in the Index published by the Holy Office. From 1738 on, the edict of faith also included a paragraph on freemasonry.

For many years the edict of faith prompted many denunciations and enabled the inquisitors to exercise strict control over the people. However, it possessed one drawback that did not escape the notice of perspicacious minds: it described heterodox opinions and practices in such minute detail that, paradoxically, it might well serve to propagate among the faithful types of heresy that, until then, they had never even imagined. For example, second- and third-generation *conversos*, deprived of all instruction in the faith of Moses, could discover what the Jewish rites (prayers, fasts and so on) were – just by listening to the edict read aloud by the inquisitors! An anonymous letter to Charles V, in 1538, pointed out this danger and suggested suppressing the declaiming of the edict, since in fact it disseminated knowledge of precisely what it condemned. A little later, Francisco de Borja developed a similar line of reasoning: he advised preachers not to allude to heresies and offences against the faith, for fear of teaching simple souls things of which they should remain ignorant: 'It is best to pass over them in silence,' he said. Following the Logroño trial of 1611, Inquisitor Alonso Salazar y Frías declared without hesitation that witchcraft had been unknown until people began to talk about it. The judges had themselves created the crime by bringing it to the notice of poor and ignorant folk. However, such observations had no effect. Up until at least the mid seventeenth century, the edict of faith continued to be read out every year. Then changes set in. In Valladolid, the custom was abandoned in 1660. Little by little, other districts followed suit. By the eighteenth century, the edict was a pure formality that was no longer taken seriously. Some inquisitors, among them those of Seville, regretted this. At the beginning of the eighteenth century they were complaining that it was a long time since any heretics had been tracked down. The trouble was that they were no longer being denounced. The practice of reading out edicts of faith ought to be revived to encourage the faithful to denounce to the commissioners of the Holy Office all those suspected of professing Judaism, Protestantism, Illuminism and other heresies.

The arrest

Within the period of grace indicated by the edict of faith, and before and after it too, the inquisitors would record a great number of denunciations. By no means all were prompted by zealous faith. Some simply targeted non-conformists, people whose attitudes distanced them from the usual customs. Others reflected petty preoccupations such as a desire to injure a neighbour or rid oneself of a rival. Nor was it solely the masses who resorted to malicious denunciations, for members of the social elite were equally capable of such baseness.

In 1572, Fray Luis de León was denounced to the Inquisition by his own colleagues at the University of Salamanca: Bartolomé de Medina, 'master of holy theology' and León de Castro, 'professor of Greek'. They were jealous of Fray Luis, envied his popularity among the students, thought him arrogant and cocksure. In the Spain of the Ancien Régime, denunciation to the Inquisition was a convenient means to dispose of a rival. The case of Fray Luis was not the only one of its kind. Lucienne Domergue has cited similar examples in the eighteenth century, such as the case of the mathematicians of the University of Valencia who were brought to trial in about 1750 and who protested, 'They seek to harm us in order to occupy our

University Chairs'. Another case worth mentioning is the arrest in 1787 of Friar Gonzalo Soto in the Canaries, which was prompted by an argument over experimental physics and had very much the air of a settling of old scores between Augustinians and Dominicans.[9] Could it be that the Spanish temperament particularly lent itself to such warped behaviour? Unamuno came close to such a conclusion. In 1918 he declared that it was not religious zeal that inspired the Inquisition, but envy, 'that terrible Hispanic envy, born of incompetence and pettiness. People could not bear to see anyone distinguishing himself, not thinking as others did, standing out from the herd. They could not tolerate heresy, personal opinions, thinking for oneself. By the very force of things, one had to stick to orthodoxy, the central dogma, the general opinion – or rather non-opinion, routine, common sense, non-thought ...'[10]

The inquisitors were not dupes; they knew that many denunciations related to declarations and attitudes that had nothing to do with orthodox faith. They therefore undertook a preliminary sifting operation in order to set aside any reports that clearly stemmed from malice and had no concrete basis. When denunciations seemed more serious, the prosecutor (*fiscal*) would seek to corroborate them by appealing for more testimony. As has been noted above, inquisitors and prosecutors were recruited in preference among jurists, and these were not always qualified to decide whether the statements or behaviour ascribed to a suspect really implied an unorthodox position. This was particularly true when they had to examine theological questions, sometimes of a quite subtle nature. When this was the case, the prosecutor would appeal to external advisers whose task it was to clarify the issue. In delicate situations, when persons of quality were involved for instance, the Supreme Council would be asked for its opinion. This is what happened between 1525 and 1540, with the Illuminists. Some were connected with figures of note such as canons of Toledo and university professors, and this made prudence advisable; and even more so in the Carranza affair of 1559.

Carranza, after all, was the primate of Spain and a theologian of great repute. The Inquisition accordingly took precautions. It did not immediately declare Carranza to be a heretic, but merely suggested that, possibly accidentally, he might have spoken as a heretic. In order to verify this, the Inquisition insisted that his writings be investigated impartially, with phrases taken out of context and examined *per se*, *in rigore ut jacent*. The question should be what meaning particular words and phrases might convey to the simple faithful masses. There is something terrifying about such a procedure, for it may result in totally twisting a thought. If Carranza spoke particularly of faith, it could be deduced that he held a low opinion of good works and so on. Carranza scented danger and protested: the works of Arius and Mohammed had never been treated in such a manner; common sense dictated that a book's propositions should be replaced in context; adopting the methods recommended by Valdés, it would not be hard to condemn even the works of Saint John Chrysostom and Saint Augustine, or to detect heresy in the Gospel of Saint John.[11] His efforts were in vain. The Inquisition ordered Domingo de Soto, a theologian regarded as an authority, to give his opinion of certain phrases in Carranza's *Catechism* and to judge them *in rigore ut jacent*. With a heavy heart, Soto found himself bound to admit that certain passages were indeed imprudent, to say the least, and called for correction or clarification. That was quite enough for the Inquisition to find Carranza guilty.[12]

The compilation of a file containing the testimony of witnesses and the qualifiers' reports (the *sumaria*, as it was called in the Inquisition's jargon) constituted the preliminary phase of the trial. Next, the prosecutor would officially request the arrest of the suspect. This operation was known as the *clamorosa*. The inquisitors would not decide on an arrest until they sounded out consultants and, above all, until they were convinced that they were dealing with a heretic. If the slightest doubt remained, Torquemada's instructions were to defer the arrest and wait until more conclusive testimony and evidence had been gathered. They warned that to summon a suspect simply to interrogate him was to set him on his guard and give him the chance to prepare a defence. They then added that experience showed that in such circumstances a heretic never confessed.

The arrest was acompanied by the sequestration of enough of the detainee's possessions to pay for his upkeep and food. Persons of high standing had the right to special treatment: if they had sufficient means, they were allowed to be attended by one or two servants who would, for example, prepare their meals – at the detainee's expense, of course. But those servants would have to remain imprisoned with their master throughout the latter's detention. A prisoner was allowed neither money nor paper. Valdés's instructions (1561) were particularly precise about the paper. If a detainee asked for paper in order to prepare his defence, all the pages were to be counted and numbered; those not used had to be returned.[13] A detainee was not allowed to communicate with other detainees. It sometimes happened that, owing to lack of space, several people had to be held in the same cell. In such a case, they were not to be separated later; if they had to be moved to a different cell, they all had to move together, to prevent them communicating information to other prisoners. No visits were allowed, except from lawyers. Detainees did not have a right to take communion. They were deprived of the comforts of religion in general on the grounds that, since they were presumed guilty of heresy, they were excommunicated. They could make confessions, but not receive absolution, except if they fell gravely ill and were in danger of dying.

Much has been written, particularly in the nineteenth century, about the Inquisition's prisons. They were called secret because, like everything to do with the Holy Office, they were indeed subject to the most absolute secrecy. They were no more sordid than other prisons, but no less so either. One, in Cuenca, is still standing, built according to the plans of the Italian architect Andrea Rodi, a pupil of Juan de Herrera, on the site of an ancient fortress. It seems to have been the only building constructed specifically as the headquarters of an inquisitorial court. In most towns, the Holy Office was based in old buildings that had not been designed for the purpose and that had to be renovated, in particular so as to accommodate prison cells.

The Instruction

Once in prison, the suspect was at the disposal of the court until such time as it saw fit to interrogate him. That could take weeks, or even months. During this time, which seemed to him interminable, the detainee was held in isolation from the outside world. He did not even know who was accusing him nor of what, for the rule was that everything to do with the Inquisition must remain secret. There could be no exceptions. Denouncers were guaranteed anonymity, in theory to protect them from pressures and possible future vengeance. All confrontation between accused and accusers was deliberately avoided. But of course if a confrontation did occur, the former inevitably set eyes on the latter, and the secrecy was gone. Naturally, the moment would eventually come when the suspect had to be told of what he was accused and would be read the charges laid against him, but every precaution was taken to prevent him, if possible, from identifying the witnesses. A detainee was allowed no visitors. Only the jailer was allowed to enter his cell. The inquisitors knew exactly what they were about when they surrounded themselves with absolute secrecy and a certain mystery. It was a way of inspiring respect for, and fear of, the Holy Office and to reinforce its sacred nature. The obsession with secrecy was carried so far that it was not even possible to obtain copies of the statutes, instructions and other documents relating to the Inquisition. Collections of texts and ordinances were certainly printed, but they were strictly for internal use; only the inquisitors themselves could hold and consult them. In 1556, the *Suprema* forbade the courts to communicate any information at all concerning the deliberations of the Holy Office, without first obtaining permission. It was forbidden, for example, to certify that an individual had never been found guilty or arrested by the Inquisition, which meant that it was impossible for anyone to prove that he had never had charges laid against him.

Finally, ('on the day that suited the inquisitors', as Torquemada's instructions specified), the detainee was brought before his judges. He was seated, having stood only to hear the accusation read out to him. This first hearing was designed to establish the identity and past history of the accused. He was questioned about his parents, his grandparents, the trades that he had plied, the towns where he had lived, his spouse and their children. He then had to explain where he was raised and by whom, what studies he had pursued, any travels he had engaged in abroad and in whose company. He was tested to see if he knew the principal prayers of Catholicism and the catechism, and he was required to say where and when and to whom he last made his confession.

This was but the preliminary phase of the trial. Immediately after, the inquisitors entered upon the nub of the matter. Giving no details, they invited the accused to tell them why he had been arrested and to make a full confession. This formal request (or admonition) was repeated three times over a period of several days. The trial, in the strict sense, had begun. It was characterised by two features:

1 Unlike modern practice in western societies, the accused who appeared before the Inquisition were presumed not innocent, but guilty. It was up to them to prove the contrary.
2 The inquisitors wanted confessions. The whole procedure was geared to this end. Whatever the testimony and evidence presented against the accused, that was not judged to be sufficient; it was essential that the accused acknowledge his guilt and that he do so publicly, just as he was expected to express his repentance in public: this was one of the purposes of an auto da fé.

If, following the third admonition, the detainee still refused to confess, the prosecutor told him what charges he faced. In principle, the court was concerned only with offences against the faith, but if the detainee happened to have committed other crimes or offences, these would certainly be included in the bill of indictment: the inquisitors had no authority to penalise him for such offences, but they were aggravating circumstances. The prosecutor then left the audience chamber, leaving the accused to reply point by point to the inquisitors. These appointed one lawyer, or several, whose task it was not to defend the accused, but to persuade him to confess. The lawyer was not allowed to remain alone with the accused; an inquisitor always had to be present. Seldom, and only in special cases, were the accused allowed to choose their lawyers freely. Carranza, for example, appealed to an eminent university professor, Martín de Azpilcueta ('the doctor from Navarre'), who agreed to defend him. Philip II never forgave him for doing so.

The inquisitors then invited both parties, the prosecutor and the accused, to present their arguments. The former produced the testimony against the prisoner and asked the witnesses to confirm their statements and, if necessary, add to them. The accused, for his part, had three means of defence at his disposal. He could reject certain witnesses (*proceso de tachas*). But as he did not know who they were, he had to list the names of all those he suspected of wishing to harm him; then, if any of the witnesses did appear on the list, they were automatically rejected. The second means (*proceso de abonos*) consisted in presenting witnesses who could testify to his morality. The third (*proceso de indirectas*) was to produce statements or evidence that indirectly showed that the charges brought against him were without basis.

Torture

The Inquisition, like other courts under the Ancien Régime, resorted to the torture of prisoners to make them confess, but it did so far less than other courts, not out of humanity or repugnance for such methods, but simply because it reckoned the procedure to be fallible and inefficient. '*Quaestiones sunt fallaces et inefficaces*', Eymerich wrote in his *Handbook for Inquisitors*, and commented, 'Torture itself is not a certain means of discovering the truth. There are weak men who, at the slightest pain, confess even to crimes that they did not commit, and others, stronger and more stubborn, who will bear the greatest torments.' In the *Instructions* that Valdés published in 1561, he likewise hid none of his scepticism. He declared that physical and moral strength is unequally distributed among men, which is why torture must be regarded as a very uncertain means of prising the truth from the accused.

However, this did not stop the Inquisition from torturing individuals of every kind, including nobles since, as Eymerich points out, in matters of heresy there are no privileges and privileged. Members of both the clergy and the nobility were subject to common inquisitorial law.[14] The prosecutor would present a request to apply torture and the whole court, both the inquisitors and the representatives of civil justice, would then decide whether or not to do so. A doctor was detailed to examine the prisoner and state whether or not he could bear such an ordeal. Torquemada dispensed inquisitors from attending torture sessions, authorising them to send a representative in their stead. Valdés, however, was more insistent and required the inquisitors to be present in person. Only the inquisitors, the clerk and the torturer could enter the torture chamber. It was forbidden to shed blood or to mutilate the accused during a torture session.

The Inquisition practised three methods of torture. The first was the ordeal by water. The prisoner was tied to a sloped ladder, his head lower than his heels; his mouth was propped open and a cloth was placed over it. On to this water was poured, which the prisoner was forced to swallow. The water jug contained one litre of liquid. During a single session as many as eight jugfuls could be administered to the prisoner. Another form of torture consisted in suspending the accused from a pulley by a rope that fastened his wrists together and to attach weights to his feet. The body was gradually raised, then abruptly dropped. In the third kind of torture, the rack was used. The prisoner's wrists and ankles were bound together by ropes that were then twisted tighter and tighter by means of a lever. According to Henningsen, 90 per cent of the accused brought before the Inquisition were never subjected to torture.[15]

The verdict

The 'instruction' continued until such time as the accused himself asked that it be closed. Why him, rather than the prosecutor? Valdés's *Instructions* provide the reason: if the prosecutor declared that the instruction was over, the implication would be that he had exhausted all his arguments and had no more to add, whereas if it was the accused who made the request, it was still possible, right up until the very last moment, for the prosecutor to present new arguments. A mixed commission composed of the inquisitors, representatives of episcopal jurisdiction and the consultants examined the file together; then each member was invited to express his opinion. They did so in the following order: first the consultants, then the representatives of episcopal jurisdiction, then the inquisitors. The prosecutor was not present at this debate.

When it came to delivering their verdict, the inquisitors had two concerns. The first was never explicitly formulated, but is detectable in almost all the trials, with very few exceptions: it was never to acquit the accused unless there really was no way of avoiding this. As has been said above, all the accused brought before the Inquisition were presumed guilty. The single objective of the whole procedure and instruction of the trial was to persuade the accused to recognise his guilt. So the final verdict's sole purpose was to regularise the prisoner's detention, *a posteriori*. Eymerich could see but one reason for acquitting the accused: if he had been the victim of false testimony. In any other circumstances he must be convicted. If a conviction really seemed too hard to justify, the court declared an adjournment (*suspensión*), which made it possible to reopen the case at any time. Eymerich insisted that a verdict should never state that the accused was innocent; it was better simply to say that nothing had been proven against him, thereby leaving open the possibility of bringing new charges if new facts came to light. Even when an adjournment was declared, it was accompanied by a minor penalty, for example an official warning. Why such severity? Because it was essential that the Holy Office was never seen to be in the wrong. Above all, no one should ever be able to claim that it had wronged the innocent.

Nevertheless, in the early years, the Inquisition did sometimes pronounce acquittals. Lea lists eighty-six in Toledo between 1484 and 1531 (fewer than two a year, on average).[16] Subsequently though, it was extremely rare for an inquisitorial trial to end with a verdict of acquittal. The most famous example was that of Fray Luis de León. On 28 September 1576, a mixed Valladolid commission recommended, by a majority vote, that the accused be subjected to torture and the case against him be reviewed. The other members of the commission favoured a simple warning in humiliating circumstances: Fray Luis would have to acknowledge his mistakes in the great amphitheatre of the University of Salamanca, before its professors and students, and would be banned from teaching. Following an appeal and a decisive intervention by Grand Inquisitor Quiroga, on 7 December, the *Suprema* opposed torture and insisted that Fray Luis be acquitted. The Valladolid court acquiesced. On 11 December it acquitted Fray Luis, but not without incurring considerable criticism: such a verdict constituted an encouragement to stray from healthy doctrine and placed professors who did hold fast to strict orthodoxy in an embarrassing position.

The second preoccupation of the inquisitors was part and parcel of the official *Instructions*: the accused himself must declare himself to be guilty and express his repentance. According to the degree of culpability and the accused's attitude, three categories of accused were defined:

1 those who were reasonably believed to be guilty of heresy but against whom insufficient proof was available and who, furthermore, denied the offences with which they were charged;
2 those who were guilty and who confessed (*convictos y confitentes*)
3 those who were classed, in Holy Office jargon, as *pertinaces* (obstinate). These fell into two groups: those who committed further offences after being found guilty, and those who refused to confess despite the evidence produced against them.

The first two categories were granted what was called a 'reconciliation': they would be reintegrated into the church once they had abjured their errors. Such an abjuration could take three different forms:

1 a *de levi* abjuration was required of those slightly suspected of heresy: bigamists, blasphemers, imposters;
2 a *de vehementi* abjuration was required of those seriously suspected of guilt – those who, despite the proofs produced against them, refused to confess, and those with no more than two witnesses testifying against them;
3 what was called a formal (*en forma*) abjuration was demanded from the accused known to be guilty and who had confessed. Judaisers fell into this category.

The *de vehementi* and the formal abjurations were further characterised by the fact that in the event of a second offence, the person was considered to be a relapsed heretic and as such could expect the death penalty. Such individuals were thus given a serious warning. On the other hand, a relapse after a *de levi* abjuration was not subject to any specified penalty.

The accused who were found guilty and who confessed (*convictos y confitentes*) were sentenced either to a spiritual act of penance or to a fine, or to other penalties of varying degrees of severity.

A spiritual penitence would consist of an obligation to undertake a pilgrimage to some specified sanctuary, or to retire to a monastery for a while, or to fast in particular circumstances or to recite a certain number of prayers.

A fine was not to be confused with the confiscation of property which, according to canon law, was the regular procedure where heresy was concerned. The Inquisition imposed fines only in cases where the crime of heresy was not proven.

The penalties that the Holy Office imposed on those who were 'reconciled' varied considerably. They might consist simply of exile from one's place of domicile (*destierro*), or a public flogging (a specified number of lashes administered by the official executioner), or a sentence to serve in the galleys (a penalty frequently imposed in the second half of the sixteenth century, when the king's service required many galley-slaves). And then there were prison sentences either for a specified length of time or else for life. In fact, however, a life sentence was a pure formality; it was never applied, and for a very concrete reason: the Inquisition was short of prisons and the upkeep of prisoners was too costly. In his 1561 *Instructions*, Valdés complained bitterly about this: many courts had no premises that could serve as prisons. Such buildings should therefore either be purchased or constructed. However, as we have seen, the Inquisition had never been opulent. Right from the start, this had posed a problem for the Holy Office. The chronicler Bernáldez, possibly exaggerating somewhat, wrote that, around 1488, in Seville, there were 5,000 detainees sentenced to life imprisonment. Because of lack of space, they had to be set free after four years. In the mid sixteenth century, the legal expert Diego de Simancas introduced the following guidelines: life imprisonment meant three years if the detainee had shown signs of repentance; otherwise eight years. In the medieval period, Eymerich had gone even further: when a prisoner appeared to have repented in all sincerity, he saw no reason why he should not be set at liberty under surveillance; when both husband and wife had been convicted, they could be lodged in the same cell; and if one of them had been declared innocent, he/she should be allowed to visit his/her spouse freely.

Those who had been declared 'reconciled' were *ipso facto* declared unfit to occupy ecclesiastical livings and public posts and also to exercise certain professions: for instance, those of tax-collector, pharmacist, doctor, surgeon and courtiers. That inelegibility extended to their children and their grandchildren. But as we have noted above, it was possible to avoid the ban by paying what was known as a composition fine.

The third category of accused, those whom the Holy Office considered to be obstinate (*pertinaces*), fell into three groups, according to the criteria laid down by Eymerich: relapsed 'penitents', non-relapsed 'impenitents' and those who were both impenitent and relapsed. Relapsed 'penitents' were recidivists: they had already been convicted as heretics, had admitted their mistakes, had been reconciled, had abjured and done penance, but had then relapsed into heresy. Non-relapsed 'impenitents' had been judged for the first time and proved to be heretics, but refused to confess and repent. The most grave case was that of relapsed 'impenitents'. Canon law assimilated heresy to a crime of treason that was committed against God. Just as treason against the king was punishable by death, so was treason against God. Capital punishment was the fate that awaited all those who relapsed, but there was one important difference between 'penitents' and 'impenitents': the former were strangled before being burnt; the latter were burnt alive. However, because the Holy Office was an ecclesiastical court, it could neither pass the death sentence nor execute it. With great hypocrisy, ever since the Middle Ages, inquisitors had therefore been accustomed to hand heretics over to royal justice, 'passing them to the secular branch' for it to carry out the sentence laid down for the crime of treason. The inquisitorial court had to be unanimous in taking this decision and, from the mid sixteenth century on, had then to have it ratified by the *Suprema*.

Relapsed 'impenitents' posed a problem for the inquisitors, for these felt they had partially failed in their task if they had not managed to convince such prisoners of their errors. The instructions for inquisitors urged them to make every effort to obtain the 'conversion' of 'impenitents', so that the latter would at least die reconciled with God. They would resort to every possible means to arrive at this result. For example, they would first try the utmost rigour, incarcerating the prisoner in a dark, narrow cell, with his hands and feet in chains. If this proved ineffective, they would switch to gentleness, move him to a better cell, improve his food and allow him to receive visits from his children, particularly the youngest ones, in the hope that they would touch his heart. Sometimes their efforts would be rewarded and the condemned man would eventually acknowledge the error of his ways and convert, either because he was truly convinced or because he was anxious to avoid a most horrible death: strangulation before the fire was better than being burnt alive. These last-minute conversions, even during the auto da fé or at the very stake, might commute his penalty; at the very least, he would not be burnt alive. The inquisitors' greatest dread was that those condemned would hold out against conversion to the very end. Eymerich wrote as follows: 'They insist upon the fire; if they are sentenced to be burnt alive, they are convinced they will die as martyrs and go to heaven.' Above all else, the Inquisition wished to avoid heretics presenting themselves as martyrs to their faith and, as we shall see, it took the greatest precautions, at the auto da fé and at the execution, to prevent this category of heretics from expressing their feelings.

Appeals against the sentence passed by the inquisitors could be made only to the Supreme Council. As has been noted, in principle the *Suprema* was supposed to confirm the gravest sentences, those that meant capital punishment. In other cases, however, the courts tried to prevent those convicted from making any appeal. The most effective way of doing this was to leave them in ignorance of their fate for as long as possible and to inform them of it only at the very last moment, at the auto da fé itself, when they had no time to make any move. Appeals to the court in Rome were strictly forbidden. On this point, the position of the Spanish sovereigns never wavered. A document dating from the time of Philip II was absolutely explicit: 'No affair judged by the Spanish Inquisition must be communicated to Rome, to be examined there as a last resort. Everything must be judged within the [Spanish] realm, by virtue of the apostolic delegation received by the grand inquisitor. The prelates and men of law of our kingdom know the *mores* and customs of their compatriots better than all others. It is therefore perfectly normal that Spaniards be judged by Spaniards and not by foreigners unacquainted with national and local particularities.'[17]

The auto da fé

In 1578, when completing and commenting upon Eymerich's *Handbook*, the legal expert Francisco Peña pointed out that the prime purpose of a trial and a death sentence was not to save a heretic's soul, but to ensure the public good and to strike terror into the people. He then went on to declare that sentences and abjurations must be read out publicly, 'for the education of one and all and also to terrify'. For the inquisitors, it was not enough to get the heretic to admit that he had sinned and declare that he had repented. He must be made to do so in public, so that it served as a lesson to all the faithful, who would be invited solemnly also to take this opportunity to declare their own attachment to the faith. This was the object of the ceremony known as the auto da fé, the nature of which is often misunderstood. In the course of an auto da fé nobody was executed; only after the ceremony were those sentenced to death handed over to royal justice and taken to the place of execution.

As the words indicate, the auto da fé was an act of faith, a public and solemn demonstration of commitment to Catholicism, as well as an equally public expression of the revulsion felt for heresy. For an auto da fé to convey its full meaning, it had to be reserved for circumstances that were out of the ordinary, when serious kinds of heresy were to be denounced. Minor delinquents were, to be sure, also paraded (blasphemers, bigamists, witches) but only as extras, for, on their own, such crimes did not justify an auto da fé. Furthermore, any crimes that might harm the reputation and prestige of the clergy, such as solicitations in the confessional, were kept right out of the limelight. The auto da fé was not uniquely Spanish. The medieval Inquisition had practised it in the form of a *Sermo Publicus* or *Sermo Generalis de Fide*. At the time of the repression of the Cathar heresy, such ceremonies would now and again be held in the Toulouse region. Also in Toulouse, the ceremony's name reflected the reality: it would begin with an appropriate sermon, as Bernard Gui, the local inquisitor from 1307 to 1323 mentions in his writings. The first auto da fé known to have been celebrated in Spain took place on 6 February 1481, in Seville.

According to the definition given by Llorente, an auto da fé consisted in 'a public and solemn reading of the trial and the sentences passed, which the inquisitors pronounced in the presence of the guilty or before their effigies and in the midst of all the authorities and the most respectable town corporations, in particular the royal judge of civil justice, into whose custody the convicted and the effigies were at this point transferred, so that he could immediately pronounce the sentence of death and fire in accordance with the laws applying to heretics, and order their execution. Acting upon an earlier and secret warning from the inquisitors, he would already have prepared the scaffold, the wood, the garrotting machine and the civil executioners.'

Llorente distinguishes several different forms of the auto da fé:

1 a general auto da fé, in which a large number of the guilty, from all classes, appeared;

2 a private auto da fé, lacking the apparatus and solemnity of a general auto da fé, at which the authorities were not present;

3 a single auto da fé, featuring only one guilty individual, which would be organised either in the church or in the public square, depending on the circumstances;

4 and finally, a small auto da fé (*autillo*), held discreetly within the premises of the Holy Office.

In the early days, autos da fé were rather sober and austere and were soon over. But, with the passing of time, by the sixteenth century the ceremony had become much more solemn and lengthy. The autos da fé of 1559, designed to eliminate the Lutheran groups of Valladolid and Seville, introduced significant changes. They now took on a form that was codified two years later by Grand Inquisitor Valdés and was thereafter definitive. The *Instructions* published in 1561 run as follows: 'When the trials are over and the verdicts have been decided, the inquisitors shall fix the festive day when the auto da fé will be celebrated. The date will be communicated to the canons and the municipal authorities and, if necessary, to the president and judges of the court of justice, to invite them to attend the ceremony. The inquisitors must be sure not to start too late, so that the execution of those whom they hand over can take place in daylight and without incident.'[18]

That said it all. The auto da fé would be held on a Sunday or some other holiday so that the entire population of the town and its surroundings could be present. Invitations would be issued to all the religious, civil, and legal authorities and to other official bodies and corporations. In 1598, the Holy Office went even further, insisting that the authorities and officials be present, on pain of excommunication. When an auto da fé was held away from the Court, a member of the high nobility would preside over it. In Granada, for example, in 1672, the first choice for this position was Don Rodrigo Ponce de León, the fourth Duke of Arcos; as he was unwell, he was replaced by the town's next most important figure, the marquis of Valenzuela, Don Antonio Domingo Fernández de Córdoba. At Court, of course, the Inquisition endeavoured to have the sovereign in person attend the auto da fé. We know of no autos da fé held in the presence of the Catholic sovereigns. But in 1528, the Inquisition decided to celebrate one in Valencia, to mark the visit of Charles V. The first of the great autos da fé of Valladolid, held on 21 May 1559, was presided over by the regent, Princess Joanna. Philip II, who arrived in the Iberian peninsula at the end of September, presided over the second one, on 8 October 1559. On 25 February 1560, the court of Toledo organised an auto da fé to mark the occasion of the marriage of Philip II and Isabella of Valois. When Philip visited Barcelona, in February–March 1564, for the Cortes of Catalonia, another auto da fé was held in his honour. He also presided over autos da fé in Lisbon, on 11 April 1582, and Toledo, on 25 February 1591. He seems to have particularly relished these ceremonies not out of sadism, as has sometimes been suggested (we should remember that those condemned to death were not executed until after the ceremony, when the authorities were no longer present), but on account of their great pomp: the procession, the Mass, the sermon and so on. Philip III then carried on the tradition, with the auto da fé of 6 March 1600, in Toledo. In 1632, Philip IV asked for one to be organised in Madrid, to celebrate the recovery of his wife, Isabella de Bourbon. The auto da fé of 1680, in Madrid, brought this string of ceremonies to a close, the official pretext this time being the marriage of Charles II and Louise Marie of Orleans. Grand Inquisitor Sarmiento de Valladares had intended to organise it in Toledo, but Charles II insisted on Madrid and himself fixed the date for it: 30 June, the festival of Saint Paul, 'so as to mark the great triumph of the Catholic faith and the rout of Judaiser obstinacy'. Under the Bourbon dynasty, there were changes. According to Llorente, Philip V refused to attend an auto da fé that had been planned for the occasion of his accession to the throne, but he was clearly not dead-set against such ceremonies as he did preside over one in 1720. After this, autos da fé were few and far between, but this was not because the monarchy had changed its attitude; rather, the Inquisition was no longer what it had been. In the sixteenth and seventeenth centuries, the auto da fé was one of many religious ceremonies. It was used to bestow importance upon special events, as is testified by the fact that the Catalans, who had seceded and placed themselves under the protection of France, saw fit to honour the prince de Condé, then their viceroy, by offering him an auto da fé on 7 November 1647, on the eve of his departure for Paris.

In the mid sixteenth century, descriptions of autos da fé began to be circulated, initially in a spontaneous manner. Improvising correspondents would send them to relatives or friends, to keep them up to date with the news. Subsequently talented writers would be requested to report them and their accounts would be printed. They became so popular that booksellers would provide special catalogues of them for their clients. The account of the 1610 auto da fé of Logrono (*Relación de las personas que salieron al auto de fee de [. . .] Logroño, 7 y 8 de noviembre de 1610*) ran to numerous reprints right up to the beginning of the nineteenth century. The most famous of these accounts was probably that which described the 1680 auto da fé in Madrid (*Relación del auto general de la fee que se celebró en Madrid en presencia de sus majestades el día 30 de junio de 1680 [. . .] por Joseph del Olmo, ayuda de la fuerriela de su majestad, alcaide y familiar del Santo Oficio*). The author had discharged important responsibilities in the town of Madrid; he had been one of the masterminds of the Buen Retiro Palace; and, as a Holy Office familiar, he was made responsible for drawing up the plans for the platform and planning the scheduling of the ceremony.

It was not long before painters, too, were helping to publicise the ceremonies surrounding an auto da fé. The painting by Pedro Berruguete, *The Auto da fé of Saint Dominic de Guzman*, at present in the Prado Museum, was the first of many. It was commissioned by Grand Inquisitor Torquemada, for the altarpiece of the monastery of Saint Thomas of Avila. The composition (154 x 92 cm) was designed to heighten the drama of the scene. Saint Dominic is shown standing on the rostrum, flanked by six inquisitors, among them a Dominican and another man holding the Holy Office banner; the group is completed by twelve other inquisitors. Two heretics, stripped naked, are burning on the pyre, two others awaiting their turn. The Inquisition commissioned several such works. A late example is provided by the auto da fé celebrated in the square of San Francisco, in Seville, on 13 April 1660. It was of an exceptionally spectacular nature. The *Suprema* commissioned a painting that would depict the platform, the inquisitors, the condemned men, the soldiers of the guard, and everything that was of note, 'in order to preserve the memory of the ceremony'. This painting was to grace the *Suprema*'s collection. Francisco de Herrera, 'the town's most famous painter', was the *Suprema*'s first choice, but he wanted 200 pesos for the work, a sum that was considered excessive. In the end, a less well-known painter executed the commission for 120 pesos.[19] The 1680 auto da fé in Madrid was depicted by Francesco Rizzi, and the picture was intended to be placed in the Buen Retiro Palace. It now hangs in the Prado.

The organisation of an auto da fé was a lengthy and costly operation that required the cooperation of the municipality, the police (to maintain order during the ceremony and to oversee the execution of the sentences after it) and many other groups and corporations: the Holy Office familiars, naturally, but also the diocesan chapters, religious orders and brotherhoods. Material preparations started at least a month before the appointed date. A platform had to be constructed in the town square or in some ecclesiastical building, with benches on which the condemned would be seated in full view of all present; a rostrum for the authorities, and one reserved for the inquisitors, which would be covered by a dais; also terraced seats that the would-be spectators reserved well in advance. The *sambenitos* to be worn by the prisoners had to be made, as did the effigies of those who had taken to flight or were already dead, banners, and the urns in which the sentences would be deposited. Seats and draperies had to be set in place, a meal prepared for the authorities in the event of the ceremony lasting longer than expected; various processions needed to be organised (that of the Green Cross, that of the White Cross), and the familiars who would have the honour of accompanying the inquisitors had to be designated, as did the detachments of soldiers that would mount guard. For the auto da fé of 2 December 1625, in Cordova, the preparations began on 30 October with an appeal for an offer to build the platform to carry an altar, seats for the seventy-two condemned individuals who were to appear, and other seats for the canons and municipal authorities. Everything had to be completed by 29 November. For the auto da fé of 2 June 1680, in the Plaza Mayor of Madrid, an awning was also planned, to provide shade for those attending. Added to the expense that all this incurred were many extra costs: remuneration for the subordinate staff, carpets, seats, benches and candles. It all added up to huge sums of money, especially if the ceremony was supposed to be outstandingly brilliant, for example if particularly important figures or the king himself were to be present. As has been noted, the finances of the Holy Office were never very flourishing, so the Inquisition always ran into difficulties when organising autos da fé. Local municipalities were not always disposed to make contributions, particularly in times of crisis, when their own revenues diminished. That is why, as time passed, fewer great autos da fé were held. There had been many in the second half of the sixteenth century: between 1549 and 1599, in Seville, there were at least twenty-three. In the seventeenth century the numbers were noticeably lower. The Holy Office would defer organising an auto da fé until there was a sufficiently large number of convicted prisoners, or would group together those from several courts. For fifty years, from 1632 to 1680, not one auto da fé took place in Madrid.

A few days before the appointed date, the Holy Office had a public proclamation read out, to invite the population to attend the auto da fé. To avoid any possible competition, other religious ceremonies were forbidden on that day. For the auto da fé of 30 June 1680 in Madrid, the proclamation had been made one month earlier, on 30 May. At three o'clock in the afternoon, the standard of the Holy Office was hoisted above the grand inquisitor's residence. The public crier read out the text in the main streets and squares of the town: 'The inhabitants of Madrid, the seat of His Majesty's Court, are informed that the Holy Office of the Inquisition of the town and of the kingdom of Toledo will celebrate a public auto da fé in the Plaza Mayor, on Sunday 30 June. On this occasion, the sovereign pontiff will grant particular pardons and indulgences to all those who attend.'

On the day before the auto da fé, at two o'clock in the afternoon, what was known as the procession of the Green Cross, the Holy Office's coat-of-arms, took place. It was considered a great honour to carry this standard. On 30 June 1680, in Madrid, the privilege fell to the first minister, the duke of Medinaceli. The object of the procession (which included the familiars, lawyers and commissioners of the Holy Office, as well as representatives of the secular and the regular clergy) was to convey the standard to the place selected for the auto da fé. It was placed at the highest spot on the platform and was covered by a black veil. All night long, familiars and monks kept watch around it, under the protection of a detachment of soldiers.

The next morning, at dawn, the crowd gathered to watch another procession, that which accompanied the detainees from the prison to the place of the auto da fé. In the early days of the Inquisition, the sentences of those to be 'relaxed', that is to say those condemned to death, had been made known at midnight. If they had up until then refused to recognise the error of their ways, they were now pressed urgently to confess and convert and thereby save their souls. However, the inquisitors later realised that the time allowed for this was too short, so the announcement of the sentences was made three days earlier.

During the night before the auto da fé, extraordinary precautions were taken: no one was allowed into the prison except confessors and the familiars detailed to keep the condemned under surveillance. At five in the morning, the convicted prisoners left the prison in a procession, flanked by two rows of familiars and soldiers. Behind the White Cross, also known as the Bush, because it was symbolically composed of several pieces of the wood to be used on the pyre, marched the clergy, followed by the effigies of the condemned who had taken to flight, the coffins containing those who had died before they could be judged and, finally, the condemned themselves, with special caps on their heads, carrying quenched candles, and wearing the clothing that indicated the nature of their respective sentences. This consisted of that famous tunic of infamy, the *sambenito*, which had also been a feature of the medieval Inquisition. Eymerich's *Handbook* describes it as a tunic made from two lengths of cloth, one in front and one behind, in the form of a scapular, but without any hood, on to which red crosses were sewn. The condemned prisoners did not all wear identical *sambenitos*. The colour and cut varied according to their respective crimes and sentences. Those to be 'relaxed' wore a black *sambenito* bearing a design of flames or sometimes demons, dragons and snakes, signifying the Hell that awaited them. They also wore red caps. The *sambenito* worn by those who were 'reconciled' was yellow, marked with two red crosses of Saint Andrew; the flames on their clothing were upside down, because they were spared being burnt at the stake. Imposters and bigamists had a rope tied round their necks, twisted into as many knots as the hundreds of lashes that they were to receive. Those who were 'reconciled' subsequently had to wear the *sambenito* whenever they went out, throughout the period of their sentence; they could only remove it in their own homes. When no longer in use, the *sambenitos* of both those condemned to death and those who were 'reconciled' would be hung on the walls of the parish churches, to perpetuate the memory of their infamy.

The Inquisition set the greatest store by these *sambenitos*, considering them to be the hardest penalty that could be inflicted on heretics: the tunic served to perpetuate the memory of the infamy attached to those found guilty. Their descendants were the first to suffer, but others too were shocked by the practice, as is testified by the long conflict which, from 1582 on, set the canons of Granada in opposition to the inquisitors. The latter had decided to hang the *sambenitos* in the principal chapel of the cathedral, without taking the trouble to request permission to do so from the canons or even to inform them. The chapter protested and insisted that what the archbishop himself considered an indecent practice be halted. Everywhere else, the *sambenitos* were hung in a cloister or some out-of-the-way corner, never in the principal chapel. On 22 May 1594, the king was obliged to intervene and order that the *sambenitos* be placed elsewhere, but the inquisitors turned a deaf ear. Eventually they did comply, but not until May 1611, a full thirty years later.[20]

Once the convicted had been clad in their caps and tunics and supplied with their candles, the procession left the prison and moved towards the place where the auto da fé was to be held, which was usually the main town square. When the inquisitors, the sovereign, the canons, the municipal authorities, the nobility and the clergy had all taken their allotted places, the ceremony could begin. A preacher delivered a sermon exalting the Catholic faith, rejecting heresy, and urging the accused who still persisted in their errors to repent before dying. It should be remembered that the inquisitors made strenuous efforts to persuade all the condemned to convert, wishing no one to die without having confessed and received the Eucharist. Those sentenced to death who repented were strangled before being tossed on to the pyre. Only those who refused to recognise their errors were burnt alive. The Holy Office attached great importance to the public confessions and the repentance that heretics would express, also publicly, once they had confessed. One striking example is provided by the account left by Luis Zapata of the retraction of Doctor Agustín Cazalla, preacher to Charles V, who was sentenced to death as a Lutheran at the auto da fé of 21 May 1559. Zapata reproduces a letter from Friar Pedro de Mendoza to Grand Inquisitor Valdés, to inform the latter that at the last moment he had obtained the 'conversion' of Cazalla. Upon the orders of the inquisitors, he had visited Cazalla in his cell, to tell him that he would be sentenced to death and to urge him to acknowledge his errors. Cazalla appeared at the auto da fé with a rope round his neck and wearing a cap of infamy. He tried to speak and address the crowd, but was silenced. He then asked for the archbishop of Santiago de Compostela's blessing, after which he was degraded and stripped of his insignia of priesthood and his former functions. He listened to his sentence and declared that he accepted death as a means of atoning for his sins. On the way to execution he tried in vain to persuade another man sentenced to death, one Herreruelo, likewise to retract. Cazalla was garrotted before being burnt. Herreruelo was burnt alive.

Whenever one of the condemned converted at the last moment, before the sentence had been pronounced, the proceedings of the auto da fé were interrupted. Candles were lit, canticles were sung, and the black draperies covering the crosses were removed. This happened in Madrid, in 1680, when a man and a woman condemned to death retracted when they reached the square. They were immediately taken to a small room set aside for the purpose beneath the platform, where their declarations were recorded. They escaped the death sentence and everyone present applauded. However, the inquisitors were wary of such last-minute conversions. They feared they might be the effect not of regret for having offended God, but of fear of the fire that was ignited before their very eyes. But they took precautions above all to prevent obstinate heretics from causing a scandal: at all costs, these were to prevented from addressing the crowd. It was a fear that had already been expressed, in the Middle Ages, in the *Sermo Publicus* that set the tone for the autos da fé of the Spanish Inquisition: one could not take the risk of seeing a heretic who had confessed his sin recant in public. Eymerich's *Handbook for Inquisitors* recommended tying up the tongue of prisoners who gave cause for concern or gagging them 'so that they could not scandalize those attending, with their impieties'. At the 1680 Madrid auto da fé, twelve prisoners sentenced to death were presented gagged. Those recommendations suggest that we should doubt the veracity of certain anecdotes. One example is that of Carlos de Seso's exchange with Philip II, at the auto da fé in Valladolid, on 8 October 1559.[21] Another concerns what was said to have happened in Madrid in 1680: a beautiful girl of seventeen, condemned to death as a Judaiser, was said to have called out to the queen, begging her to save her, for why should she die for having remained faithful to the religion in which her mother had raised her from the cradle?

After the sermon, the sentences were read out. Each convicted prisoner stepped forward to hear the accusations that concerned him and the verdict pronounced against him. If he was among the 'reconciled', he abjured publicly and promised never again to fall into such errors. He had to confirm and sign this declaration on the following day; if he could not write, an inquisitor or a lawyer signed for him. An inquisitor would then ask a number of questions relating to the principal points of Catholic dogma, and the accused and the public answered together: 'Yes, I believe.' The psalm *Miserere Mei* was then sung, a few prayers were recited, and as the *Veni Creator* was chanted, the Green Cross, up until then veiled by a black cloth, was uncovered. More prayers followed; then, finally, the inquisitor granted absolution to the 'reconciled' and handed over those sentenced to death to the secular branch.

An auto da fé lasted several hours, especially if, as became customary in the seventeenth century, batches of prisoners convicted by various courts all appeared together. The ceremony began very early and might end very late. The Cordova auto da fé in which the *beata* Magdalena de la Cruz was sentenced lasted from six o'clock in the morning to four in the afternoon. In Logrono, on 7 November 1610, the ceremony had to be adjourned after the reading of the death sentences, to be continued the following morning. The entire proceedings were completed at nightfall. One of the largest autos da fé in the entire history of the Holy Office was that of 30 June 1680, in Madrid. It had started at five o'clock in the morning. By about four in the afternoon, the death sentences had only just been read, and those condemned then left, to be conducted to the place of execution. The ceremony then continued with the reading of the sentences of the 'reconciled' and a solemn mass, which was not over until half past nine in the evening. Only then did King Charles II withdraw, first asking whether it was all over and he could leave. He had arrived at eight o'clock that morning and had not left his place for more than a quarter of an hour. When the organisers foresaw that the ceremony might be protracted, they took certain precautions. In Madrid, one of the familiars had been detailed to prepare a meal for the members of the Supreme Council. Food and drink were also available for the commissioners and the inquisitors from elsewhere; and even the prisoners were catered for, 'to take account of the anxiety and disquiet of the condemned and the fatigue of the monks and priests who accompanied them, the court, in its wisdom, had provided a large supply of biscuits, chocolates, jams, and drinks, so that those in need could replenish their strength'.

As we have noted, those condemned to death were not executed at the auto da fé itself, but immediately after it, in another place. The Inquisition handed them over to royal justice, which had to apply the penalty that was prescribed for the crime of divine treason: death at the stake. As soon as the sentences had been read out, a detachment of police took charge of the condemned and escorted them to the place of execution. A large crowd surrounded and followed this funeral procession. Juan Páez de Valenzuela left an account of an execution in Cordova, following the auto da fé of 2 December 1625, commenting, 'The crowd that had come to see this sad spectacle, on foot, by carriage, or on horseback was so large that you could hardly move in this huge square, even after two in the morning.' First those who had repented were garrotted. Joseph del Olmo's account of what happened in Madrid in 1680 is horrifying. There had been set up 'on the place of execution, twenty or so posts equipped with large rings to which to attach the condemned, then garrotte them, and then set fire to them as is customary, but avoiding the horror and violence that frequently attends this kind of execution'. The bodies, other remains and the effigies of those condemned in their absence were then immediately cast into the fire. Meanwhile the priests were busy among the obstinate, trying to persuade them to abjure and thereby avoid the atrocious death that awaited them. Often enough, fear had its effect; in Madrid, on 30 June 1680, six of the condemned converted a few moments before being executed, but on that day several others persisted and were burnt alive. The crowd watching was horrified but also felt a certain admiration for the courage of those who preferred to die in this way rather than abjure their faith.

Writing of these mixed feelings, Joseph del Olmo urged his readers not to confuse true courage with an obstinate blindness that closely resembled suicide. He wrote, 'It is not death that makes a martyr, but the cause for which he dies,' adding, 'In Malabar, noble women cast themselves, apparently joyfully, into the flames in order, they believe, to follow the fate of their husbands ... That is a gross illusion of blind idolatry. In the first auto da fé organised to punish the Albigensians, in 1206, at least 300 of those "relaxed" cast themselves into the flames rather than listen to the miraculous sermons of the glorious patriarch Saint Dominic, who was exhorting them.' In the mindset of the time, it seemed beyond belief that an individual could refuse to admit the truth of the Catholic faith, once all his problems with it had been clarified. Repulsing grace could be explained only by some mental derangement, a lack of intelligence or perversion. It did not occur to people that it is possible to refuse to believe out of scruples of conscience and intellectual honesty. In the twentieth century, in the Soviet Union, dissidents were likewise assimilated to the mentally sick and were shut away in psychiatric hospitals.[22] In

1680, Joseph del Olmo's thinking ran along similar lines: 'When one sees the means employed by the Holy Office to disabuse heretics, and the proofs that it gives in order to convince them – proofs drawn from the writings of men full of wisdom, virtue, and knowledge, only wilful obstinacy can explain a refusal to embrace the Christian religion. Among the people of that nation (the Jews), heredity wins out. Through pride, they set the blindness of their ancestors above the wisdom of the Christian doctors, and those feelings of theirs, exacerbated by sensuality and cupidity, the sources of all evils, blind their eyes to reason.'

According to tradition, the laymen who carried the wood to the pyre received special indulgences, but the clergy did not because, for them, that would have been an offence. At the end of the six-teenth century, this wood, which symbolised Catholic intransigency towards heresy, seems to have been strongly associated with Ferdi-nand III, the king of Castile. In 1595, in his treatise on the Chris-tian prince, *Tratado del príncipe cristiano*, which he dedicated to the crown prince, Philip, the future Philip III, Pedro de Ribadeneyra referred to that tradition: 'Some serious authors maintain that King Ferdinand carried his desire to keep the faith pure, intact and uncon-taminated to such lengths that he was not content simply to have heretics punished. When the time came to burn them, he insisted on himself bringing wood for the sacrifice.' Joseph del Olmo also refers to this in his account of the 1680 Madrid auto da fé, and adds: 'At the moment when the ceremony in the square was starting, the captain of the soldiers of the faith presented a fagot to the king; the king showed it to the queen, then returned it to the captain, requesting him to carry it to the pyre in his name, in memory of the holy King Ferdinand.'

When all the 'relaxed' were dead, the executioners still kept the fire going, in order to reduce the bodies to ashes. Sometimes this operation took all night. Meanwhile the soldiers of the faith took up the White Cross that had presided over the execution and carried it away, in a procession. A few days later, it would again be placed next to the Green Cross. On the following day, the sentences passed on the 'reconciled' were carried out: whippings, after which the victims were paraded through the main streets, for all to see. Those who had received prison sentences were then taken to their cells.

The victims of the Holy Office

The Inquisition was the only Ancien Régime institution that exercised power over every social order. It ignored the usual privileges of the clergy and the nobility. So it should have been as hard on the privileged classes as on the populace. In reality, though, it is noticeable that, except when they were charged with heresy, the nobles and other elites were spared physical penalties considered to be degrading, such as whipping and forced labour. The tendency was, rather, to sentence them to financial penalties or to prison.

Where the clergy was concerned, the Inquisition's attitude varied depending on whether it was dealing with heretics or other categories of offenders. The Holy Office showed heretics (Judaisers, Protestants and Illuminists) no indulgence at all. It considered that individuals from elites ought to be models of orthodoxy for the Christian populace, and that any failings on their part should be punished severely, to set an example. The masses must be convinced that even priests were not spared punishment when they proved themselves unworthy. This was one of Menéndez Pelayo's arguments in defence of the Inquisition: even those who criticised it as a tyrannical institution must surely recognise that it was at least a popular tyranny, a 'monastic democracy' (*democracia frailuna*) that struck down all who stepped out of line. That is one way of looking at the situation; but another is to detect demagogy and a process of levelling-down.

It is quite true that nobody was beyond the reach of the Holy Office. Bishops constituted the sole exception. In cases of heresy, they were answerable to the pope, not to the Spanish Inquisition. That was the situation in 1506, when Lucero, the inquisitor for Cordova, laid charges against Talavera, the archbishop of Granada. The pope asked to see the file on the case, examined the charges and acquitted the prelate. In 1559, in order to arrest Carranza, the archbishop of Toledo, Grand Inquisitor Valdés had to request special permission from the pope, but the brief that he obtained from Paul IV contained one important restriction: although the sovereign pontiff authorised the grand inquisitor to prepare proceedings against bishops suspected of heresy, he reserved the exclusive right to pronounce definitive judgement. In the end, after the pope threatened to proscribe and excommunicate him, Philip II resigned himself and agreed that Carranza be transferred to Rome for judgement.

When the charges against clerics did not include heresy, the situation was quite different and the Inquisition showed far greater indulgence: the penalties for soliciting priests, for instance, were extremely discreet. The Holy Office considered that a public scandal would be graver than the sin that had been committed. It would therefore avoid any publicity that would attract attention to the shortcomings of the clergy, so as not to damage its prestige among the people.

How many victims suffered at the hands of the Inquisition? Works that have appeared over the past thirty years make it possible to tackle this question, if not with confidence, at least with objectivity. At the beginning of the nineteenth century, Llorente, in his *Critical History of the Spanish Inquisition*, was the first to attempt a precise answer. He was well familiar with the archives of the Holy Office, as he had worked within the institution. The overall figure that he provides is 340,592 victims from the very beginning (1480) until 1815, a total that breaks down as follows: 31,913 individuals actually burnt, 17,659 burnt in effigy and 291,021 reconciled or given minor sentences. Llorente adds that the repression was particularly severe during the 1483–98 period, during which Torquemada was grand inquisitor: at this time 8,800 victims perished at the stake and 9,654 were subjected to a variety of other penalties.

By the mid nineteenth century, Llorente's figures were being challenged as being much too high. In his book on *Cardinal Ximénès* (Cisneros),[23] a Catholic author such as Joseph Karl Hefele, who is regarded as something of an apologist for the Holy Office, agreed on this point with a Protestant such as Peschel[24] and with the Jewish historian Graetz. Peschel believed that the number of individuals burnt between 1481 and the death of Queen Isabella (1504) was no more than 2,000. Graetz too wrote of 2,000 victims who perished at the stake, but in Torquemada's time alone. At the beginning of the twentieth century, Lea criticized Llorente's methods. As he did not possess continuous series of the relevant documents, he had relied on the data provided by the chronicler Bernáldez and, later, the historian Mariana. From these he calculated the yearly average of victims and, for the years for which no information at all was available, he simply extrapolated. He assumed that the activity of the Holy Office had been uniform during those early years. However, that was far from being the case. Without deliberately doing so, Llorente had grossly exaggerated the number of victims.[25]

There are no precise statistical data until about 1560, as most of the relevant archives have disappeared. Contemporary chroniclers record fragmentary information that is not always correct about the activities of the earliest inquisitorial courts. Other more reliable sources do exist, for example the notes that Klaus Wagner found in the margins of the notarial registers of Seville, which frequently refer to events such as the autos da fé and record the number of victims.[26] We know that the repression was particularly harsh and murderous while the Inquisition was being set up. According to the chronicler Pulgar, between 1481 and 1488, in the kingdom of Castile, at least 2,000 Judaisers were sentenced to death and 15,000 were 'reconciled'. In the district of Seville alone, between 1481 and 1488, 700 individuals were 'relaxed' to the secular branch, although it is true that some had fled and so were burnt 'in effigy'. In the course of a single auto da fé celebrated in Ciudad Real in February 1484, thirty-four Judaisers were burnt alive. In the Hieronymite monastery of

Guadalupe, during 1485, fifty-two were executed, twenty-five burnt in effigy, and forty-six corpses were exhumed in order to be cast into the flames. In Toledo, between 1486 and 1490, about 100 individuals were sentenced to death and executed. To the north of the Guadarrama, the figures are lower: 100 capital executions in Avila, up to 1500; fifty-six in Valladolid between 1489 and 1492. Ricardo García Cárcel, who studied the early days of the court of Valencia, up until 1530, mentions 2,354 trials, for which the judgements on 1,997 cases are known: there were 754 capital executions, 155 condemnations in effigy, and 1,076 'reconciled'.

From 1560 until the end of the seventeenth century, the courts were required to send periodical reports (*relaciones de causas*) to the *Suprema*. These briefly described the trials that were proceeding, stating the names of the accused, the nature of their crimes, the judgements that were delivered and so on. In the eighteenth century, the allegations of the prosecutors (*alegaciones fiscales*) were of a similar nature. Although the statistics provided by these sources are not always rigorously accurate, they do make it possible to calculate the number of victims reasonably precisely.

As we have seen, within about twenty years, between 1481 and 1500, the Inquisition eliminated the Spanish Judaisers, at the cost of a terrible repression. That was, indeed, the purpose for which it had been created. From 1500 on, that category of heretics figures only residually in the activities of the courts. However, with the arrival of the Portuguese *conversos* in the last years of the sixteenth century, it once again became a prime concern. In the meantime, the Holy Office had directed its attentions either to minority groups, essentially Illuminists and Protestants, or else to the many Old Christians against whom it laid charges for unseemly talk, blasphemy, bigamy, homosexuality, superstition and witchcraft, but such offences received only light penalties. Moriscos accused of reverting to Islam were punished less harshly than Judaisers. All this explains the decline in the number of death sentences between 1500 and 1580. After 1580 down to the last decades of the eighteenth century, Judaisers of Portuguese origin were the object of a repression which, although savage, by no means reached the level of the years from 1480 to 1500.

The credit for the most serious efforts to calculate the number of victims of the Spanish Inquisition must go to Jaime Contreras and Gustav Henningsen. On the basis of the *relaciones de causas*, these two historians estimate that between 1540 and 1700 the Holy Office arrested 49,092 individuals. Working from prudent extrapolations for the periods immediately preceding and following these years, they calculate that a total of 125,000 trials took place. That is one third of the number that Llorente suggested. In those trials, unseemly talk and blasphemy head the list, representing 27 per cent of all the charges; next come 'Mohammedanism' (24 per cent), Judaism (10 per cent), Lutheranism (8 per cent) and, lastly, superstitions of various kinds, including witchcraft (8 per cent). As to the sentences imposed, Contreras and Henningsen calculate that the death penalty was passed in 3.5 per cent of the cases, but only 1.8 per cent of those condemned were actually executed, the rest being burnt in effigy. In other words, between 1540 and 1700, 810 individuals were executed. We know that death sentences were numerous before 1500 and a few more were passed after 1700. So it is reasonable to suppose that, in the course of its history, the Inquisition was responsible for fewer than 10,000 death sentences followed by execution.

That is a far lower figure than is usually suggested. By way of comparison, the Religious Wars in Europe accounted for tens of thousands of victims. Saint Bartholomew's Day (24 August 1572) alone resulted in 3,000 deaths in Paris, not to mention those recorded in other French towns. At the end of the nineteenth century, the novelist Juan Valera exclaimed, 'All the Moors, Jews, and heretics arrested and burnt in Spain in the course of three hundred years by no means equal the number of witches burnt in Germany.' These days, such considerations are voiced increasingly often in the press and serious works of scholarship. When all the evidence is taken into account, the context suggests that the Spanish Inquisition was but one of the many manifestations of the intolerance characteristic of the period of the Religious Wars, and so there is no reason to single it out in particular. The pontifical declaration *Memory and Reconciliation*, in which the Catholic Church asks to be pardoned for the excesses committed by the Inquisition, testifies to this tendency to relativise and underplay the activities of the Holy Office. John Paul II points out that the Inquisition was created and operated during a painful phase in the history of the Church. A reading of this document leaves one with the impression that the abuses committed, regrettable in themselves, were, after all, less numerous than those of other religions during the same period.

But the problem posed by the Inquisition cannot be reduced to statistics and the macabre score of its horrors. In the sixteenth century, liberty of thought existed nowhere; every State practised intolerance. Should we conclude that the Spanish Inquisition does not deserve its sinister reputation, since it was less murderous than the many manifestations of intolerance in other European countries and also, where witch-hunts were concerned, in Anglo-Saxon America? In opposition to this tendency to belittle, and so – like it or not – excuse the Spanish Inquisition, we should do well to remember a few facts. The Spanish Holy Office does not constitute the same kind of manifestation of intolerance as many others in Europe. Even if we accept that the Spanish Inquisition was less murderous than has been claimed (which is indeed true), the fact remains that it had no equivalent in Europe. From this point of view, Marcel Bataillon set the record straight in his thesis on Erasmus, published in 1937: 'The Spanish repression was distinct not so much through its cruelty as through the power of the bureaucratic, policing, and judicial apparatus at its disposal. Its centralized organisation covered the whole peninsula in a relatively tight network; it even had antennae abroad [...] Through the edict of faith that enjoined everyone to denounce all noticed offences against the common faith, the entire Spanish people found itself, willy-nilly, associated in the actions of the Inquisition.'[27] It is because of those characteristics that comparisons with other countries are not convincing. Everywhere else, flare-ups of intolerance would produce thousands of victims – flare-ups that were preceded and followed by more or less long periods of peace. In Spain, one finds an intolerance admittedly less deadly, but institutionalised, organised and bureaucratised, which lasted far longer, from 1480 to 1820. The very formula of the Holy Office rendered it redoubtable. With its mixed jurisdiction, designed for religious purposes but placed under the authority of the State, it in some ways constituted an anticipation of modern totalitarianism.

5   The Inquisition and society

In 1813, when the Cortes of Cadiz were thinking of suppressing the Inquisition, one of those who spoke was not afraid to attribute the decadence of Spain to that institution: 'The obscurantism, the backwardness of science, the ruination of the arts, trade, and agriculture, and the depopulation and poverty of Spain all stem largely from the Inquisition. For industry, the sciences, and even religion to prosper, what is needed is great men to cultivate, enrich and teach them, through their knowledge, eloquence and example.' The tone was set. Those were the principal arguments voiced in what, in the second half of the nineteenth century, was to be called the science quarrel. 'Why had Spain fallen so low under the rule of the last Hapsburgs?', the poet Gaspar Núñez de Arce asked, in his inaugural speech to the Spanish Academy, on 21 May 1876: because of despotism – despotism both political and religious. A week later, reporting that speech, another liberal, Manuel de la Revilla, agreed with those statements but qualified them: 'It is intolerance, even more than despotism, that has ruined the culture of our land.' However, he believed that it was true that 'the decadence of the sciences and that of letters has not been equal. In Spain, there are no men of the stature of Copernicus, Galileo, Kepler, Newton, Pascal or Descartes to be found [...] Hard though it is to acknowledge, the facts are there: in the history of literature, Spain counts for a great deal; in the history of the sciences, she means nothing [...] The fault lies with our ferocious religious intolerance.' Other commentators were equally categorical: 'The

Inquisition paralysed the scientific energies of the nation' (José del Perojo). It was at this point that the young Menéndez Pelayo – at the age of twenty! – startlingly chose to make his name by launching into an attack on the 'liberaloid clique' (*la estirpe liberalesca*) that was denigrating Spanish culture, out of its hatred for the Inquisition and 'the men in soutanes': 'What fashionable philosophers cannot bear to acknowledge is that educated Spaniards of the past could be Catholic and could write under a regime of religious and monarchical unity.' Menéndez Pelayo then went on to declare that in truth, 'Religious intolerance had no influence at all on the sciences so long as they did not call dogma into question. No useful book was ever proscribed. No scholars were ever persecuted.'

One hundred years after this polemic, the debate has lost none of its relevance; in fact, it has been extended to every aspect of Spain's development. The claim now is that intolerance not only slowed down, when it did not actually block, scientific progress and intellectual liberty, but furthermore, by expelling and persecuting Spain's most dynamic elements (the Jews and the *conversos*), it precipitated the economic decline of the country which, as a result, became marginalised in the modern world. What is really the fact of the matter? Can the Inquisition be blamed for all the misfortunes of Spain?

The Inquisition and economic development

Did the religious policy inaugurated by the sovereigns in 1480 cause the ruin of the Spanish economy? That is what a long historiographic tradition has been repeating until recently: after the expulsion of the Jews, and having deprived itself of the most dynamic elements of its population, Spain, bogged down in the fanaticism and prejudices of a bygone age, turned its back on productive activities, despised manual labour, used the Inquisition to persecute what was left of its bourgeoisie, and took refuge in a haughty caste-fixated attitude, displaying interest solely in military values and those of the nobility and all that went with them: land, income from real estate, in fact just plain income.

There is no need to dwell on the remarks made in the Introduction to the present work: the creation of the Inquisition and the expulsion of the Jews did provoke a passing slump here and there, but they did not lead to catastrophe. Before 1480, as after, Spain, or more precisely Castile, pursued the expansion that had begun at the beginning of the fifteenth century and continued into the mid seventeenth, an expansion that was strengthened by the discovery of America but predated it. All historians of the Spanish economy – Hamilton, Carande, Lapeyre, Pierre Vilar, Felipe Ruiz Martín among others – are in agreement: Castile profited from the American market. Its businessmen manifested a competence, efficiency and dynamism that bear comparison with the greatest examples of similar qualities to be found in the Europe of that time. Contrary to what is often assumed, throughout most of the sixteenth century Spain grew increasingly rich. The American market contributed greatly to its success. Prices rose, but so did salaries; and entrepreneurs, farmers and merchants all profited. There is no other way to explain the fortunes that went into building, to which so many monuments, palaces and private houses testify – all of them constructed in those fine days of prosperity.

Not until the last third of the sixteenth century did the expansion slow down and the tendency become reversed, as I have tried to explain in another work.[1] Initially, the rise in prices had encouraged agriculture, industry and commerce. As the century proceeded, the American market continued to exert strong pressure on demand; Spanish prices remained the highest in Europe, but wages soon matched the rising curve of prices, whereas elsewhere the disparity between the two increased. According to Hamilton, this is the explanation for Spain's atypical development. Everywhere else the wide disparity between prices and wages made it possible to accumulate profits that could then be reinvested; capital was created, hence the rise of capitalism. In Spain this did not happen. With wages keeping pace with prices, profits were lower, as was the accumulation of capital and, for that reason, Spain did not move into the capitalist era.[2] Despite Spain's commercial monopoly, more competitive foreign goods swamped the Spanish and American markets, and recession took over.

Not all historians agree with Hamilton's thesis,[3] but whatever judgement is passed on it, it is remarkable in that it attempts to account for the economic phenomena without resorting to arguments of an ideological order. This shows that it is perfectly possible to propose a plausible interpretation for Spain's economic evolution without feeling obliged to evoke the expulsion of the Jews, the Inquisition, and blood purity. It was not because of their temperament, but as a result of the circumstances that Spaniards ended up preferring sure incomes, guaranteed by the State, to the risks of commercial or manufacturing enterprises. The Inquisition's influence on the evolution of economic attitudes was no more than incidental.

The Inquisition and books[4]

Right from the start, the printing press was recognised to be an effective means for diffusing knowledge. In Spain, a 1480 edict exempted imported books from customs duty on account of the services that they could render. In 1502, another edict ruled that works printed in the territories of the kingdom of Castile be subject to prior authorisation. Such authorisation could be given by the courts of justice (*Chancillerías*) of Valladolid and Ciudad Real (transferred to Granada a few years later), the archbishops of Toledo and Seville, and the bishops of Granada, Burgos and Salamanca. It was a matter not of establishing any kind of censorship, but rather of guaranteeing the intellectual proprietorship of the authors. This is certainly what is suggested by the declarations of the statement that accompanied the edict: a book was protected by an exclusive privilege, usually for a period of ten years. That exclusivity was valid only in the kingdom of Castile. In the kingdom of Aragon any book could be printed freely, even without the consent of its author. These measures remained more or less effective right up to the end of the Ancien Régime. From 1554 on, it was the Council of Castile that granted the necessary authorisations, on the basis of a report provided by the censor; but in principle the job of a censor was not to prevent the diffusion of immoral or dangerous works.

Authorisation did not signify approval of the printed text, but the populace was often convinced that it did. In his *Theological Matters*, Melchor Cano relates the case of a priest who was convinced that anything that was published was true or, at the very least, inoffensive. He claimed that the king's agents would never commit the crime of allowing lies to circulate – certainly not by granting them privileged rights. He therefore believed in the authenticity of the adventures of Amadis of Gaul. Melchor Cano concluded from this that vigilance with regard to published matter should address not only religious ideas and good *mores*, but also deter the diffusion of useless books of no interest. Most Humanists of the time shared that point of view. In this way, Melchor Cano drew attention to the danger that certain works might present.

The printing press made it possible to diffuse works which, until then, had been accessible to only a limited elite. Many books – not only recreational literature, but also bibles and treatises on spirituality – were now beginning to appear in the vernacular. To be sure, the limited nature of the editions (between 250 and 1,600 copies), the high prices and the illiteracy of most of the population all combined to reduce the impact of the book revolution. All the same, progress was spectacular. It is estimated that three quarters of the books published between 1445 and 1520 were works of a religious nature: bibles, psalms, gospels and the like. This success alarmed the religious authorities. The *Inter sollicitudinis* papal bull of 4 May 1515 certainly praised the printing press, but immediately went on to recommend measures designed to prevent thorns from growing among the good plants and poison from mixing with medicine.

In Spain, the Inquisition soon busied itself destroying books that might provide new converts with information about Judaism or Islam. On 7 November 1497, the *Suprema* ordered the court of Valencia publicly to burn books written in Hebrew and relating to Judaism, medicine, surgery and other sciences, and also bibles in the vernacular. This order appears to have been revoked subsequently, but a similar one was obeyed to the letter in Barcelona. In the following year, the *Suprema* entrusted a number of well-known theologians with the task of examining bibles, Korans and other Muslim texts before burning them. In 1500, in Granada, Cisneros is said to have consigned to the flames over one million books in Arabic (the figure seems much inflated), sparing only those on medicine, which were destined for the future university of Alcala. On 12 October 1501, the sovereigns ordered the destruction of all Korans found in the former emirate of Granada; but again books on medicine, philosophy and history were spared. Finally, in 1511, another official text confirmed the previous measures and forbade the publication and reading of all books written in Arabic.

The above measures applied to books that were possibly related to Judaism (books in the vernacular were included in this category) or to Islam. Where all other types of work were concerned, the Inquisition waited fifty or so years before intervening. Spain was neither the only nor the first of the Catholic nations to draw up a list of works that the faithful were forbidden either to read or to possess. In this domain, the Sorbonne led the way in 1544, followed by the University of Louvain (1546) and the Republic of Venice (1549). The first Index issued by Rome dated from 1551. In that same year, the first Index produced by the Spanish Inquisition appeared. There was nothing original about it. It was simply a new and expanded edition of the Index published in Louvain in 1550. The second Spanish Index (1554) was exclusively devoted to editions of the Bible. The third, produced by Valdés in 1559, was far more ambitious. It was typical of the anti-mystical trend then current in Spain. It listed 701 titles, classified into six categories:

- books in Latin;
- books in the vernacular (170 titles);
- books in Flemish (fifty titles, reproduced from the Louvain Indexes of 1546 and 1550);
- books in German (thirteen titles, reproduced from the Louvain Indexes of 1546 and 1550);
- books in French (ten titles, reproduced from the Louvain Indexes of 1546 and 1550);
- books in Portuguese (twelve titles, reproduced from the Portuguese Index of 1551).

The second category (books in the vernacular) was the largest. It comprised twenty or so Italian works, fourteen works by Erasmus, eighteen translations of the Holy Scriptures, thirteen catechisms (including Carranza's), twenty Books of Hours, ten or so prayer books, five books of religious polemics, four books on history, one on medicine, one on botany, thirty-six on spirituality (including Luis de Granada's *Book of Prayer*, *Guide for sinners*, and *Handbook of Various Prayers*, and Juan de Avila's *Audi filia*) and nineteen works of a literary nature (plays by Torres Naharro, Gil Vicente and Juan del Encina, the *Lazarillo de Tormes*, and the *Diálogo de Mercurio y Carón* by Alfonso de Valdés, etc. What prompted the Inquisition to ban some of these plays and the *Lazarillo de Tormes* remains unclear: possibly the anticlerical tone of several passages. On the other hand, it is not hard to see why Alfonso de Valdés's *Dialogue* was proscribed, for it constitutes a hard-hitting attack on the Church and a fervent plea for a spiritual Christianity.

The Council of Trent had advised Rome to publish an Index of proscribed books, but Spain always refused to take account of this document, considering that only the Inquisition was competent to deal with such matters. In 1572, for example, the *Suprema* declared that it did not need to consult the pope on such questions and would abide by its own criteria. As a result, paradoxical situations sometimes developed: some books put on the Index by Rome would be authorised in Spain! In 1583, Quiroga, Valdés's successor, published a new Index which reproduced that of 1559 but expanded it and was more specific. This document filled two volumes. The first listed books that were totally proscribed. Unless indicated otherwise, all these prohibited books were in the vernacular; for some books in Latin a special licence was required. The second volume listed the corrections to be made in a whole series of works: entire paragraphs and pages that were to be blacked out and rendered illegible. Quiroga's Index featured 1,315 works. They included works by Thomas More, Francisco de Borja, Luis de Granada, Juan de Avila, and also many books on witchcraft and magic. In 1612, Grand Inquisitor Sandoval took a new initiative when he added to his Index books that undermined decent *mores* and works of a political nature. In the eighteenth century, works by Grotius, Pufendorf and Bayle and Voltaire's *Henriade* were banned, and so was the *Critical Theatre* by the Spanish Benedictine Feijóo. The Inquisition took another initiative in 1790: it would now classify all proscribed authors in alphabetical order, to make consultation of the Index easier.

To perfect their Indexes, the inquisitors turned to qualified consultants whose influence inevitably reflected their own temperaments and personalities. The great theologian Melchor Cano, who was obsessed with Illuminism, was probably responsible for the antimystical orientation of the 1559 Index. Collaborators in the preparation of the 1583 Index included the historian Mariana and university professors such as Diego de Zúñiga and Alvar Gómez de Castro. It was apparently the latter who banned, as undermining decent *mores*, the works of Catullus, Martial and Ovid, certain odes by Horace, Terence's *Eunuch*, Boccaccio's *Decameron*,

Montemayor's *Diana* and all chivalric novels, with the exception of the first four books of the *Amadis*. On the other hand, Gómez de Castro had opposed the inclusion of the *Celestina* and the poems of Boscan and Garcilaso. Mariana was far more strict, wanting to ban all obscene books, starting with the *Celestina*, and also all chivalric novels, 'if only to force the public to read useful books and true histories'. We possess one exceptional document relating to these matters, the *Notice on the prohibition of literary works by the Holy Office (Dictamen acerca de la prohibición de obras literarias por el Santo Oficio)*, probably written by Jerónimo Zurita at the time when he was preparing the 1583 Index. 'With regard to books that run contrary to good *mores*', the author draws a distinction between those written in Latin and those written in the vernacular. The former – Catullus, Martial, Ovid, Tibillus, Propertius, Plautus, Terence and so on – should not be banned, because of their unquestionable literary merits: 'In any society one needs doctors; one also needs poets, for if men were always healthy, doctors would be useless; and similarly, if one did not need to relax after one's graver occupations, one would have no need of poets.' On the other hand, Zurita is intransigent where chivalric novels are concerned: 'Because they are written without skill [*sin artificio*] and are full of improbabilities, it is a waste of time to read them. It is better to suppress them, with the exception of the first four books of *Amadis*. Because these are extemely well written and tell of chaste loves and the misfortunes that befall a king, a very wise king, because he did not appreciate a knight who was exceptional, and because they also purvey other lessons, those four books of *Amadis* have been translated into every language.' Zurita favoured the authorisation of the *Celestina* but not *Diana* – 'which is no great loss'. It is not hard to see that the creation of an Index involved preoccupations that had nothing to do with defending the faith and good *mores*. It was also a matter of preventing Spaniards from wasting their time reading works of fiction. That was a point of view close enough to that of the Humanists, who were hostile to any kind of recreational literature. Even the exception made for the *Celestina* and *Amadis* were typical of such an attitude; they were already to be found in the *Dialogue on Language* by Juan de Valdés, written in 1535.

That being said, it is still hard to see exactly why this or that work was banned. The preface to the 1583 Index provides a few clues. It lists fourteen general rules, subsequently reproduced (with a few corrections and additions) in later Indexes:

1   Of course all books condemned by popes and councils before 1515 were banned.

2 *and* 3   All books written by heretics were banned.

4   All books written by Jews or Muslims or of a kind to oppose Catholic dogma were banned.

5 *and* 6   Translations of the Bible into the vernacular, in particular those produced by heretics, were banned.

7   Books of Hours in the vernacular were banned.

8   'Disputes and controversies of a religious nature between Catholics and heretics, and refutations of Mahomet's Koran in the vernacular' were banned, because such polemics enabled people to form some idea of what infidels believed.

9   Books on occult knowledge that served to invoke demons and books of judicial astrology were banned.

10   Books that used the Holy Scriptures for profane ends were banned, as were poems that interpreted the Holy Scriptures in a disrespectful manner, contrary to the teachings of the Catholic Church.

11   All books that did not display the name of the author and publisher and the date and place of publication were banned.

12   All interpretations disrespectful to the saints and members of the ecclesiastical hierarchy were banned.

13   All future books that came to be published and that contained theses that ran counter to those taught by the Catholic Church were banned.

14   Whenever a book was banned in a specific language, it should be understood that it was also banned in whatever other language it appeared, except where the contrary was indicated.

So it was not simply books that opposed Catholic dogma that were banned or expurgated; also proscribed were those that contained attacks against the clergy or comments disrespectful of the Church. The 1559 Index specified that books in the vernacular 'were proscribed either because it was not good to read them in the vernacular or because their content was full of vain, useless, apochryphal and superstitious things, or because they were full of errors and heresies'. The 1583 Index confirmed that trend. The reason why books by Thomas More, Francisco de Borja, Luis de Granada, and Juan de Avila among others were proscribed was 'not because their authors had distanced themselves from the Holy Roman Church [...], but either because they were wrongly attributed to them or contained quotations from other authors [...] or else because it was not a good thing that certain theses be accessible in the vernacular [...]: even if the authors in question had written in good faith and were faithful to the holy Catholic doctrine, malice might incite enemies of the faith to interpret them incorrectly'. In 1584, the works mentioned above were joined by others by Erasmus, Vivés, Lefèvre d'Étaples, Scaliger, Valla ... and also by *La Vita dell'imperatore Carlos Quinto* by Alfonso de Ulloa, because the latter had dared to praise Constantino Ponce de la Fuente, who had been condemned in his absence as a Lutheran. But incoherences – or what appear to be such – were common. Molinos's *Spiritual Guide*, dated 1675, did not appear in the 1707 Index, possibly because the Spanish inquisitors did not wish to seem to be reproducing a decision taken in Rome. In Spain, this book was not officially banned until 1747.

The Inquisition's policies produced grave consequences. By dint of setting the faithful on their guard against certain dangerous books, it eventually put them off reading altogether. This was deplored by Alonso de Cabrera, one of the most fashionable preachers during the reign of Philip II. He warned that, for fear of being thought a heretic, a person no longer dared to pray or to speak of God in a conversation; people even preferred not to learn to read at all. This calls to mind an observation made by the poet Góngora, the canon of Cordova, in 1588: better by far to be thought a libertine than a heretic.

The Inquisition and science

In principle, there was no reason why the Inquisition should ban scientific books for, as Father Mersenne pointed out in 1625, it was perfectly possible to be at the same time a good Catholic and a good mathematician. Yet, at an early date, the Holy Office was putting such books on the Index, for no obvious reason. In some cases what bothered the censors seemed to be not the subject – medicine, biology, botany, geography – but the presumed Protestantism of the authors or commentators. No doubt that was why the botanist Fuchs, for example, suffered: he was believed to be a Lutheran. In other cases, such far from impartial censorship seems to have been justified in the name of the struggle against superstition. The 1632 Index thus ordered the expurgation of the translation of *Dioscorides* published by Laguna in 1555. Certain passages were censored because, it was claimed, they might put false ideas in the minds of naïve readers – for instance, ideas about the influence of the stars and about destiny.[5] In 1654, the Holy Office was alarmed to find the doctor Huarte de San Juan, in his *Examination of Men's Wits (Examen de ingenios)*, explaining that it is not possible to prove the immortality of the soul or the reality of miracles. On those questions, only faith could bring certainty. The author had to agree to remove such bold assertions from the second edition of 1594.

Rome's condemnation of Galileo, in 1634, has passed into history as being symbolic of the conflict between science and the Catholic Church. Galileo's theory seemed incompatible with what the Bible taught, so the Church rejected it. However, the 1640 Spanish Index ignored that censorship. Why? Because the same Roman decree that condemned Galileo also proscribed a book by an Italian jurist, Rocco Pirro, which justified the king of Spain's right to rule over Sicily. The Holy Office decided to ignore a document that dared to attack the interests of the Spanish crown. Although the Spanish Inquisition did not immediately confirm the proscription of Galileo, in 1632 it had certainly followed the Roman congregation which, in 1616, had condemned the theories of Copernicus, thereby bringing a long period of scientific openness to a close. For in 1561, the University of Salamanca had authorised the teaching of Copernicus's theories as an optional subject for study (*ad vota audientium*) and it had confirmed that decision in 1625, nine years after Rome had condemned those theories. In 1574, a professor in Salamanca, Diego de Zúñiga, also well known as an adviser to the Holy Office on the preparation of its Indexes, declared in a commentary on the Book of Job published that year that, from a scientific point of view, the Copernican system seemed more satisfactory than that of Ptolemy. Zúñiga did not hesitate to state openly, in black and white, that Copernicus's system was not contrary to the Bible: *Motus terrae non est contra Scripturam*. A few years later, in 1585, the Spanish Jesuit José de Acosta took a similar line: did the Holy Scriptures appear to stand in opposition to science? 'One thing is certain: in the Holy Scriptures one should follow, not the literal sense that kills, but the spirit that gives life.' Despite these precedents, however, eventually the Spanish Inquisition gave in. In 1632 it placed both Copernicus and Zúñiga on the Index. It was later also to censure the works of Kepler, but that was because they referred to the king of England as a defender of the faith, *fidei defensor*.

In the domain of the exact and natural sciences, the Spanish Inquisition was guided above all by a profound mistrust of anything done or printed in the Protestant countries. Now, the scientific revolution began and developed in northern Europe, that is to say in regions that coincided with the area in which Protestantism spread: not something likely to favour the acceptance of its innovations in Spain. So should Spain's scientific backwardness really be blamed on the Inquisition? I think not, or at least not directly, and for two good reasons. In the first place, because the scientific revolution, with its three stages represented respectively by Galileo, Descartes and Newton, took place in the seventeenth century, in a period when Spain, weakened by more than a century of imperialistic activities, no longer had the dynamism that it had possessed at the end of the fifteenth century. Secondly, it should be remembered that that scientific revolution was essentially the fruit of theoretical thinking. So Spain was hardly prepared for it. In the sixteenth century, it had been mainly preoccupied with practical applications of science: for example, how to perfect nautical instruments that would make it possible to calculate longitude and latitude more accurately. It was because it had neglected fundamental research almost exclusively in favour of applied research that Spain fell so far behind in its scientific development. In this respect, the responsibility of the Inquisition was strictly limited.[6]

The Inquisition and literature

In 1559, nineteen works were placed on the Index on account of their more or less declared anti-clericalism. They included plays by Torres Naharro, Juan del Encina and Gil Vicente, and also the *Lazarillo de Tormes*. Eventually, in 1584, this novel was authorised, but only in an expurgated version. However, it is hard to see why the *Divine Comedy* and the *Decameron* were proscribed: possibly out of puritanism, a reaction that was to become more noticeable in the seventeenth century. In 1632, the Inquisition confirmed an earlier rule: 'Books that evoke, describe or teach lascivious things – amorous and other themes – mingled with heresies and errors against the faith are proscribed [...] It should be remembered that the apostolic Roman Holy See likewise censures the kind of books that deliberately evoke, describe and teach lascivious and obscene things, even when these are not intermingled with heresies and errors against the faith.' Yet in 1632, the *Celestina* was merely expurgated, not banned, which suggests that for three centuries the Inquisition believed that the author had intended it to be a moralising work. In *Don Quixote*, only one sentence was censored, the one that declared that 'charitable works performed with tepid enthusiasm and laxity have no merit and no value'.

From 1612 on, the Inquisition took to placing on the Index books that had very little to do with dogma or upright *mores*. Political reasons became increasingly important. Suspicion fell upon everything published in northern Europe on the subject of natural law and everything that diverged from the theories developed by the Spanish jurist-theologians of the sixteenth century. Jean Bodin was placed on the Index very early on, Hugo Grotius and Pufendorf in 1747. In the eighteenth century, the critical spirit became increasingly suspect: Bayle, Montesquieu, Voltaire, the Encyclopaedia, Rousseau, Diderot were all banned, and Feijóo's *Critical Theatre* was expurgated.

The Inquisition's censorship probably harmed Spanish spirituality more than it did literature. Even Manuel de la Revilla, who was a virulent opponent of the Inquisition in the second half of the nineteenth century, felt bound to admit that literature had been affected by the censorship hardly at all: 'It cannot be denied that the period when our country most suffered from intolerance and despotism was also that in which literature attained the peak of its splendour.' Manuel de la Revilla explained this paradox as follows: religious intolerance certainly was a cause of decadence for literature, but it was not the sole cause and its action was no more than indirect. Furthermore, he suggested, the Inquisition regarded literature as an inoffensive kind of derivative. However, this explanation is hardly convincing.

It was not literature *per se* that suffered from the inquisitorial censorship, but criticism in all its forms: social, political, anti-clerical, philological. The Inquisition deliberately discouraged intellectuals from writing works of a critical nature. It, so to speak, confined them to purely aesthetic themes.

The Inquisition and intellectual life

Was the censorship imposed by the Holy Office effective? To possess a banned book in one's house or to buy or sell one without authorisation (authorisation that might be granted to professionals, such as university teachers, for example) was not without danger; and many must have hesitated to run the risks. Nevertheless, there have always been men who try to procure proscribed works, partly out of interest for the subject and perhaps also because they are attracted by the very idea of breaking the rules. Booksellers were well aware of this and always made sure that such books were available in their shops. The Holy Office was equally aware of the situation and from time to time it took measures to enforce respect for its edicts. The most effective of those measures, and also the most barbaric, was the burning of proscribed books. As we have seen, at the end of the fifteenth century and the beginning of the sixteenth, the Inquisition had destroyed many works on Judaism and Islam in this manner, and subsequently such operations continued. In January 1558, in Valladolid, the *Suprema* organised a burning of the books that it had confiscated from heretics and that were accumulating in its offices. One of the last operations of this kind that we know of took place in Toledo on 29 June 1634, when a number of books and documents that were dated the previous 9 March were burnt on orders from the *Suprema*.

Another way of enforcing prohibitions was to make spot-checks on bookshops from time to time. This was the procedure that Páramo, in 1578, advised the inquisitors of Cordova to adopt, explaining that they should entrust to competent and trustworthy individuals the task of inspecting the bookshops of the town and the surrounding district, in particular those of Baeza, which was a university town. In 1605, the Inquisition went even further, insisting that bookshops keep a register of the names of their clients: even the buying of a book and reading it now became suspect.

Despite these precautions, cultural contacts between Spain and other countries were never discontinued. We have seen how Protestant propaganda managed to penetrate the Iberian peninsula despite the vigilance of the Holy Office's commissioners. In all periods and whatever the regime, people have always found ways to discover what was happening on the other side of the political frontiers. If that is true today, when policing techniques are so much more sophisticated, it was certainly the case in the societies of the Ancien Régime. Despite the Inquisition, foreign publications never ceased to enter Spain. Reading the works written by the Humanist Palmireno, in the mid sixteenth century, one does not have the impression that the author is a man ignorant of what was being published in the rest of Europe. Quevedo wrote in praise of Montaigne's *Essays*, which were theoretically proscribed. Antonio Domínguez Ortiz has drawn attention to the trial of Diego Mateo Zapata (1664–1738), Philip V's doctor, who, in 1725, was found guilty of Judaism. Zapata's library included many proscribed or suspect authors: Gassendi, Descartes, Malebranche, Bacon, Bayle, Hobbes; and he admitted that he willingly lent books to his friends. In 1757, when Curiel, a highly placed official responsible for the censorship of books, wanted to draw up a list of the kingdom's printing works and bookshops, he had to appoint specially recruited agents for the purpose, for the Inquisition was unable to provide the information: a remarkable indication of its inefficiency. In 1789, it was in vain that Floridablanca ordered the Holy Office to establish a *cordon sanitaire* along the frontiers of Spain: Spaniards still managed to find out what was happening in Paris, just as in the sixteenth century they had never been ignorant of what was thought, said and published in circles won over to the Reformation.

All the same, the Inquisition did constitute a redoubtable obstacle to free research and the critical spirit. Humanism, far more than science or literature, attracted the suspicion and hostility of the inquisitors because it tended to submit ancient texts to rigorous criticism and to free them from the errors and all the scholia and glosses that had accumulated around them in the course of time, in order to discover what they really, literally, meant. The Humanists applied the methods of philology to the whole of literature, including the authors of Graeco-Latin antiquity and the Bible. In the fifteenth century, Lorenzo Valla had blazed the trail, discovering in vernacular versions mistakes of transcription introduced by copyists, errors of translation, inexactitudes and even misinterpretations. Nebrija, a disciple of Valla's, took a similar view: a grammarian's calling is to study the Bible as he would any other text, and to apply the usual methods of philology to it. Nebrija affected modesty, claiming to make no more than minor adjustments to the spelling and emphasis and to specify the meaning of a word here or there, but the scholastics were not fooled: it was not just the form, but the very meaning of the Bible that risked modification, and that was what provoked their indignation – Nebrija was introducing a secular perspective in a domain that until then had been the exclusive preserve of theologians.

The implications of such an attitude are not hard to see. If everything rests upon the literal meaning and if the key to this lies in a knowledge of Hebrew, what is the standing of all the interpretations of the Bible produced since the origins of Christianity? It has to be admitted that some are erroneous, even though a venerable tradition has perpetuated them and accustomed us to them. In the last analysis, one realises that the discipline of philology is indispensable to a theologian, and where philology and theology diverge, philology must have the last word. That was certainly the deep conviction of the Humanists, even if they were careful to play down its implications. The indignant exclamation of one monk, in 1571, sums up the whole debate: 'But if that is the case, a knowledge of grammar is all that is needed to explain the Holy Scriptures, and theology serves no purpose at all!'

It was indeed a battle between the grammarians and the theologians. The former always criticized the ignorance of the latter and often held them up to ridicule. In his trial, Fray Luis de León did not mince his words. Although broken by four years of incarceration, he still found the courage to reject the theologians consulted as experts by the Inquisition: they knew nothing! The theologians were no less severe with regard to the grammarians. Sepúlveda, for his part, regretted the scorn that theologians poured upon Humanists. It seemed to him that there was no time to be lost: they should set about studying Latin and Greek. As one Jesuit declared, the difference between grammar and theology was as great as that which separated nothingness from infinity.[7] Arias Montano, the editor of the monumental Bible printed in Antwerp by Plantin between 1568 and 1572, was declared by his critics to be a good theologian but rather too much of a grammarian (*muy gramático*), to which Montano retorted that it was certainly not a criticism that could be levelled at any of them; it could not be said that any one of them knew more grammar than he, Montano, did.[8] When Domingo Báñez, the great theologian, was asked what he thought of Hebrew studies, he replied without hesitation that they served no purpose; in fact they were dangerous.[9] That was also the view expressed one century later by Bossuet, in reply to Richard Simon: when interpreting the Holy Scriptures, it was not indispensable to understand philology, indeed it was probably even dangerous.[10]

It was dangerous. That was the point: Humanists were suspect; a critical mind led to heresy.[11] Friar Antonio de Arce, one of Fray Luis de León's judges, boasted of knowing neither Greek nor Hebrew, and maintained that Humanists were arrogant and sarcastic.[12] Bartolomé de Medina denounced his colleagues, the Hebrew and Bible

professors of Salamanca, because of their fondness for the humanities and innovations.[13] That was precisely the fear expressed by the
Valencian Humanist Pedro Juan Núñez in a letter written ten or so
years earlier to the historian Jerónimo Zurita: some people do not
want anybody to take an interest in the humanities, because they
consider them dangerous: a Humanist who corrects a sentence of
Cicero's may be tempted to do as much for a passage in the Bible;
and if anyone disagrees with the commentaries on Aristotle, what is
to prevent him casting doubt upon the authority of the doctors of the
Church?[14] Such an attitude was still outraging some intellectuals at the
end of the century,[15] but most capitulated more or less cravenly, and
gave up doing their jobs. Among the latter was Baltasar de Céspedes,
the son-in-law of Sánchez de las Brozas. He had learned his lesson:
he now limited himself solely to matters of form. He made much of
the authority of the saints and took care never to suggest the slightest interpretation of his own. In this way, research and thought in
inquisitorial Spain were eventually sterilised. Only a few great minds,
sure of their knowledge and courageous, were capable of taking the
risks. The rest preferred to stop using their critical faculties. They
were, after all, only human.

6   The Inquisition and the political authorities

For the legal expert Páramo, writing at the end of the sixteenth century, heretics represented a threat not only to religion, as went without saying, but also to the State.[1] Under the Ancien Régime, in Europe, the notion that a ruler's subjects might not all profess the same religion was not acceptable. The idea of declaring oneself neutral, that is to say indifferent with regard to a truth that could only be unique and exclusive, was repugnant. On this point, Catholics and Protestants were in agreement, as were Jews, even though the latter did not dispose of the means to apply that principle. When Spinoza was judged guilty of atheism, the reason why he was not condemned to death was simply that the rabbis of Amsterdam were less powerful than Torquemada. At the time, it was generally agreed that unity of belief within a nation was necessary for the cohesion of the State and social peace. For sovereigns, a heretic was bound to represent a potential rebel. It is worth remembering how Charles V reacted, in his Yuste retreat, when he learned that Lutheran circles had been discovered in Valladolid. He urged his daughter Joanna, then in charge of the government, to clamp down with severity: 'These heretics must be treated as rebels, agitators ready to create disorder and upset society, as men prepared to undermine the security of the State.' Similarly, the gist of Philip II's comment on the situation in the Netherlands in 1565 was that he had no intention of reigning over heretical subjects. It would be inaccurate to label such reactions as fanaticism, for all the rulers of the day, whether Catholic or Protestant, took the same view and applied the same principle in the States subject to their authority: subjects could have no religion other than that of their sovereign (*cujus regio, ejus religio*). In France, in 1598, it was lassitude on the part of the combatants that led to the Edict of Nantes: a success for the pragmatists, that is to say those who put the State first and sought above all to re-establish peace. Tolerance was limited to a non-belligerent coexistence. The State remained Roman Catholic. Liberty of worship was established, but with restrictions. Above all, it was guaranteed not by the State, but by the relinquishment of a degree of sovereignty: the Protestants had a hundred or so strongholds at their disposal and could be judged only by mixed (Catholic/Protestant) courts. It was in this same spirit that Chancellor Bacon, horrified by the bloody religious quarrels that he had witnessed, advised the temporal authorities to observe the greatest circumspection before intervening in spiritual matters; sovereigns should not insist on too much conformity for their subjects, for it could push the latter to the end of their tether and lead them into desperate action. An absence of disorders and rebellions was, from now on, one of the objectives of politics. It was some time before authorities moved on from the affirmation of the rights of truth to a declaration of the rights of man and the adoption of State moral and religious indifference (theoretical secularism) as an end to be aimed for, and before *de facto* neutrality was recognised as the most expedient means of guaranteeing public welfare in a city whose members were split between different religions (practical secularism). As late as 1815, Joseph de Maistre, steeped in the maxims of the Ancien Régime, was writing, 'Heresiarchs, stubborn heretics and propagators of heresy should unquestionably be classified among the worst of criminals [...] Modern sophists, arguing in comfort at their desks, are unconcerned that Luther's arguments brought about the Thirty Years War. But earlier legislators, aware of what those fateful doctrines could cost mankind, most justifiably employed the ultimate penalty for a crime capable of shaking society to its very foundations and plunging it into a bloodbath [...] When one considers the fact that the court of the Inquisition would certainly have prevented the French Revolution, one suspects that a sovereign who deprived himself totally of that instrument could well deliver a fatal blow to humanity.'[2] In France, it was not until 24 December 1789 and 27 September 1791 that Protestants and Jews, respectively, received recognition as full citizens. A little later, England followed the same evolution. Up until 1828, 'Nonconformists' had been disqualified from public appointments; Catholics had to wait a further year, until 13 April 1829, before they were granted the same rights as Anglicans.

For centuries it was thought that temporal authorities were obliged to support the Church, but at the same time those authorities did not hesitate to exploit religion to their own advantage. The fact was that, if it was accepted that heretics disturbed social order, religion could easily be used as a pretext to eliminate political opponents. For evidence of this, in France one has only to think of the crusades against the Albigensians, the trial of the Templars and the death of Joan of Arc. In every case, politics and religion were almost inextricably intertwined. The Catholic Church regarded the Cathars as heretics; it needed the temporal authorities to restore order; and the battle for the Catholic faith took on the air of a crusade. But it was a crusade that offered the king of France a pretext to relieve the count of Toulouse of his southern possessions and reattach them to the crown. It was this political motive that led King Pedro II of Aragon (who had no sympathy for the Cathars) to come to the aid of his relatives and vassals to the north of the Pyrenees. The victory of Catholicism was also a political success for the king of France. What was the determining element in this affair: the desire to crush heresy or the wish to expand the French kingdom? Similar questions could be asked in relation to the Templars, at the beginning of the fourteenth century. It was inquisitors who forced the dignitaries of the order, under torture, to confess to abominable crimes and inquisitors who had the Grand Master of the order, Jacques de Molay, burnt alive in March 1314; but it was Philip the Fair who acquired the order's immense riches. The case of Joan of Arc provides another example of the confusion of politics and religion. It was at the request of the English that French inquisitors declared the Maid to be idolatrous, apostate and relapsed and had her burnt alive in 1431. Twenty years later, circumstances had changed and the king of France, Charles VII, had no difficulty in persuading other inquisitors to review the trial and rehabilitate Joan of Arc.

In medieval Spain, the Church had stirred up a hatred of the Jews that political parties had exploited to their own advantage; but it was the temporal authorities who decided to set up the Inquisition. They saw it as the most effective means to remodel Spanish society and eliminate all traces of Semitism (both Judaism and Mohammedanism) and to put an end to the medieval multiculturalism in which minority and autonomous religious communities had existed alongside the dominant Christian community of the majority – in short to make Spain a country like the rest of Christendom. Christian countries were characterised by three terms, one faith, one law and one king. In the case of the Hispanic monarchy, that formula was reduced to two terms, one faith and one king, since the law varied from one kingdom to another (from Castile to Aragon) and from one territory to another. It was not identical for the inhabitants of Castile, Navarre, Aragon, Catalonia, Valencia, etc. On the other hand, they all recognised a single king and were now to profess a single religion. The Inquisition's task was to ensure the ideological homogeneity of the monarchy; and that was an eminently political objective.

The Holy Office was a mixed institution, an ecclesiastical court but one appointed by the temporal power, to which it was answerable. It nevertheless sometimes happened that the defence of ecclesiastical prerogatives overrode all the rest of the inquisitors' preoccupations.

In 1608, for example, the Holy Office insisted on the correction of a number of passages in Castillo de Bobadilla's treatise *Política para corregidores*. The subject of the book was entirely profane: it explained how to administer and manage the domains of the crown and those of local lords, and how to administer justice in them. The author himself was an Old Christian and was under no suspicion. However, the Inquisition found certain phrases unacceptable as they seemed to call into question the pre-eminence of the clergy. One example was: 'The ecclesiastical judge and the secular judge are equal, but in some circumstances the latter may take precedence over the former.'

However, such cases were exceptional. Most of the time, the temporal authorities dictated the behaviour of the Inquisition in domains that had nothing to do with the defence of the faith, to such an extent, indeed, that some historians have considered the Holy Office to represent an early manifestation of regalism. The preface to the code of procedure published in 1484 contains a telling sentence. Torquemada expresses himself as follows: 'By order of their most serene majesties, the king and the queen ..., I the prior of the Holy Cross [...], the grand inquisitor, etc.' By order of the sovereigns! At other points too, Torquemada uses a similar expression: 'Their highnesses order that ...' Nothing could be clearer: the grand inquisitor explicitly claimed to represent the temporal power although, formally speaking, his authority stemmed from the pope. Ferdinand, for his part, did not hesitate to issue direct orders to the inquisitorial courts, without passing through the intermediary of the grand inquisitor. Nor did he have the slightest scruple about entrusting profane tasks to the inquisitors: in November 1480, for example, Friar Diego Magdalena, appointed inquisitor to Valencia, was ordered to keep all the king's agents under surveillance, from the grand inquisitor himself right down to the least of his subordinates.

After Ferdinand, all the kings continued to use the Inquisition for political ends. At the death of the king of Aragon, in January 1516, opponents, trying to make the most of the situation, conspired to restore the Albret family to the throne of Navarre. The two regents, Cisneros and Adrian of Utrecht, placed the inquiry in the hands of not the institutions of royal justice, but the Inquisition, making the latter responsible for punishing the guilty parties. The reason for this appears to be that the Inquisition recognised neither personal privileges nor any forms of regional autonomy. Under the Ancien Régime, it was the only court with the right to lay charges against anyone within the territory of the monarchy. It was thus the easiest way to take action, even in cases only remotely related to religion. Four years later, on 11 October 1520, at the request of Charles V, Pope Leo X authorised Grand Inquisitor Adrian to lay charges against members of the clergy who took the side of rebel *comuneros*. These ecclesiastics were guilty of conspiracy against the royal power, certainly not of heresy. Nevertheless, in this case too, the inquisitors were given a far freer hand than ordinary judges, even episcopal ones: they were not obliged to respect ecclesiastical regulations and so could act more effectively and more swiftly.

In 1541, Charles V convened the Imperial Diet in Ratisbonne. If opponents saw fit to express reservations concerning the policies adopted, Grand Inquisitor Valdés simply placed on the Index any critiques that were published 'whether in verse or in prose, and whatever the language'. Whatever did a nation's monetary policies have to do with religious orthodoxy? Apparently nothing. The duke of Lerma, Philip III's prime minister, nevertheless asked the Inquisition to take the Jesuit Mariana to court, because he had been imprudent enough to publish a treatise entitled *De mutatione monetae* in Latin (which limited its diffusion). In it, he criticised the huge issues of *vellon* (coins of copper alloy) which, he claimed, led to inflation, higher prices, food shortages and discontent. It is true that Mariana was not found guilty, but it is significant that Lerma considered it normal to turn to the Inquisition in order to silence an opponent. Similarly, in 1606, the town of Medina del Campo wanted to entrust the Inquisition with inquiries into cases of smuggling and counterfeiting. In

1619, the writer Sancho de Moncada expressed his approval: why should the Inquisition not intervene? It was, after all, a State matter! A decree of 9 February 1627 ratified that interpretation: all cases of counterfeiting were in future to be handled by the Inquisition.

Startling use was again made of the Holy Office for political ends on the occasion of the Catalan rebellion of 1640. The Inquisition banned political pamphlets such as the *Proclamación católica* by Gaspar Sala which, from the point of view of dogma, was completely innocuous (the document concerned what we today would call fundamentalism), but which was at fault because it challenged Philip IV's rights to Catalonia. The lampoon attacking colonisation produced by Las Casas (*La Destrucción de las Indias*) had provoked no doctrinal objections when it had appeared at the end of Charles V's reign. In fact, the great theologians of the day and the whole Dominican order had supported Las Casas's arguments against Sepúlveda who, at that same point, was defending the right of colonisation. The trouble, however, was that the works of Las Casas were providing arguments for the enemies of Spain (the Dutch, the English and the French). That is why the Inquisition placed them on the Index in 1660 – not because they were judged heretical, but because they were damaging Spain's international reputation: 'The book records horrifying and monstrous facts. The histories of other nations contain nothing like them [...] Even if the facts are exact and not too exaggerated, it would have been quite enough to bring them to the attention of the king and his ministers so that they could be remedied. There was no need to broadcast them throughout the world. Spain's enemies and heretics have seized the opportunity to accuse Spain of savagery and cruelty.'[3] At the time of the War of Succession, Philip V used every possible means to defeat his opponents, and the Inquisition lent him its support. An edict dated 9 October 1706 made it obligatory to denounce all priests who advised their penitents not to be loyal to the Bourbon: 'This concerns all confessors who commit such an execrable crime in the course of penitent's confession. We order that they be denounced within nine days, under pain of excommunication *latae sententiae ipso facto incurrenda* [automatically incurred]'.[4]

What should we make of such efforts to disguise the monarchy's foreign policy beneath a cloak of ideology? In 1516, in *The Prince*, Machiavelli was already accusing King Ferdinand of acting 'under the cover of religion' when he dispossessed the Jews and the Moors and, 'still under the same cloak', of attacking Africa, conquering the kingdom of Naples, and launching himself against France at the head of the Holy League. It was above all Charles V and his successors who attracted criticism for aspiring to a universal monarchy – in other words, adopting an imperialist policy by systematically dressing up such ambitions as a defence of Christianity against both his external enemies (the Turks) and his internal opponents (the Protestants). The French manifesto of 1635, inspired by Richelieu, to justify the declaration of war against Spain, makes the same accusation. There can be no doubt that Philip II, possibly even more than Charles V, used the argument that the Spanish monarchy was operating as the champion of Catholicism. The Moriscos, for example, were presented as a kind of fifth column, ready to support a Turkish invasion when the time was ripe, while the Protestants were said to be natural allies of the Flemish rebels. Even today, that idea is widely accepted: the Hispanic monarchy is held to offer an example of a State that set itself a spiritual mission, considering its role to be to ensure the unity of Christendom abroad and to preserve orthodoxy within its own frontiers. In short, this was an empire at the service of the Counter-Reformation, and a power pledged to religion.

So was it part of the sovereign's role to intervene in disagreements of a religious nature? In the Salamanca of the 1530s, the Dominican professor Francisco de Vitoria, qualified to speak for both the natural and the supernatural orders, thought not: he argued that grace cannot suppress nature; the spiritual should not interfere in the temporal, except in certain overlapping domains and even then not without taking certain precautions. In about 1556, the Valencian

Fadrique Furió Ceriol, who was hoping that Philip II would introduce more tolerant and 'secular' policies, reckoned that kingship was
a profession that had to be learned and practised correctly; virtue
and religion were not enough, in fact were not even necessary: 'It
can be said of someone that he is a good prince, just as it can be said
of another that he is a good musician; even if he is an arrant knave,
he will continue to be called a good musician, simply because he is
perfectly skilled in his profession.'[5]

All the same, it must be recognised that in Spain such principles
ran counter to a mindset and a current of opinion that favoured the
civil authorities' interventions in religious affairs. This is where the
Inquisition came in: it was unique in that it entrusted the repression of heresy to the civil authorities. That transfer of responsibility
involved weighty consequences, for it introduced a confusion between
the sphere of politics and that of religion. To be a good Spaniard, it
was not enough to respect the laws of the kingdom, it was also necessary to profess the Catholic faith; and it was up to the State to
suppress any deviation from orthodoxy. Sixteenth-century Spain thus
combined conditions that favoured the emergence and development
of what is sometimes called the theocracy temptation: the expectation
that the political authority will in effect realise the kingdom of God.
The State assumes the mission of ensuring the triumph of virtue, the
faith and religion by employing the means available to the political
authorities – means which, when necessary, include constraint. This
is a world such as that evoked by Dostoevsky (in *The Brothers Kar-
amozov*) in his fable about the Grand Inquisitor who dreams of using
political means to make people happy and to win eternal salvation for
their souls.

In the last years of the sixteenth century, this kind of providential-
ism was gaining ground. Mariana was the first to express his fears
regarding Protestant nations. In his view, heresy justified going to
war as it divided nations and peoples. The quarrel over Machiavellianism helped to harden attitudes. In less than fifty years the situation

was completely turned around. In 1550, Charles V had granted royal privileges to a translation of Machiavelli's *Speeches* on Livy's first decade and had recommended it to the future Philip II as extremely profitable reading. In 1584–5, the Duke of Sesa was insisting to the Council of the Inquisition that *The Prince* should be translated into Spanish and was even prepared to pay the costs of its publication. But by this time, the battle was already lost, for the *Speeches* had been placed on the Index in the previous year. The order of the day now was refutation of Machiavellianism, which was considered to be a subtle form of heresy. The title of a book by the Jesuit Rivadeneira, published in 1595, speaks for itself: *A Treatise on the religion and virtues that a Christian prince must possess in order to govern and preserve his States. An attack on the teaching of Nicolas Machiavelli and the pragmatists of our age*. Rivadeneira countered the reasons of State that turned the State into a religion by reasons of State that turned religion into a State.

In opposition to Machiavelli and his followers, Spanish thinkers refused to consider politics as a technique whose ends have nothing to do with morality and religion. For them, morality could not be reduced to individual morality; it must also inform political activity. For most of the seventeenth-century authors who took an interest in political problems, the king of Spain was the Christian prince *par excellence*, so his behaviour was inevitably inspired by the maxims of the strictest Christian morality. On those grounds, he was the natural defender of Catholicism, the opponent of heresy and the protector of the Church. As we have seen, that view was shared abroad where, however, it also aroused indignation. In reality the situation was more complex. The foreign policy of the Hapsburgs cannot be reduced to its ideological aspects. Other considerations also come into play, such as solidarity with the House of Austria and the desire to preserve Spain's rank as the hegemonic power. Nevertheless, for centuries the ambiguity remained and continued to fuel the idea of Spain as the champion of Catholicism.

The mysterious Antonio Pérez affair presents the most striking example of the way in which the political power made use of the Inquisition to get round legal and constitutional obstacles. Antonio Pérez was one of the *letrados* (school graduates of the lettered class) chosen by Philip II as a close collaborator. Since 1566 he had served as secretary to the king, with special responsibility for Italian affairs. In the course of his duties he met with the king several times a day. He enjoyed the latter's trust, knew all the State secrets and was familiar with all the Court intrigues. In 1578, public rumour accused Antonio Pérez of having arranged the assassination of Escobedo, an agent of Don Juan of Austria. Philip II soon became convinced that Pérez had not only committed this crime but had also falsified documents, communicated State secrets to third parties and involved himself in influence-peddling. On 28 July 1579, Antonio Pérez was arrested for high treason. Fearing the worst, he tried to flee. His first attempt, on 31 January 1585, was unsuccessful; a second attempt was better prepared and succeeded. On 15 April 1590, Antonio Pérez reached Aragon. Upon arrival, he applied to benefit from the guarantees that the *fueros* granted to natives of the kingdom, for he was a citizen of Saragossa. Until such time as his case could be examined, he was therefore placed under the protection of the *Justicia*, a magistrate responsible for seeing that the *fueros* were respected. Philip II demanded his extradition. It was refused. There could be no better example of the limits of sixteenth-century absolutism and royal centralism: the king could not get an individual accused of high treason and *lèse-majesté* handed over to him, because the legislation of Castile did not apply to Aragon.

To get around this difficulty, Philip II then turned to the Inquisition which, for its part, did exercise jurisdiction over the entire territory and did not recognise the *fueros*. Any pretext would now serve. One of his servants declared that Pérez was given to blasphemy; another accused him of homosexuality. The king's confessor, Diego de Chaves, certified that Pérez must be a heretic. However, when the inquisitors tried to seize the prisoner, a popular demonstration prevented them from doing so (24 May 1591). Six months later, on 24 September, the Inquisition tried again, but another riot gave Antonio Pérez the chance to flee abroad. During 1592, the Inquisition found new charges to level against Antonio Pérez: he had close contacts with Protestants in Bearn and so was guilty of complicity with heretics; in texts published in exile, he had declared that the Holy Office could not flout the *fueros*. In January 1593, the Inquisition condemned him to death in his absence. Pérez died in Paris on 3 November 1611. In 1615, at the request of his widow, the Inquisition agreed to revoke the sentence passed in 1593: proof, if proof were needed, that this had all along been a political trial.

The Inquisition was prepared to put itself at the service of the political authorities except when it was asked to act openly in opposition to the objective initially assigned to it: the repression of crypto-Judaism. Between 1621 and 1643, the count-duke of Olivares sought to eliminate certain Genoese bankers whom he considered too grasping, and to replace them with Portuguese businessmen, mostly converted Jews, who offered a double advantage: they were subjects of the monarchy and many had contacts with relatives and friends settled in northern Europe and well established in commerce and finance. Olivares accordingly asked the Inquisition to turn a blind eye in a number of cases. It was probably he who inspired the memorandum mentioned earlier: its author (possibly a member of the Council of the Inquisition, Hernando de Salazar or Diego Serrano de Silva) suggested that the Inquisition show indulgence towards the Portuguese *marranos*, since their emigration would deprive the monarchy of experienced merchants. Such recommendations were no more than partially successful. They were considered shocking in that they presupposed an over-radical change in the religious policies of the past. In a letter dated 8 August 1634, Father Pereyra took offence: 'The favourite wants to recall Jews to Spain. Some are already here. They are received by the king, to whom they deliver memoranda.

This very day I myself have seen one, wearing a white hat, waiting in the Palace anteroom.'

In 1644, the great writer Quevedo also attacked this policy when he added to the text of his *Dreams* an extremely violent pamphlet entitled *The Island of the Monopantos (La isla de los Monopantos)*. It tells of influential Jews secretly meeting in Salonica to study the best means of imposing their domination over the world, with the support of Monopantos, that is to say Christians ready to collaborate with them, easily recognisable as the count-duke of Olivares and his friends. This treatise may have been a distant model for *The Protocol of the Sages of Zion*. In it Quevedo lambasts the modern techniques for manipulating money and banking, the mechanisms of which he does not understand but the suspected implications of which alarm him. He targets the burgeoning capitalism that has already become cosmopolitan and anonymous and is the more disquieting on that very account, and the primacy of economics over moral and spiritual values. A few years earlier, on 12 March 1641, Pellicer had noted in his newsletter *Avisos*: 'I am reliably informed that efforts are being made to bring Jews in from Holland [...] Fortunately, the Inquisition is on the watch.' The Inquisition was indeed on the watch. So long as Olivares remained in power, it limited itself to taking action only in the most flagrant cases, but it never gave up what had, since the start, been its principal objective. To urge it to favour the return of Judaisers was clearly somewhat to overstep the mark.

Whenever the temporal power sought to emphasise its supremacy over the ecclesiastical power, it called upon the services of the Inquisition, as is clearly illustrated by what is known as the Jansenism quarrel. Over and above its doctrinal aspects (its insistence on greater theological and moral rigour in the face of the laxity attributed to the Jesuits), in Spain Jansenism was seen as a manifestation of regalism. That was very clear at the point when there was a change of dynasty, in 1700. In the War of Succession, Rome had appeared to side with the archduke of Austria against the Bourbons. This gave Philip V a pretext to try to limit the influence of the pope.

No sooner was he enthroned than Philip V dismissed Grand Inquisitor Baltasar de Mendoza, whom he considered to be too well disposed towards the pope, and asked a member of the *Suprema*, Lorenzo Folch de Cardona, to submit a report on the powers of the grand inquisitor and the Supreme Council of the Inquisition. This was a question that masked another, far more important one concerning the respective powers of the pope and the king, for while it was the pope who appointed the grand inquisitor, he did so in accordance with the king's recommendation. It was therefore a matter of knowing who – the king or the pope – would have the last word in the event of a conflict. Cardona's memorandum, *A Historico-Juridical Discourse on the Bases of the Jurisdiction Delegated by the Supreme Council of the Inquisition, which is dependent on his Holiness the Pope in Apostolic Matters, but on His Majesty the King in all others*, sought to establish that every member of the Inquisition Council possessed a deliberative as well as a consultative vote and that the grand inquisitor's role was solely to preside over meetings of the Council. The vote that he cast following the Council's deliberations carried no more weight than that of any other councillor. In other words, whatever the circumstances, the king could impose his will upon the Inquisition, without referring to the pope.

Cardona's memorandum was submitted to Macanaz for his opinion. Macanaz, who in 1711 was the administrator of finance of Aragon, was one of the leading theorists of the *Nueva Planta*, that is to say the organisation of the kingdom so as to make it more centralised and to strengthen the powers of the king. On the strength of his successes in the field of administrative reform, Macanaz thought he could attack the Inquisition with impunity. On 19 December 1713, he presented the king with a memorandum, *Plan for the Reform of the Inquisitorial Court*, which took over the arguments elaborated by Cardona and went on to spell out their consequences: the Inquisition was subject to the authority of the crown; it should exercise jurisdiction solely in spiritual matters; the censorship of books, for example, ought to revert to the crown. Macanaz was later to admit that, in writing this memorandum, he was pursuing a most precise objective. His aim was to have done with the errors to which Spain had become accustomed and to refute the notion that the king was obliged to accept the decisions of the Inquisition. To insist that it was the king who appointed the grand inquisitor, while the pope did no more than approve his choice, was tantamount to limiting the pope's influence over the Church of Spain. Regalism was the order of the day.

That was certainly how the pope himself interpreted the situation. Diplomatic relations between Rome and Philip V's Spain had broken down as early as 1709, but the Holy See was not without its supporters in the government. In August 1714, Grand Inquisitor Cardinal Giudice, then on an ambassadorial mission in Paris, made his position quite clear and denounced Macanaz. Philip V recalled him immediately, but at this point the government underwent an important change. Philip V's new wife, Isabella Farnese, grew close to the Jesuits in Rome. In February 1715, Macanaz was dismissed and entered upon a life of exile that lasted until 1748. He was then permitted to return to Spain, only to find himself incarcerated in the dungeons of Corunna. There he remained until his death in 1760.

Macanaz was a forerunner of the enlightened ministers of the second half of the eighteenth century. Like them, he was convinced of the need to strengthen the king's authority vis-à-vis the Church and the Inquisition. Was he a victim of Jesuits who saw him as a rival and opponent? If that was indeed the case, he was to be dramatically avenged only a few years after his death. Ever since the Catholic sovereigns, Spanish monarchs had constantly been interfering in ecclesiastical affairs and trying to impose their authority in matters of discipline, if necessary in opposition to the bishops and the pope. The concordat of 1753 was the outcome of more than two centuries of attempts to secure for the crown effective control over the Church of Spain. Bishops and, to a lesser degree, parish priests, who were appointed by the king, were considered officials in the employ of the State authorities. They were expected to support the views of the government and to collaborate loyally and effectively in its reformist policies. The reformists had no liking for the regular clergy, over whom they exerted no control. Above all, they distrusted the Society of Jesus, because of its vow of blind obedience to the pope. They tended to overestimate its influence within the State (the king's confessor was frequently a Jesuit), in society (because of the Jesuits' dominant role in education), and also in South America (where the missions of Paraguay, for example, constituted a vast territory over which the Jesuits exercised an authority deemed to be incompatible with that of the king).

The 1766 uprising against the minister Esquilache provided the desired pretext for a reaction. Following an inquiry, ordered by Campomanes, the influential procurator of the Council of Castile, the government became convinced that the Jesuits had been largely responsible for organising the 1766 demonstrations. They believed that the Imperial College of Madrid had been the hub of all the agitation, which had been entirely plotted by two Jesuits (one of whom was confessor to the queen mother, Isabella Farnese). It was assumed that their purpose had been to force a change of government, and possibly even the abdication of Charles III. The Jesuits were also accused of having covertly circulated a mass of brochures, lampoons and pamphlets hostile to the authorities and of having thereby created and encouraged subversion. The memory of theses defended by certain Jesuits, such as Suaréz and Mariana, on the subject of the people's right to oppose tyrannical power (what men of the Enlightenment described as regicidal and *bloodthirsty* doctrines) probably helped to set most of the reformers in opposition to the Society of Jesus. In 1767, the 2,641 Jesuits of Spain and the 2,630 resident in South America were all expelled. Their possessions were confiscated and passed to the State. But that was not the end of their misfortunes. In

1772, José Moñino, ambassador to the Vatican and future count of Floridablanca, persuaded the pope to dissolve the Society of Jesus.

As we have seen, the attitude of enlightened ministers towards the Inquisition was ambiguous. They did not like it but thought it might come in useful. For one thing, they were depending on it, alongside the bishops, to help wipe out superstition and to advance the Enlightenment. They accordingly did no more than limit the powers of the Inquisition by, for example, in 1770 transferring cases of bigamy from its jurisdiction to that of the bishops. In the meantime they kept the institution in reserve. During the reign of Charles IV, it was the Inquisition that Floridablanca made responsible for opposing the spread of revolutionary ideas in Spain. All the same, the reformist ministers could not do entirely as they pleased and the Inquisition retained a solid enough position in a number of fields, as is testified by the trial of Olavide, which took everyone by surprise.

Pablo de Olavide was a Peruvian Creole who, in 1750, at the age of twenty-five, left his native land to travel in France and Italy. For one whole week, he was privileged to be Voltaire's house-guest in Fernay. In Paris, where he resided for several months, he was able to enjoy the life of high society, thanks to the fortune of his wife (he had married an extremely wealthy widow). He thus frequented the fashionable salons, where he met many figures from the world of the sciences, arts and letters. He also purchased all the books that were the talk of the town (literary, scientific and philosophical works), thereby acquiring a first-rate library which he sent to Spain in 1765, when he decided to settle there. Steeped in French culture, a voracious reader and interested in everything new, as he was, he soon won the trust of the reformist ministers who, in 1767, appointed him as an assistant with the post of *corregidor* in Seville. In this role, he proved extremely active; in particular, he introduced a programme of university reform. Many local figures of note frequented his salon, and he placed his extensive library at the disposal of his friends. Jovellanos, then a young magistrate, benefited hugely from his contact with such an open mind. Next, Olavide was entrusted with organising the colonisation of the Sierra Morena, upon which the government had decided. He took his task extremely seriously and made rapid and encouraging progress. But his success and his highly placed protectors made him imprudent. He declared himself a Copernican; his library contained impious and lascivious books; he ignored the fasts prescribed by the Church; he indulged in sarcastic comments about popular devotional practices, which he dismissed as superstitions; he prohibited the burial of the dead in churches and the sale of indulgences; he criticised alms-giving, insisting that the best way to help the poor was to create more jobs; he advised nobles who were considering building chapels to put their money to better use, for example by introducing agricultural improvements; and he mocked the monks, deploring their ignorance.

The monks never forgave him. One, in particular, resented Olavide's behaviour and sarcastic comments: the Capuchin friar Romualdo of Friburg, who was responsible for encouraging the integration of colonists of German or Swiss origin who did not understand Spanish. He complained to the archbishop of Seville and the bishop of Jaen. Both were friends of Olavide and neither took his denunciations seriously. The disappointed Capuchin monk then, on 31 October 1775, appealed directly to King Charles III's own confessor. His timing was good. Among the *philosophes* and *encyclopédistes* of Europe, it was currently rumoured that the Inquisition was about to be suppressed and all the credit for its suppression was ascribed to the count of Aranda, recently appointed ambassador to Paris and (wrongly) said to be a Voltairian. However, Charles III, who was extremely devout, not to say bigoted, was by no means in favour of the idea and his confessor, Elata, encouraged his attitude with two arguments favouring the maintenance of the Inquisition: in the first place, the inquisitors were at the service of the monarchy; and secondly, the Inquisition could conveniently be used against freethinkers, atheists and freemasons.

Elata had no difficulty persuading the king that it was time to give pause for thought and a warning to those in the government or the higher echelons of the administration who thoughtlessly indulged in criticism of religion and its ministers. On 12 November 1775, Roda, the minister of justice wrote as follows to Grand Inquisitor Felipe Beltrán, on the subject of the Olavide affair: 'By order of the king, it is my duty to inform you that, not only does His Majesty give his permission and consent that the Holy Office freely act and proceed according to its duty and powers, but also that His Majesty is prepared to offer you his protection and any necessary aid and, so that the Holy Court may immediately proceed with all the necessary enquiries and in order to remove any obstacles that may arise, His Majesty has decided to summon Pablo de Olavide to the Court.'

Ever since the eighteenth century, most historians have avoided laying the blame on Charles III and Grand Inquisitor Beltrán. They have favoured the hypothesis that the initiative for the arrest of Olavide came from subordinate inquisitors, and the king, faced with a *fait accompli*, simply allowed things to take their course. It has even been suggested that Olavide's trial was a deliberate provocation, a challenge to Grand Inquisitor Beltrán, well-known for his open-mindedness and his sympathy for the Enlightenment: not daring to attack the highly placed reformist ministers in person, the inquisitors, alarmed by the new tendencies, decided to make an example of a second-rank official. However, the document cited above (as well as others of a similar nature that José Luis Gómez Urdáñez has published and commented upon)[6] proves irrefutably that Charles III was indeed directly responsible for the persecution to which Olavide was to fall victim. It was he who summoned Olavide to Madrid, in order to facilitate his arrest by the Inquisition. Grand Inquisitor Beltrán acted upon the orders of the king. At the time, all this was perfectly clear to everyone. It explains why the count of Aranda made no move even when the affair became a talking point in Europe, where it was considered to constitute decisive proof that Spain was finding it hard to become a well-run State. Aranda kept quiet because he feared not the Inquisition, but the king. He must certainly have blamed the stubbornness and bigotry of Charles III for the misfortunes that befell his friend, for he and his reformist friends were all too well aware that their pious sovereign was perfectly capable of taking the matter even further. They were no doubt considerably relieved that there was to be only one victim.

Olavide was arrested on 14 November 1776. For two years he was subjected to particularly harsh treatment, incarcerated in an unheated cell (there was a stove in it, but this was removed lest he set the place on fire), with no servant, and totally cut off from the outside world. The grand inquisitor never replied to any of his letters. On 24 November 1778, his fate was at last sealed. The Inquisition spared him the humiliation of a public auto da fé, but a hundred or so of his former friends and acquaintances were invited to attend the private ceremony (*autillo*) in the course of which a list of his crimes was read out. The court formally declared him a heretic and sentenced him to two years' imprisonment followed by eight years of seclusion in a monastery, the forfeit of all his privileges and the confiscation of all his possessions. Two days later, Grand Inquisitor Beltrán sent the minister of justice a letter that leaves Charles III's attitude in no doubt. Beltrán states unequivocally that the ceremony of the 24th 'was organised in accordance with His Majesty's wishes, as your Excellency was informed'.

Olavide spent the winter of 1778–9 in a Benedictine monastery in Sahagun (in the province of Leon), where he suffered greatly from the cold. He asked to be transferred to a more clement region. In June 1779, he was allowed to spend a while in the thermal spas of Puertollano and Almagro and then move to a Capuchin monastery in Murcia. There, Olavide complained of the heat: 'If I am left here, I shall die for lack of the appropriate care,' he wrote to the grand inquisitor. The doctors recommended the sulphurous waters of Caldets, in the province of Gerona. This was very close to the French frontier, but Beltrán nevertheless gave the required permission. No sooner did Olavide arrive in Caldets than he obtained a false passport and fled to France (November 1780). He settled first in Toulouse, then in Paris, where he presented himself as the count of Pilos. He had managed to transfer most of his fortune to France, so was able to resume the sumptuous high-society life that he so much enjoyed and receive his friends and be received in the smartest salons of the capital. In the eyes of one and all, he was a victim of fanaticism, but he was careful to make little of this. In fact, he refused to be considered a martyr of the Inquisition and made a show of the most edifying piety, attending daily mass, performing good works, observing fast days and abstinence. Was he sincere?

Olavide witnessed all the major events of the French Revolution: the meeting of the States General, the taking of the Bastille, the king's flight, the Terror and so on. In 1791, realising that the situation was becoming critical, he decided to leave the capital and move to Meung-sur-Loire, a small town close to Orleans. Even there, he was not out of harm's way. In the eyes of the Jacobins, his fortune, lifestyle and connections all made him suspect, despite his having been a victim of 'fanaticism and despotism'. On 16 April 1794, the Committee of Public Safety placed him under arrest. Olavide managed to convince the revolutionary authorities that he presented no threat. He was set free, but prudently decided to move slightly further away from Paris, to Cheverny, on the banks of the Loire. Here, he produced the four volumes of a work entitled *El evangelio en triunfo (The Triumph of the Gospel)*, which was published in Valencia in 1797. The work enjoyed an immediate success. Olavide now requested permission to return to Spain. Charles IV authorised this and, in return for a few concessions of a formal nature, the Inquisition raised no objections. In early October 1798, Olavide arrived in Madrid. He abjured his past errors in private, and the king restored all his privileges and furthermore allotted him an annuity. Olavide settled in Baeza, where he continued to lead a pious life. He died on 25 February 1803.

The Triumph of the Gospel tells the story of a debauchee who, when assailed by God's grace, returns to a religious life. By dint of focusing on the tragic events that had occurred in France since 1789, Olavide took the opportunity to deplore a revolution that had attacked the two pillars of society: the throne and the altar. In the preface, he declared that he had witnessed the birth of the horrifying revolution which, in a short space of time, consumed 'one of the finest and most opulent kingdoms of Europe'. Was Olavide's purpose in publishing this book simply to ingratiate himself in order to be allowed to return to Spain? That question is prompted by the fact that, for the essential points of his thesis, the author simply produced a free adaptation of French works on the same subject, merely adding a few comments of his own. All the same, Olavide did not totally repudiate the 'Enlightenment', his past and the ideas that he formed in Madrid, Seville and the Sierra Morena on reform in the fields of agrarian development, education and the provision of welfare. His book was far less original than was believed at the time, but that does not prove that its author was not sincere. After all, as we have noted above, when Olavide had settled in France in 1780, although free there from all inquisitorial constraints, from the Christian point of view he had nevertheless led an exemplary life, respecting the sacraments and observing all the precepts of Roman Catholicism.

There is really nothing particularly surprising about his attitude. In the circles of the Spanish *ilustrados* (Enlightened thinkers), Olavide was no exception. He subscribed to the ideas of men such as Campomanes, Aranda and Jovellanos, ideas that by no means coincided with those of the French *philosophes*, particularly in the domain of religion. That is a fact that makes it easier to understand how it was that, under the reign of Charles III, the reformers seemed in no hurry to abolish the Inquisition. At the very most, they wished to reform its methods and missions in order for it to become a docile instrument in the hands of the royal power. At the end of the eighteenth century, a rift definitely opened up between, on the one hand, the higher echelons of the Holy Office composed of enlightened prelates, keen to fight against the superstitions of the masses, and, on the other, those who constituted its base, the district inquisitors, the commissioners and the familiars: a kind of proletariat of ignorant clerics clinging to their meagre pittances and their privileges. The former group had difficulty in obtaining obedience from the latter which, often enough, it despised. Two more or less contemporary anecdotes reflect the situation in the early years of the nineteenth century. In 1805, a young student from Valencia made a number of imprudent remarks that caused him to be denounced to the Holy Office. The local inquisitor, Nicolás Laso, summoned him, congratulated him, and proceeded to show him his library, in which the works of Voltaire, Rousseau and Helvetius held pride of place. He dismissed him saying, 'Well now, young man, off with you: continue your studies in peace and remember that the Inquisition of our country is less vindictive and persecutes people less than is reported.'[7]

In his *Memories of an Old Man*, Alcalá Galiano, one of the most distinguished liberals of the age, tells the story of his arrival in Madrid in early 1808. He was barely seventeen years old. The inquisitors stationed at the town gates came upon a copy of Robertson's *The History of Charles V* in his luggage. They examined the book, which was in English – most suspicious! – with mistrust and, being in doubt, decided to confiscate it. A few days later, Alcalá Galiano was summoned to present himself to Grand Inquisitor Arce, who returned his book to him with a smile, saying, 'Well, young man! So this is the kind of book that you read. Be careful!' The two anecdotes speak volumes about what the Holy Office had become and the contrast that separated its leaders from its rank and file.

Clearly, the Spanish sovereigns had no compunction about using the Inquisition for political ends. Was one of those ends to impose upon the whole realm homogenous legal norms modelled on those applied in Castile? And was the Inquisition called upon to promote Castilian as the language of culture and communication generally, throughout the realm? In other words, was the Holy Office regarded as an instrument of centralisation?

Right from the start, Castile had definitely stood apart in the combination of territories that constituted the Hispanic monarchy. To point to Castilian expansionism in order to explain the situation is clearly absurd, as a glance at the map immediately shows. Castile represented two thirds of the double monarchy's territory. It was also the most densely populated and the richest, and for a long time, up until the mid 1650s, it was furthermore the most dynamic. Those factors are quite enough to justify the pre-eminence of Castile. The first Hapsburgs noted the situation and made Castile their base, a move that presented an added advantage since Castile offered by far the least legal resistance to their demands for funds and troops. At no point did they try to use force to overcome the opposition that they encountered in the territories of the kingdom of Aragon. In the seventeenth century, Olivares, realising that Castile was exhausted, tried to strengthen the union of the territories of the Iberian peninsula by bringing them all under the same law, the same taxation system and a single administration; and he envisaged this unification according to the Castilian model. In short, he wanted to merge the different components of the realm into a national community, so that Philip IV would be the king of Spain, not the king of Castile, Portugal, Aragon and Valencia, and the count of Barcelona, etc. It was not a new idea. In 1598, the jurist Alamos de Barrientos had made similar recommendations, suggesting that the existing structure of the realm be replaced by another, in which there would be 'one kingdom formed of several provinces, but unified: the king would be the king of all of them together'. Olivares modified that idea, recommending retaining the separate kingdoms but unifying their legislation: *multa regna sed una lex*. In 1640, Catalonia rebelled against the plan. When it rejoined the realm, it resumed its former status.

Fifty years later, the situation was reversed. The abolition of the autonomous regime in the territories of the crown of Aragon was the work of the first Bourbon king, Philip V, but it is by no means certain that it was part of a deliberate policy of centralisation. It seems, rather, that it was a matter of a series of *ad hoc* measures taken to cope with the territories that had rallied to the archduke of Austria during the War of Succession. This is borne out by the fact that the Basque provinces and Navarre, which remained loyal to the Bourbon cause, both preserved their status. The unification process made some progress in the eighteenth century, but was still not completed.

The Hapsburgs had made no attempt to impose the general use of the Castilian language. In the sixteenth century, the Portuguese, Catalan and Valencian elites progressively adopted Castilian as the language of culture, in a spontaneous movement to which no political pressure was applied. Throughout the Hapsburg period, Catalan remained the language of the administration and the people. But with the arrival of the Bourbons, things began to change. In 1717, the Court advised the representatives of the central power to encourage the use of Castilian, but to do so with the utmost discretion: 'We must attain the objective without seeming to aim for it.' In the second half of the century, that tendency was confirmed and became more focused. A 1768 decree stated that only works in Castilian should be published, so as to speed up the linguistic integration. However, the Catalan university of Cervera noticeably continued to publish catechisms and other works in Catalan, and the authorities made no objection. In 1780, new instructions from the government recommended that the use of Castilian be generalised, but issued no formal directive banning regional languages.

The Church does not seem to have been concerned to use Castilian to the detriment of the regional languages. In their colleges in Catalonia and Valencia, the Jesuits taught in Castilian, but that was because the local elites insisted they do so: they wished to give their children a Castilian education. However, those same Jesuits preached in Catalan, because they wished to be understood. In doing so, they were simply following the usual practice of the Church, which was always in favour of using the language of the people. Children living in the principality of Catalonia were taught in Catalan, even if they were Castilian or French. In the 1636 and 1637 council assemblies in Tarragona, the Catalan bishops declared that it was obligatory to preach and to teach the catechism in Catalan.

The Holy Office certainly made no attempt to innovate in these domains. In the territories of the crown of Aragon, in the early days at least, many of the inquisitors were Castilian, but the commissioners, familiars and subordinate personnel were recruited from among local inhabitants. Interrogations and minutes were usually recorded in Catalan. The transcripts of the statements of Blanquina March, the mother of Luis Vives, arrested, judged and convicted in the early sixteenth century, were all in Valencian. From 1560 on, however, the *Suprema* recommended the use of Castilian not for ideological reasons, but simply in the interests of efficiency. Soto Salazar, who in 1568 made an inspection of the courts of Catalonia, explained his position in this matter very clearly: 'When documents are written in several languages – Latin, Catalan and Castilian – it is hard to find one's way around them.' In that same year, the secretary Agustín Malo noted that outside Barcelona – and probably within it too – nine-tenths of the inhabitants understood nothing that was set out in an edict of faith written in Castilian. Efficiency and common sense dictated that Catalan be used.

We are bound to conclude that the Inquisition was certainly an instrument in the service of the political power, but it was not used to promote the linguistic unification of the realm.

Conclusion

From 1480 to 1834, the Spanish Inquisition was placed under the authority of the royal power. That is what distinguished it from the forms of intolerance to be found in other countries during this period. Everywhere else, the civil power supported the spiritual power's campaign to punish attacks against religion, and frequently brought considerable zeal to the task. It acted, quite literally, as the secular arm of the Church.[1] In Spain, the civil power was not content simply to back the Church. It took the initiative in repression and itself appointed the agents whose task it was to pursue it; and it also granted those agents privileged status. The Council of the Inquisition was one of the great State bodies on a par with the Council for Finances and the Council for the Indies. The confusion of the temporal and spiritual spheres contained the seed of one of the most dangerous temptations of the modern world: the tendency to make ideology the obligatory complement of politics. In Nazi Germany and in the Communist regimes, to be considered a good citizen it was not enough to pay one's taxes and obey the country's laws; it was also necessary to adhere to the dominant ideology, on pain of being regarded as suspect. Similarly, in the Spain of the Ancien Régime, it was inadvisable to stray from Catholic doctrine. A good Spaniard obviously had to be a good Catholic; woe betide anyone who forgot that! In a book published in 1927, *Religión y Estado en la España del siglo XVI,* Fernando de los Ríos compared the Spanish Inquisition to the Soviet secret police known as the GPU (an earlier form of the NKVD, which later became the KGB). As he saw it, the Soviet Union, an heir to Byzantine Caesaro-Papism, was a Party-State, just as Hapsburg Spain had almost become a Church-State. [2] The way in which both rid themselves of deviationists is instructive. When one reads Koestler's *Zero and the Infinite* or *L'Aveu (The Confession)* by Arthur London, one cannot fail to be struck by the similarities between an inquisitorial trial and a Stalinist one. Four fundamental common features should suffice to make the point.

1 The mania for secrecy. Brought face to face with the inquisitor, a detainee knew neither what he was accused of nor by whom. He himself was invited to say why he found himself there. If he persisted in confessing to nothing, the evidence against him was read out to him, but the witnesses were not named. In Prague, London found himself in exactly the same situation: 'My accuser then picked up other notes and began to read out certain passages from the statements recorded there, without telling me who had made them [...] Until dawn, he continued reading me more reports and denunciations [...] without revealing the names of their authors.'[3]

2 The notion of objective complicity. We have noted this in the case of Carranza. In the course of missions entrusted to him, the archbishop of Toledo had travelled abroad, in the Netherlands, Germany, Italy and England. He had therefore probably met heretics and, without realising it, had adopted some of their ways of thinking and speaking. As a result, he may sometimes have expressed himself objectively as a heretic. When the Inquisition had certain passages from his works examined *in rigore ut jacent*, taking them out of context, it came upon many instances of wording which, objectively, seemed suspect or, at the very least, ambiguous. The risk of such contamination was not underestimated in the countries of the Eastern bloc. 'For them [the accusers], anyone who had travelled abroad was at the very least shady, a potential

spy.'⁴ The notion of objectivity made it possible to set in opposition to the interlocutor's subjective intentions, which were declared to be beyond reproach or at least innocent, what was called his objective thought.⁵

3 The connivance between the accused and his judges. In Spain, the latter tried to get the accused to recognise his own faults and to agree to be punished for them. He was required to confess in public, before the Christian people he had scandalised with his attitude. The punishment, too, had to be public, and for the same reason: the edification of the faithful. That was the whole point of an auto da fé. The trial of Doctor Cazalla, condemned to death on 21 May 1559, provides a particularly clear example. On the day before, he was told that he was to die at the stake; he was now expected to express his repentance publicly, before the assembled crowd. Cazalla allowed himself to be persuaded: 'What can I do to perform my duties to the Holy Office?' he asked. In similar fashion, a Communist arrested for dissidence would try to perform a last service for the Party. 'At first you tried, with all your might, to help the Party by answering all the questions meticulously, giving all possible details. You wanted to help the Party to see clearly; you wanted to see yourself clearly and to see others clearly. You wanted to understand why you found yourself there, what unknown offence had brought you there. The years of struggle and discipline in the Party ranks and your entire past education had taught you that the Party was never wrong, the USSR was always right. You were perfectly prepared to criticise yourself and admit that you had accidentally made mistakes in your work and had thereby harmed the Party.'⁶ The public trial and the confessions broadcast by the press and the radio were modern forms of the auto da fé.

4 Finally, the dishonour that befell the accused and his family. In Spain the convicted man was obliged to wear the *sambenito* and was banned from certain professions, and that dishonour and discrimination extended to his entire family. In the countries of

Eastern Europe, likewise, for the wife and children of a 'traitor', life was not easy.

It was this amalgamation of politics and religion and the determining role reserved for the temporal power that constituted the specificity of the Spanish Inquisition and rendered it irreducible to other forms of religious intolerance.

Notes

Introduction: From the Spain of three religions to inquisitorial Spain

1 The difference in the rates of interest indicates that in Castile silver was rare, and therefore expensive.

2 'The three sacraments of baptism, confirmation and ordination confer, as well as grace, a sacramental "seal" through which the Christian participates in the Christian vocation and belongs to the Church according to a variety of states and functions. This configuration of Christ and the Church, realised through the Holy Spirit, is indelible and remains for ever in the Christian as a positive disposition for grace, a promise and guarantee of divine protection and a vocation to the divine cult and the service of the Church. These sacraments can therefore never be repeated' (*Catéchisme de l'Église catholique*, Paris, Mame-Plon, 1992, p. 246, para 1230).

3 On 23 June 1858, on the orders of the inquisitor, police tore a six-year-old child from his Jewish family in Bologna on the pretext that, unknown to his parents, he had been baptised by a Catholic servant a few years earlier. Despite a campaign by the international press, the child was never returned to his family. He died, a Catholic priest, in 1940. See David Kertzer, *Pie IX et l'enfant juif. L'enlèvement d'Edgardo Mortara*, Paris, Perrin, 2001.

4 The children Robert and Gérald Finaly, born respectively in 1941 and 1942 to a Jewish family that had emigrated from Austria to France, were entrusted by their parents, who feared they would be rounded up by the Germans, to the Grenoble municipal crêche, run by Mlle Brun. The parents, who were arrested by the Gestapo, were then deported and died. Mlle Brun refused to return the children to their aunts, who demanded them back in February 1945. In 1948 she had had them baptised, a step that had not until then been taken, as they had been considered to be protected by a false certificate

of baptism. Mlle Brun then appealed to the Church, which seemed to offer its support. Many by no means unimportant Catholics also thought that, by virtue of canon law, given that they had been baptised, the Finaly children should remain Catholics, but it was known that their family's intention was to raise them as Jews. Not until 1953 was the matter resolved, with the children being returned to their natural family. See André Kaspi, 'L'affaire des enfants Finaly', in *L'Histoire*, no. 76, 1985, pp. 40–53.

5 We know of this pamphlet and its main lines of argument through the reply to it written by Talavera, entitled *Católica Impugnación*.

6 The history of the Soviet Union provides a striking example. Its leaders knew perfectly well that the abolition of the free peasantry and the establishment of a State-controlled economy would, in the immediate future, probably entail chaos that would slow down the development of production. They nevertheless persisted in this course for decades because their aim was to establish a new type of society based on collectivism: 'They subordinated economic rationality to ideological rationality' (Raymond Aron, *Plaidoyer pour l'Europe décadente*, Paris, 1977, p. 85).

1 The eradication of Semitism

1 It was not long before the event became the stuff of legend. It was said that on the night of the crime, the church bell of Velilla, a hamlet thirty or so kilometres from Saragossa, began to toll of its own accord, as it did every time something extraordinary occurred, and the ox's pizzle that secured the clapper snapped. The victim's blood in the cathedral was said to have liquefied two weeks after the crime, and people rushed to soak their handkerchiefs and scapulars in it. Pedro Arbués was canonised by Pius IX on 29 June 1867.

2 Esther Benbassa, 'Les marranes, juifs du secret', in *L'Histoire*, no. 232, May 1999.

3 See José Martínez Millán, 'La persecución inquisitorial contra los criptojudíos en el siglo XVIII. El tribunal de Llerena (1700–1730)', in Joaquín Pérez Villanueva and Bartolomé Escandell Bonet, *Historia de la Inquisición en España y América. III. Temas y problemas*, Madrid, BAC, 2000, pp. 557–656; Marina Torres Arce, 'Los judaizantes y el santo oficio de Logroño en el reinado de Felipe V', in ibid. pp. 657–93; Marina Torres Arce, *La Inquisición en su entorno. Servidores del Santo Oficio de Logroño en el reinado de*

Felipe V, Santander, Universidad de Cantabria, 2001, and Angel del Prado Moura, 'El tribunal de la Inquisición de Valladolid en la crisis del antiguo régimen (1700–1834)' (thesis, University of Valladolid, 1994).

4 Antonio Domínguez Ortiz, 'La Inquisición en Andalucía', in *Estudios sobre Iglesia y sociedad en Andalucía en la Edad Moderna*, Granada, 1999.

5 Julio Caro Baroja, *Los judíos en la España moderna y contemporánea*, Vol. III, Madrid, Ed. Arion, 1961, p. 143.

6 J. Cavaignac, *Dictionnaire du judaïsme bordelais aux XVIIIe et XIXe siècles*, Bordeaux, Archives départementales de la Gironde, 1987.

7 Julio Caro Baroja, *op. cit.*, p. 157.

8 The misfortunes of the *chuetas* were not over. In the twentieth century they were still the victims of various forms of discrimination. In one incident, they were ejected from a public ball; a canon of *chueta* origin was banned from hearing confession and preaching; in 1904, the leader of the government, Antonio Maura, was insulted in Parliament itself: 'Silence, *chueta*!' Not until 1955 did Bishop Enciso Viana abolish all distinctions between *chuetas* and 'the pure' within the clergy of Majorca. See Angela Selke, *Los chuetas y la Inquisición*, Madrid, 1972.

9 'It sometimes happens that a criminal Jew becomes an even more criminal Christian, as is testified by Spain' (cited by S. Markish, *Erasme et les Juifs*, S.I., L'Age d'homme, 1979, pp. 96–8).

10 Antonio Domínguez Ortiz, *Los judeoconversos en España y América*, Madrid, Éd. Istmo, 1971, p. 98.

2 Defending the faith

1 J. E. Longhurst, 'Los primeros luteranos ingleses en España (1539). La Inquisición en San Sebastián y Bilbao', *Boletín de estudios históricos sobre San Sebastián*, 1967, no. 1, pp. 20–21.

2 Luis Vives was from a family of *conversos*. His father was condemned to death as a Judaiser and was executed in September 1524. The human remains of his mother were to be burnt in effigy following a posthumous trial, in 1528–30. Vives, who had left Spain in 1509, never returned; he died in Bruges in 1540. Was he fleeing from the Inquisition? Possibly, but it is worth noting that he did not make the most of his exile to rally people to Judaism; he lived and died as a Christian.

3 Marcel Bataillon, *Erasme et l'Espagne. Recherches sur l'histoire spirituelle du XVIe siècle*, Paris, E. Droz, 1937.

4 J. C. Nieto, *Juan de Valdés and the origins of the Spanish and Italian Reforma-tion*, Geneva, Droz, 1970.

5 C. Gilly, 'Juan de Valdés: Übersetzer und Bearbeiter von Luthers Schriften in seine *Diálogo de doctrina*, *Archiv für Reformationsgeschichte*, 74, 1983.

6 In 1562, his remains were exhumed and burnt.

7 One of the earliest reprinted editions of John Fox's *Book of Martyrs* states that Dr Gil and Constantino Ponce were 'the first who, almost at the same time, discovered the shadows of Spain ... They preached in Seville with great zeal and much success' (as Bayle also notes in his *Dictionnaire*). The nineteenth century was equally certain: one of the earliest historians of Spanish Protestantism, Adolfo de Castro, regarded the 1559 victims as martyrs. See *Historia de los Protestantes Españoles y de su persecución por Felipe II*, Cadiz Imp. de la Revista Médica, 1851. An apologist for the Inquisi-tion, Marcelino Menéndez Pelayo was equally certain that these people were indeed Lutherans.

8 The first two works attacking the Inquisition were *De statu Belgico, atque religione Hispanicae, Historia Francisci Enzinas Burgensis* by Francisco de Enzinas, written in 1545 and published in Strasbourg in 1558, in a French translation, under the name François du Chesne, and *Acts and Monuments* by John Foxe, who had fled to Flanders to escape persecu-tion by Mary Tudor. A manuscript version was circulating in 1554 and in 1563 it was published in London. The most famous of the books against the Spanish Inquisition is the *Sanctae Inquisitionis Hispanicae Artes* (Heidelberg, 1567, translated the following year into first French and English, then Dutch and German) by the mysterious Reginaldus Gon-salvius Montanus, who claimed to have been a member of the Lutheran community of Seville.

9 *Reprobación de las supersticiones y hechicerías*.

10 An ointment made of mandragora, henbane, belladonna, etc. caused hallu-cinations, as Dr Laguna learned for himself in 1545, in Nancy and also in Metz, from the testimony of old men accused of sorcery. Medieval Arabic medicine used anaesthetics based on mandragora, hashish, henbane and opium. Variants included aconite, which produces an irregular heartbeat, and belladonna, which produces delirium. 'On the threshold of sleep, the irregular heartbeat causes an impression of falling into emptiness. The combination of the two may produce the sensation of flying' (J. Vernet, *Ce que la culture doit aux Arabes*, Paris, Sindbad, 1985, p. 418, note).

11 *A Treatise on Superstitions*, a book published in Logroño, in the heart of a province in which sorcerers abounded.

12 'In such delicate affairs, one must be indulgent rather than rigorous' (letter from the *Suprema* dated 27 March 1539).

13 Henry Kamen, 'Notas sobre brujería y sexualidad y la Inquisición', in Angel Alcalá *et al.*, *Inquisición española y mentalidad inquisitorial*, Barcelona, Ariel, 1984, p. 232.

14 H. R. Trevor-Roper, *The European Witch-Craze of the 16th and 17th Centuries*, 1967, London, Penguin Books, 1969.

15 'Que no se confunda el blasfemo con el hereje; al primero que no se le prenda, pero sí al segundo.'

16 Lucien Febvre, *The Problem of Unbelief in the 16th Century: The Religion of Rabelais*, trans. Beatrice Gottlieb, Harvard University Press, 1982.

17 See Francisco Márquez Villanueva, 'Nascer e morir como bestias', in Fernando Díaz Esteban, ed., *Los judaizantes en Europa y la literatura castellana del siglo de oro*, Madrid, Letrúmeno, 1994, 273–93.

18 See Yovel (Yirmiyahu), *Spinoza, el marrano de la razón*, Madrid, Anaya, 1995 (first English edn: *Spinoza and other heretics*, Princeton University Press, 1989).

19 Henry Kamen, 'Notas sobre brujería y sexualidad y la Inquisición', in Angel Alcalá *et al.*, *Inquisición española y mentalidad inquisitorial*, Barcelona, Ariel, 1984, p. 235.

20 After 1777, cases of bigamy could fall under any one of three different jurisdictions: royal justice, when the bigamy infringed the rights of one spouse; episcopal justice, when the validity of the marriage was in doubt; the Inquisition, only if the heresy was patent.

21 Jacques Rossiaud, in *L'Histoire*, June 1999, special edition on 'Love and sexuality'.

22 On 8 July 1787, at the request of Floridablanca, Charles IV sent instructions to this effect to the Junta de Estado; see C. Hermann, *L'Église d'Espagne sous le patronage royal (1476–1834)*, Madrid, Casa de Velázquez, 1998, p. 148.

23 The Valladolid court regretted this in 1781: there were very few spontaneous denunciations despite the fact that many prohibited books were being brought into Spain.

24 In 1812, Francisco Alvarado (who used to sign himself 'el filósofo rancio' (the old-style philosopher) wrote, on the subject of condemned detainees who were handed over to the secular branch: 'we only ever saw one; our

parents never saw any; our grandparents had only very vague memories and spoke of such individuals as being as rare as comets' (Julio Caro Baroja, *op. cit.*, p. 167).

25 The account of this auto da fé was again reprinted in 1820.

26 In 1798, Abbé Grégoire, who had become the constitutional bishop of Blois, had fired off a diatribe to Grand Inquisitor Ramon José de Arce, demanding the suppression of the Inquisition and at the same time defending the French Revolution. This document provoked a generally hostile reaction in Spain, where it had a very bad reception.

27 Blanco-White, a defrocked priest who was to end his days in exile in England, was in favour of freedom of the press, but with reservations: in 1814, he advocated the suppression of the Inquisition and also of the censorship of books and favoured the free expression of 'theological opinions', but he added, 'I am speaking of serious and discursive books, because jokes and sarcastic remarks should not be allowed in religious matters.' Cited by Lucienne Domergue, *La Censure des livres en Espagne à la fin de l'Ancien Régime*, Madrid, Casa de Velázquez, 1996, p. 296.

28 The Cortes of Cadiz also insisted on the destruction, within three days, of all the pictures and inscriptions that recorded the punishments and penalties imposed by the Inquisition in churches, monasteries and public places.

3 The administratibe apparatus of the Holy Office

1 Empress Isabella took an interest in the future of a young and wealthy heiress, Luisa de Acuña. She had placed her in a convent in Toledo until such time as a husband was found for her. Abusing his authority, Manrique procured his nephew access to the convent and had him married forthwith to Luisa de Acuña. The indignant empress ejected Manrique from Court. In 1533, Charles V, upon his return to Spain, authorised Manrique to resume his post as grand inquisitor. However, in the following year, he ordered him back to his diocese, where he died in 1538.

2 In 1869, Victor Hugo wrote a play about Torquemada (entitled *Torquemada*) that he did not publish until 1882. It portrayed three priests: François de Paule, who personified the holiness and gentleness of the Gospel but took no interest in the ways of the world; Pope Alexander Borgia, a libertine and sceptic, avid for temporal power; and Torquemada, the fanatic, convinced that by burning heretics he was purifying and saving them.

3 Charles V had authorised the work before even setting eyes on the monument. When he visited the site, on 19 May 1526, he is said to have expressed his regrets as follows: 'Had I known what was involved, I should not have agreed to it. You are making something which one can see anywhere and destroyed something to be found nowhere else.'

4 'Determinar las causas que vienen a él [el Consejo] en grado de apelación de todas las demás inquisiciones.'

5 J. Caro Baroja, *El señor inquisidor*, p. 41.

6 J. Contreras, *El Santo Oficio de la inquisición en Galicia*, Madrid, Akal, 1982.

7 Francisco Tomás y Valiente, 'Relaciones de la Inquisición con el aparato institucional del Estado', in J. Pérez Villanueva, *La Inquisición española*, Madrid, Siglo XXI de España, 1980, p. 49.

8 Ricardo García Cárcel, *Herejía y sociedad*.

9 Roberto López Vela, in J. Pérez Villanueva and B. Escandell, *Historia de la Inquisición en España y América*, vol. 2, Madrid, 1993, p. 810.

10 There were very few familiars in zones with Morisco populations, the implication being that they could not be relied upon to keep the descendants of Muslims under surveillance.

11 H. C. Lea, *Historia de la Inquisición española*, Madrid, 1983, vol. 2, pp. 76–7.

12 Miguel Ángel Ladero Quesada, 'Judeoconversos andaluces en el siglo XV', in *III Coloquio de historia medieval andaluza*, Jaen, 1984, pp. 40–1.

4 The trial

1 Bernard Gui, the inquisitor for Toulouse from 1307 to 1324, author of the *Practica Inquisitionis heretice pravitatis* (1322), a handbook republished in 1886 as *Practica inquisitionis heretice pravitatis*, author Bernardo Guidonis, a document published for the first time by Canon Célestin Douais, xii-371 p. Paris, A. Picard, 1886, and reprinted by Guillaume Mollat as *Manuel de l'inquisiteur* ... 2 vols. in-8. Paris, 1926–7 ('Les Classiques de l'histoire de France au Moyen Age', 8–9).

2 Nicolas Eymerich, grand inquisitor of Catalonia, Aragon, Valencia and Majorca in 1357. His *Directorium inquisitorum* (1376) was published by Louis Sala-Molins in 1973.

3 Perhaps the reason was that they were hard to obtain. Eymerich's handbook was not published until 1503. It was reprinted in 1578 with a commentary by the jurist Francisco Peña, a judge at the Rota (an ecclesiastical court in Rome).

4 Llorente, I, 175.

5 *Compilación de las instrucciones del Oficio de la Santa Inquisición, hechas por el muy reverendo señor fray Tomás de Torquemada [...] e por los otros reverendísimos señores inquisidores generales que después sucedieron cerca de la orden que se ha de tener en el ejercicio del Santo Oficio de la Inquisición, sumariamente, antiguas y nuevas, puestas por abecedario,* Madrid, 1630.

6 *Compilación de las instrucciones del oficio de la Santa Inquisición, hechas en Toledo, año de 1561.*

7 H. C. Lea, *A History of the Inquisition of Spain*, 4 vols, New York, 1906–8.

8 C. Amiel, 'La "mort juive"', in *Revue de l'histoire des religions*, CCVII, 4/1990, pp. 389–412.

9 Lucienne Domergue, 'Inquisición y ciencia en el siglo XVIII', in *Arbor*, no. 484–5, CXXIV, 1986, p. 111.

10 Unamuno, 'La libertad a la fuerza', article published in *La Publicidad* of 26 September 1918 and reprinted in *Artículos olvidados*, London, ed. C. Cobb, 1976, pp. 199–201.

11 The archbishop of Toledo did not realise how truly he spoke: the Inquisition did indeed seize upon notes and censure sentences that it believed to have been written by Carranza but that, in reality, were citations from Saint John Chrysostom and Saint Augustine.

12. The Spanish Inquisition was simply repeating a procedure that the medieval Inquisition had followed before it. In 1329, Master Eckhart had been found guilty of penning propositions which, when examined *ut verba sonant* (as the words sound), had a heretical ring to them.

13 In these circumstances, we must reject as highly improbable the hypothesis according to which Fray Luis de León composed his book on *The names of Christ* while in detention in Valladolid. It would have been materially impossible for him to do so.

14 'The privilege of not being subjected to torture granted by law to persons of noble birth in other cases does not apply in matters of heresy' (*Handbook for Inquisitors*).

15 Gustav Henningsen, 'La elocuencia de los números', in Ángel Alcalá *et al.*, *Inquisición española y mentalidad inquisitorial, op. cit.*, p. 221.

16 C. Lea, *Historia de la Inquisición española, op. cit.*, vol. II, p. 616.

17 Ricardo García Cárcel, 'De la Reforma protestante a la Reforma católica ...', in *Manuscrits*, 1998, no. 16, pp. 58–9.

18 Valdés was content to repeat the recommendations of Eymerich: it was preferable for the auto da fé to take place on a holiday; 'it is useful for a great crowd to be present at the ordeal and torments of the guilty so that fear deters them from evil'; 'the presence of the chapters, the churches and the magistrates makes the ceremony very striking. It is a spectacle that fills those present with terror and presents them with a horrifying image of the Last Judgement. Such fear is the most suitable sentiment for an auto da fé to inspire' (*Handbook for Inquisitors*).

19 The painting is now the property of Don Rafael Atienza, Marquis of Salvatierra.

20 Rafael Marín López, 'Notas sobre la canonjía inquisitorial en la catedral de Granada', in Antonio Luis Cortes Peña and Miguel Luis López-Guadalupe, eds, *Estudios sobre Iglesia y sociedad en Andalucía en la Edad Moderna*, Universidad de Granada, 1999, p. 61.

21 Carlos de Seso is said to have begged the king for mercy, only for the latter to reply, 'If I had a son as perverse as you, I should myself bring the wood to burn him.' The words were subsequently frequently quoted, attributed to a variety of figures, in particular François I, the king of France.

22 This custom seems to have already existed in Tsarist Russia; see N. Berdiaev (*Les Sources et le sens du communisme russe*), who cites the case of Tchaadaïev (1794–1856), who was declared to be mad and was placed in medical custody so as to silence him; later, Tchaadaïev was to publish *The Apologia of a Madman*.

23 Translated into French in 1856.

24 *Das Zeitalter der Entdeckungen*, Stuttgart, 1877.

25 See Gérard Dufour, 'Les victimes de Torquemada', in *Caravelle*, no. 25, 1975, pp. 103–18.

26 Klaus Wagner, 'La Inquisición en Sevilla (1481–1524), in *Homenaje al profesor Carriazo*, vol. III, Seville, 1973.

27 *Erasme et l'Espagne*, Paris, 1937, p. 530.

5 The Inquisition and society

1 Joseph Pérez, *L'Espagne de Philippe II*, Paris, Fayard, 1999, ch. 3.

2 E. J. Hamilton, *American Treasure and the Prince of Revolution in Spain*

1501–1605, Harvard University Press, 1934. Hamilton's thesis, set out in an article as early as 1929, partly inspired the theories of Keynes.

3 Pierre Vilar, for example, considers Hamilton's conclusion to be too hasty. The same idea had been expressed already in the eighteenth century by R. Cantillon: 'Spain's backwardness was caused by an increase in wages'; see Pierre Vilar, *Une histoire en construction*, Paris, 1982, p. 130.

4 On the relations between the Inquisition and culture, see the remarkable synthesis by Ángel Alcalá, *Literatura y ciencia ante la Inquisición española*, Madrid, 2001.

5 In 1604, Bernardino de Mendoza translated Justus Lipsius' *Republic*. The Inquisition insisted on the deletion of all the passages in which the role of divine Providence was underestimated in favour of expressions such as 'destiny' or 'fortune', which smacked too much of paganism.

6 This was the line of reasoning adopted by Acisclo Fernández Vallín in 1894, in his inaugural lecture to the Spanish Academy of Sciences: 'Theoretical astronomy has not made much progress and Spain has lost the race in this domain. We must seek the principal reasons for this situation, not in any influence the Inquisition may have exerted – for in these disciplines it had none, either good or bad – but in the enthusiasm that prompted the most gifted scholars to cultivate applied astronomy, for preference.' In his reply, Merino agreed: 'What has always been cultivated with the most enthusiasm in Spain is not pure science […] but its practical and, so to speak, utilitarian applications. In modern times, what our science has most lacked is scientific disinterestedness […] We must begin now by convincing Spaniards of the sublime usefulness of useless science.'

7 L. Gil Fernández, *Panorama social del humanismo español (1500–1800)*, Madrid, Alhambra, 1981, p. 275.

8 The anecdote is recorded by Francisco Cascales and is quoted by L. Gil Fernández, *Panorama social del humanismo español (1500–1800)*, *op. cit.*, p. 257.

9 Quoted by M. de la Pinta Llorente, *La Inquisición española y los problemas de la cultura y de la intolerancia*, Madrid, Ed. Cultura Hispánica, 1953, p. 174.

10 'As if all that mattered was knowing languages! … I confess that it is no great misfortune not to be able to discern one style from another or even not to know very much Greek. We should indeed be unfortunate if, in order to defend the truth and the legitimate interpretation of the Scriptures, especially with regard to faith, we were at the mercy of the Hebraists or the

Greek scholars, whose reasoning in all matters is usually so weak.' In his *Sermon on Honour*, Bossuet criticised the arrogance of scholars and men of letters, but without explicitly emphasising the dangers of a critical spirit: 'Those who think themselves the most rational scholars, literary men, and wits, are vainly proud of their intellectual gifts. In truth, Christians, they do deserve to be distinguished from others and are among the world's finest ornaments. But who could tolerate them when, as soon as they feel they are a little talented, they exhaust their listeners' patience with all that they have done and said and, just because they know how to arrange words, turn out a pretty line, round off a sentence, they think they have the right to be endlessly heeded and to pass sovereign judgement upon everything?'

11 'Today, Ciceronians are called Lutherans and madmen'; 'it is said that they are not very pious and are not keen on churches' (opinions recorded by Palmireno in 1573; L. Gil Fernández, *Panorama social del humanismo español, op, cit.*, p. 263.

12 E. Asensio, in *Fray Luis de León*, Salamanca, Éd. de la Universidad de Salamanca, 1981 [Academia Literaria Renacentista, 1], p. 50.

13 'They have a taste for the humanities and innovation' (M. de la Pinta Llorente, *Proceso criminal contra el hebraista salmantino Martín Martínez de Cantalapiedra*, Madrid-Barcelona, CSIC, 1946, p. lxix).

14 'Such rubbish puts me beside myself and I find it hard to take no notice of it' (letter from Pedro Juan Núñez to Jerónimo Zurita, quoted by M. de la Pinta Llorente, *Proceso Cantalapiedra, op. cit.*, p. xix).

15 'His temporibus, quidam indocti et temerarii homines leviter statim eos judaizare clamant qui non omnia in Sacra Scriptura exponenda ad sensus anagogicos referant, vel qui facilem et planam alicujus hebraei interpretationem sequantur [...]. Docti vero homines in sacris litteris vix tuto se versari posse putabant' (Diego de Zúñiga, *In Job commentaria*, Toledo, 1548, quoted by L. Gil Fernández, *Panorama social del humanismo español, op. cit.*, p. 490).

6 The Inquisition and the political authorities

1 'Heretici, non solum religionem, sed etiam statum politicum evertunt' (Paramo, *De origine et progressu officii Sanctae Inquisitionis ...*, Madrid, 1598, p. 322.

2 Letters on the Inquisition, Moscow, 20 June (2 July) 1815.

3 The ban seems to have targeted in particular a bilingual reprint of the

Brevíssima Relación de la Destrucción de la India Oriental, su autor D. Bartolomé de las Casas, impresa en Venecia por Ginami el año de 1643. Escrito en idioma castellano e Italiano (in Castilian and Italian), produced in Venice in 1643. The prohibition was repeatedly renewed in subsequent years. It still figured in a document published by the Inquisition in Seville dated 22 June 1741.

4 In similar vein, a pastoral letter from the archbishop of Saragossa, Antonio Ibañez de la Riva Herrera, dated 8 June 1707 revokes and annuls all authorisations to hear confessions or preach granted to Capuchins in the diocese. They and other ecclesiastics, both secular and regular, were suspected of inciting subjects of the crown of Aragon (Aragon, Valencia and Catalonia) to revolt against Philip V and rally to the archduke of Austria.

5 Fadrique Furió Ceriol, *Del concejo y consejeros del príncipe*, quoted by J. A. Maravalli, *La oposición política bajo los Austrias*, Madrid, Ariel, 1972, p. 58.

6 José Luis Gómez Urdáñez, 'El caso Olavide. El poder absoluto de Carlos III al descubierto', in Santiago Muñoz Machado, ed., *Los grandes procesos de la historia de España*, Barcelona, Crítica, 2002, pp. 308–34.

7 Lucienne Domergue, in *Arbor*, 484–5, CXXIV, 1986, p. 127.

Conclusion

1 The France of the Ancien Régime provides one of many examples. In his *Origines de la France contemporaine*, Taine noted the extent to which, even in the Age of Enlightenment, the royal power clamped down on impiety. The most spectacular manifestations of that zeal are provided by the Calas and the Chevalier de la Barre affairs, but there were many others. As late as 1825, the sacrilege law prescribed the penalty for parricide for those who profaned the consecrated host, so that, as Royer-Collard pointed out, the 'real presence' within the host became 'a legal fact'.

2 In his *Sociologie du communisme* (Paris, Gallimard, 1949), Jules Monnerot similarly describes Soviet Communism as 'the Islam of the twentieth century' because of its lack of distinction between politics, religion and economics. Stalin was both head of State and secretary general of the Party – in other words, the commander of the faithful.

3 Arthur London, *L'Aveu*, Paris, Gallimard, 1968 (Coll. 'Folio'), pp. 81–3.

4 Ibid., p. 107.

5 One of Rajk's co-accused, Savarius (Szaz), the author of *Volontaires pour l'échafaud* (*Volunteers for the Scaffold*) (Julliard), later, with hindsight, analysed

the mechanism of the process. During the Spanish Civil War, the members of the International Brigade for a while eluded Party control and were in contact with many different kinds of people: among them anarchists and Trotskyists. 'Contact meant possible contamination. So the accusations that were dreamed up took on a kind of substance, an "objective" truth', according to the type of reasoning that Savarius analysed. He explains how it was possible to start with a true fact and deduce a fabricated lie by means of a series of 'in shorts'. Here is an example: 'You knew so and so? One of his friends was a traitor; "in short", through so and so you were in contact with that traitor.' Here is another: 'You worked for such and such a firm; it was set up by the English; the English stuffed all their foreign branches full of Intelligence Service agents; so you must have worked alongside them; "in short", you were influenced by them; "in short", you were acting on the orders of the Intelligence Service' (Dominique Desanti, *Les Staliniens*, Paris, Fayard, p. 141).

6   Arthur London, *L'Aveu, op. cit.*, pp. 77–78.

Bibliography

The bibliography of Émile Van Der Vekene (*Bibliotheca biblio-graphica historica Sanctae Inquisitionis* ... Vaduz, Liechtenstein, Topos Verlag, 1982–92, 23 vols.), lists several thousand books devoted to the Inquisition.

There are two essential works of reference: Henry Charles Lea's *A History of the Inquisition of Spain* (4 vols, New York, 1906–08, which is still very useful. It has been translated into Spanish: *Historia de la Inquisición en España*, 3 vols, Madrid, Fundación Universitaria Española, 1983; and the three volumes of the *Historia de la Inquisición en España y América*, edited by Joaquín Pérez Villanueva and Bartolomé Escandell Bonet, which were preceded, in 1980, by another collective volume, also edited by Joaquín Pérez Villanueva, *La Inquisición española. Nueva visión, nuevos horizontes*, Madrid, Siglo XXI de España.

Despite its early date and its shortcomings, it is still worth consulting Juan Antonio Llorente's *Histoire critique de l'Inquisition espagnole* (4 vols, Paris, 1817–18). The *Memoria histórica sobre cual ha sido la opinión nacional de España acerca del tribunal de la Inquisición*, also by Llorente (Madrid, 1812) has been reprinted, edited by Gérard Dufour (Paris, PUF, 1977), who has also produced a study of the subject: *Juan Antonio Llorente en France, 1813–22: contribution à l'étude du libéralisme chrétien en France et en Espagne au début du XIXe siècle*, Paris, 1984.

Among the many general studies on the Inquisition, the following are particularly useful:

Alcalá, Ángel, *Literatura y Ciencia ante la Inquisición Española*, Madrid, 2001

—— ed., *The Spanish Inquisition and the Inquisitorial Mind*, original Spanish edition Barcelona, 1984; English translation distributed by Columbia University Press, 1987

Bennassar, Bartolomé *et al.*, *L'Inquisition espagnole*, Paris, Hachette, 1979

Bethencourt, Francisco, *L'Inquisition à l'époque moderne: Espagne, Portugal, Italie, XVe–XVIe siècle*, Paris, Fayard, 1995

Contreras, Jaime, *Historia de la Inquisición española (1478–1834)*, Madrid, 1997

Contreras, Jaime, and Henningsen, Gustav, 'Forty-four thousand cases of the Spanish Inquisition (1540–1700): analysis of a historical data bank', in Henningsen and Tedeschi (eds), *The Inquisition in Early Modern Europe*, DeKalb, Ill, Northern Illinois University Press, 1986

Cruz, A. J., and Perry, M. E., eds., *Culture and Control in Counter Reformation Spain*, Minneapolis, 1992

Dedieu, Jean-Pierre, *L'Administration de la foi. L'Inquisition de Tolède (XVIe–XVIIe siècles)*, Madrid, Casa de Velázquez, 1989

Edwards, John, *The Spanish Inquisition*, Stroud, Tempus Publishing Ltd, 1999

García Cárcel, Ricardo, and Moreno Martínez, Doris, *Inquisición. Historia crítica*, Madrid, Temas de Hoy, 2000

Haliczer, Stephen, *Inquisition and Society in the Kingdom of Valencia 1478–1834*, Berkeley, University of California Press, 1990

——, ed., *Inquisition and Society in Early Modern Europe*, London, Croom Helm, *c.* 1987

Henningsen, Gustav and Tedeschi, John, eds, *The Inquisition in Early Modern Europe*, DeKalb, Ill, Northern Illinois University Press, 1986

Kamen, Henry, *The Spanish Inquisition: An Historical Revision*, London, Phoenix, 1997

Monter, William, *Frontiers of Heresy: The Spanish Inquisition from the Basque Lands to Sicily*, Cambridge, Cambridge University Press, 1990

Perry, M. E., and Cruz, A. J., eds, *Cultural Encounters: The Impact of the Inquisition in Spain and the New World*, Berkeley, University of California Press, 1991

Further information and commentaries may be found in the following works:

Beinart, Haim, *The Expulsion of the Jews from Spain*, trans. Jeffrey M. Green, Portland, Littman Library of Jewish Civilisation, 2002

Caro Baroja, Julio, *Las brujas y su mundo*, trans. N. Glendinning, *The World of the Witches*, London, Weidenfeld, 1964

——, *El señor inquisidor*, Madrid, Altaya, 1996

Defourneaux, Marcelin, *Pablo de Olavide ou l'Afrancesado*, Paris, PUF, 1959

Christian, William, *Apparitions in Late Medieval and Renaissance Spain*, Princeton, Princeton University Press, 1981

Domínguez Ortiz, Antonio, *Los judeoconversos en la España moderna*, Madrid, Ed. Mapfre, 1992

Escamilla-Colin, M., *Crimes et châtiments dans l'Espagne inquisitoriale*, 2 vols, Paris, 1992

Escudero, José Antonio, ed., *Perfiles jurídicos de la Inquisición española*, Universidad Complutense de Madrid, 1989

Eymerich, Nicolas, *Le Manuel des inquisiteurs à l'usage des inquisitions d'Espagne et de Portugal ou Abrégé de l'ouvrage intitulé Directorium inquisitorum*, a reprint and translation into French of the *Directorium inquisitorum R. P. F. Nicolai Eymerici*, by Francisco Peña, Louis Sala Molins, Paris-The Hague, Mouton éd., 1973

García Cárcel, Ricardo, *Orígenes de la Inquisición española. El tribunal de Valencia, 1478–1530*, Barcelona, Ed. Península, 1976

—— ,*Herejía y sociedad en el siglo XVI. La Inquisición en Valencia. 1530–1609*, Barcelona, Ed. Península, 1979

Giles, Mary E., ed., *Women and the Inquisition in Spain and the New World*, Baltimore, Johns Hopkins University Press, 1999

González Novalín, J. L., *El Inquisidor general Fernando de Valdés*, 2 vols, Oviedo, 1968–70

Hamilton, Alastair, *Heresy and Mysticism in 16th Century Spain: The Alumbrados*, Cambridge, James Clarke & Co. Publishers, 1992

Henningsen, Gustav, *The Witches' Advocate: Basque Witchcraft and the Spanish Inquisition, 1609–1614*, University of Nevada Press, 1995

Jiménez Monteserín, M., *Introducción a la Inquisición española, Documentos básicos para el estudio del Santo Oficio*, Madrid, 1980

Kagan, Richard, *Lucrecia's Dreams: Politics and Prophecy in Sixteenth-Century Spain*, Berkeley, University of California Press, 1990

MacKay, Angus, 'Popular Movements and Pogroms in 15th Century Castile', *Past and Present: A Journal of Historical Studies*, 55 (1972), pp. 33–67

Martinez Millan, José, *La hacienda de la Inquisición (1478–1700)*, Madrid, 1984.

Nalle, Sara T., 'Inquisitors, priests and people during the Catholic Reformation in Spain', *Sixteenth-Century Journal*, 18 (1987)

——, *Mad for God: Bartolomé Sánchez, the Secret Messiah of Cardenete*, Charlottesville and London, University Press of Virginia, 2001

Netanyahu, Benzion, *The Origins of the Inquisition in Fifteenth Century Spain*, Random House, New York, 1995

——, *Towards the Inquisition. Essays on Jewish and Converso History in Late Medieval Spain*, Ithaca, Cornell University Press, 1997

Pérez, Joseph, *Historia de una tragedia. La expulsión de los judíos de España*, Barcelona, Crítica, 1993

Roth, Norman, *Conversos, the Inquisition and the Expulsion of the Jews from Spain*, Madison, University of Wisconsin Press, 1995

Tellechea Idigoras, José Ignacio, *El arzobispo Carranza y su tiempo*, 2 vols, Madrid, Ed. Guadarrama, 1968

Index